Hiking the Grand Canyon

Also by John Annerino

Photography

Canyon Country: A Photographic Journey

Grand Canyon Wild: A Photographic Journey

Roughstock: The Toughest Events in Rodeo

Apache: The Sacred Path to Womanhood

People of Legend: Native Americans of the Southwest

The Wild Country of Mexico: La tierra salvaje de México

Canyons of the Southwest: A Tour of the Great Canyon Country from Colorado to Northern Mexico

High Risk Photography: The Adventure Behind the Image

Nonfiction

Dead in Their Tracks: Crossing America's Desert Borderlands

Running Wild: An Extraordinary Adventure of the Human Spirit

Adventure Travel

The Photographer's Guide to Canyon Country

The Photographer's Guide to the Grand Canyon

Adventuring in Arizona

A Sierra Club Totebook®

Hiking the Grand Canyon

Third Edition

John Annerino

Sierra Club Books
San Francisco

Text copyright © 2006, 1993, 1986 by John Annerino, except for the following:
Chapter 1 (Native Peoples of the Grand Canyon) copyright © 1986 by Janet R. Balsom
Chapter 2 (Natural History) copyright © 1986 by Lawrence E. Stevens
Chapter 3 (Geology) copyright © 1986 by Michael Young

Published by Sierra Club Books
85 Second Street, San Francisco, CA 94105
www.sierraclub.org/books

Produced and distributed by
University of California Press
Berkeley and Los Angeles, California
University of California Press, Ltd.
London, England
www.ucpress.edu

SIERRA CLUB, SIERRA CLUB BOOKS, and the Sierra Club design logos are registered trademarks of the Sierra Club.

Library of Congress Cataloging-in-Publication Data

   Hiking the Grand Canyon / John Annerino—3rd ed.
      p. cm.—(A Sierra Club totebook)
   Includes bibliographical references and index.
   ISBN 1-57805-150-9 (alk. paper)
   1. Hiking—Arizona—Grand Canyon National Park—Guidebooks.   2. Grand Canyon National Park (Ariz.)—Guidebooks.   I. Series.
GV199.42.A72G7334 2006
917.91'32—dc22   2005047191

Cover design by Lynne O'Neil
Cover photograph © Tom Till
Book design by Mark Ong
Composition by David Van Ness

All interior photographs © George H. H. Huey, except for the photo on page 233, which is © John Annerino.

Printed in the United States of America on New Leaf Ecobook 50 acid-free paper, which contains a minimum of 50 percent post-consumer waste, processed chlorine free. Of the balance, 25 percent is Forest Stewardship Council certified to contain no old-growth trees and to be pulped totally chlorine free.

Third Edition
10 09 08 07 06
10 9 8 7 6 5 4 3 2 1

In memory of my father
who sacrificed it all
to move our family west
from the steel gray canyons
of the Windy City
to a new life in the sunshine
of the Grand Canyon state

Contents

Preface to the Third Edition

Since this guide was first published more than 20 years ago, the Grand Canyon's international renown has not diminished. Fêted as one of the Seven Natural Wonders of the World, it was described by *National Geographic* as "one of the greatest and most spectacular canyon systems on earth." President Theodore Roosevelt was so awed during his visit to the Grand Canyon on May 6, 1903, he said, "In the Grand Canyon, Arizona has a natural wonder which, so far as I know, is in kind absolutely unparalleled throughout the rest of the world. . . . You cannot improve on it. The ages have been at work on it, and man can only mar it. What you can do is keep it for your children, your children's children, and all who come after you, as the one great sight which every American should see." Since Grand Canyon National Park was established on February 16, 1919, more than 70 million American and foreign tourists have heeded the Rough Rider's call. In a recent year, 4½ million people visited the Grand Canyon: 270,000 hiked below the North and South Rims, 29,666 backpacked to Phantom Ranch for an overnight stay in the inner Canyon, 21,597 rafted the Colorado River (there have been 500,000 river runners to date), and 150,000 rode scenic helicopter flights. There's another, little-known, statistic for this World Heritage Site, which has been described as the "crown jewel of America's natural treasures": since records were first kept in 1867, 195 hikers and river runners have died exploring the greatest canyon on earth. That number eclipses the 170 climbers and sherpas who have perished while trying to surmount the highest mountain in the world, the 29,035-foot Mount Everest, during its 75-year climbing history. Beautiful to behold, the Grand Canyon is 277 miles long, 8 to 16 miles wide, more than 6,000 feet deep at its deepest point, and 1.8 billion years old. Many areas in the Grand Canyon, which encompasses 2,000 square miles of the Colorado Plateau, remain dangerous terra incognita for foot travelers in the 21st century. This new addition to the Sierra Club's celebrated Totebook® series is not a blueprint; it does not include paint-by-number trail descriptions or GPS waypoints; it will not replace common sense—you still have to make your own decisions. It is instead a key to opening the door to Grand Canyoneering. It describes how to prepare yourself for a safe journey through one of the most popular, rugged, and spectacular hiking destinations anywhere. And it is a handy tote-along trail guide to use once you've opened that door. (To ensure the accuracy of the trail, route, and river descriptions, I've described only those areas that I've *personally* day hiked, backpacked, canyoneered, run, climbed, or rafted.) "May the trail rise up to meet you, and the wind be always at your back."

—John Annerino
Tucson, August 2005

Acknowledgments

Many people have shown me hidden passages through the Grand Canyon I would not have discovered alone. I would like to thank: Galen Snell, who first introduced me to the Canyon with a life-changing hike down the Boucher Trail; boatwoman Suzanne Jordon, who spent a month teaching me how to run the Colorado River in a paddle raft; Dave Ganci, whose pioneering first ascents of Zoroaster Temple and Angels Gate were my inspiration for climbing the Southwest Face of Zoroaster with George Bain; George Bain, for making the daring lead of Zoroaster's Twilight Traverse during our first ascent—and for remaining an inspiration for Grand Canyoneering; Tim Ganey and Craig Hudson, for their intellect and dedication that ensured I got through the Canyon alive during three dangerous trans-Canyon runs; photojournalist Christine Keith, for boldly documenting those adventures; and the Native Americans who traveled on foot throughout the Grand Canyon—the Mojave, Hualapai, Havasupai, Hopi, Navajo, and Kaibab Paiute. Their cultures, lifeways, and fleet-footed journeys along rugged Canyon routes left an indelible mark on me.

I am grateful for editors Kristi Hein, Marilyn Schwartz, and Sharron Wood, and the contributors who generously lent their expertise: Janet R. Balsom for her essay "Native Peoples of the Grand Canyon," Lawrence E. Stevens for his essay "Natural History," Michael Young for his essay "Geology," George

H. H. Huey for his black-and-white images, and George Bain for updating "Climbers of Temples and Buttes in the Grand Canyon Region."

This book would not have become a reality without Sierra Club Books' senior editor, Jim Cohee, and publisher, Helen Sweetland. Thank you.

PART
I

WELCOME TO THE GRAND CANYON

1 | Native Peoples of the Grand Canyon

by Janet R. Balsom

Nearly 10,000 years ago, Native Peoples may have been hunting the last of the ice-age animals in the Grand Canyon. A single portion of a Folsom projectile point was found in an isolated area of the canyon, suggesting the possibility of people in the area at the end of the Pleistocene. A single artifact does not prove that Paleo-Indian hunters were living in the canyon, but it does suggest a more complicated story of human use than previously thought.

The presence of hunters and gatherers in the Grand Canyon is well documented. Between 3,000 and 4,000 years ago, the makers of split-twig figurines left their marks on the canyon. These figurines, made primarily of either willow or cottonwood, have been found in caches in caves in the Mississippian Redwall Formation. The makers of the figurines are thought to have followed a hunting-and-gathering lifestyle known as Archaic. It is thought that the figurines may have been made by people of the Pinto Basin period Desert Culture for purposes of imitative hunting magic. Projectile points characteristic of the Desert Culture have been found in the vicinity of Grand Canyon, but never in direct association with the figurines.

Further evidence of Archaic manifestations at Grand Canyon is primarily limited to the South Rim and far western reaches of the North Rim, although recent information gathered from the inner Canyon suggests limited occupation of the

Canyon itself. Adaptation most likely involved reliance on a hunting-and-gathering subsistence base. In general, subsistence would have adjusted to the environment based on the seasonal exploitation of various plant and animal resources in areas of high resource variability.

For many years it was thought that the Canyon was abandoned between the Archaic and later Puebloan occupations. Recent research suggests that limited occupation continued from Archaic times until sometime around A.D. 700 to 800, when the ancestral Puebloan tradition was fully recognized. At that time the population began to rise, and the people of the Kayenta tradition established themselves in the eastern reaches of the Canyon while a group called the Cohonina became established in the western South Rim areas. The ancestral Puebloan people were utilizing and expanding in both the South Rim and inner Canyon areas until around A.D. 1050, when they expanded to the North Rim. Evidence from research conducted on Unkar Delta and Walhalla Glades indicates that the population had increased to a point where utilization of one area was not adequate. Movement onto the North Rim provided an additional area that could be exploited for farming. Walhalla Glades supported a farming community for about 100 years, from A.D. 1050 until 1175. Mineralogic evidence from the ceramics found on both Unkar Delta and Walhalla Glades suggests that these two communities were comprised of the same people, utilizing the inner Canyon most of the year and the North Rim to supplement the Canyon resources during the summer. A gradual decline in population occurred after A.D. 1100 until around A.D. 1175, during which time most areas of Grand Canyon were abandoned. Information recently gathered suggests that abandonment of some areas of the eastern inner Canyon was not until sometime after A.D. 1175. Along the eastern South Rim there is evidence to suggest that the population remained until after A.D. 1200 to 1225. It is thought that abandonment after A.D. 1175 was due to climatic changes on the Colorado Plateau.

The ancestral Puebloan lifestyle was marked by a number of cultural traits. The earliest ancestral Puebloans lived in pit-houses characterized by upright rock slabs and a semi-subterranean floor. These early ancestral Puebloans did not make pottery. Instead they made and used baskets, usually of yucca. Because of this trait, this period of time is referred to as Basketmaker. It lasted from around A.D. 1 until A.D. 800. The economy at this time was primarily a hunting-and-gathering one. There is very little evidence of Basketmaker people in Grand Canyon.

Around A.D. 800 the ancestral Puebloan people started to build coursed masonry structures. This is the beginning of the Pueblo period, the word *pueblo* coming from the Spanish word for town. The Pueblo period is divided into stages, beginning with Pueblo I (PI), dated to around A.D. 800–900; Pueblo II (PII), dated approximately A.D. 950–1175; Pueblo III (PIII), dated A.D. 1175–1300; and Pueblo IV (PIV), dated A.D. 1300–1540. Most occupation in the Grand Canyon occurred during the PII period. At the beginning of the Pueblo period the ancestral Puebloan people started to produce pottery. Early ancestral Puebloan pottery consisted of crude gray vessels. As time progressed, designs were added until a very sophisticated ceramic tradition existed. The different designs of black-on-white, black-on-red, and the corrugated-style pottery are characteristic of the PII periods in Grand Canyon. Of the 4,300 sites recorded in Grand Canyon so far, over 1,500 date to this time period.

Subsistence during PII times was characterized by a mixed hunting-gathering and agricultural economy. In an environment as marginal as the Grand Canyon, people must rely on a number of strategies in order to be successful. Evidence for agriculture on the South Rim is limited, but evidence in the inner Canyon and on the North Rim is extensive. Agricultural features such as check dams, terraces, and grid gardens can be found in a number of areas in the inner Canyon (e.g., Unkar Delta) and on the North Rim (e.g., Walhalla Glades).

At the same time that the ancestral Puebloans were utilizing the western areas of the Canyon, a group known as the Cohonina was utilizing the western South Rim, the Esplanade, and Havasu Canyon from around A.D. 700 until A.D. 1175. The lifestyle of the Cohonina was very different from that of the neighboring ancestral Puebloan people, although it appears that the two groups did maintain close relations. On most sites found on the South Rim and on the neighboring Kaibab National Forest, artifacts will be comprised of both Kayenta and Cohonina ceramics. The Cohonina are poorly understood at this time.

Environmental conditions in the western Canyon areas would not allow an economy relying on agriculture like that of the ancestral Puebloan people. Instead, Cohonina occupation was seasonal, relying primarily on hunting and gathering. Agave was of particular importance. Roasting pits can be found in many areas occupied by the Cohonina. Abandonment by the Cohonina around A.D. 1175 was probably due to the same climatic changes that drove the ancestral Puebloan people from the Grand Canyon.

Sporadic occupation continued in and around the Canyon for many years, with significant evidence of reoccupation sometime after A.D. 1300 with the presence of the ancestors of the Southern Paiute and another archaeologically identifiable group known as the Cerbat. This later group is thought to be ancestral to the Pai (Hualapai and Havasupai) and to have occupied the same area as the Cohonina and the modern Pai. Another view

The ruins at Nankoweap. Photo © George H. H. Huey

suggests that the Cohonina were the direct ancestors of the Havasupai.

The Havasupai, Hopi, Hualapai, Southern Paiute, Navajo, Yavapai, Western Apache, and Zuni represent the modern-day Indian tribes that have historic ties to the Grand Canyon and live in and around the Canyon today. Of these, only the Havasupai live within the Grand Canyon itself. They occupy a 185,000-acre reservation bordered by Grand Canyon National Park. The word *Havasupai,* which means "people of the blue-green water," refers to the color of the water of Havasu Creek, which runs through the side canyon they inhabit. The Havasupai are primarily farmers, utilizing the Canyon for agriculture in the summer months and the rim and its resources of game and wild plants for food in the winter to supplement the food they grow. Their lifestyle is essentially unchanged since their ancestors first settled Havasu Creek around A.D. 1300.

Neighboring both the Havasupai and Grand Canyon National Park are the Hualapai, a group closely related to the Havasupai. *Hualapai* means "people of the pine trees," which refers to the tall pine trees that grow in the upper elevations of their reservation. Many changes have taken place since their ancestors first inhabited the area. The Hualapai were often at war with neighboring Yuman peoples, most notably the Yavapai. With the expansion of white settlers onto Hualapai land, hostilities began with the Anglos. In 1866, Anglos killed one of the Hualapai leaders. Retaliation was swift, but the poorly equipped Hualapai were no match for the white soldiers. By 1869, the war was over. The Hualapai were moved in 1874 to a portion of the Colorado River Indian Reservation. In 1875 they returned to their homeland. By 1883 a reservation was established, allocating the tribe approximately 1 million acres of land encompassing areas along the Colorado River and the South Rim.

Economically, the Hualapai relied on a subsistence pattern utilizing the many wild plant and animal resources. Today they rely on support from Anglo interests, namely, tourism and river rafting.

The Southern Paiute inhabit areas on the North Rim of the Grand Canyon on the Kaibab Reservation. These people are descendants of Shoshonean groups and did not move into the Grand Canyon region until around A.D. 1300. Their utilization of the Canyon was limited to the North Rim and some areas of the inner Canyon on the north side of the river in the west end of the Canyon. They were primarily hunters and gatherers, but they also practiced agriculture. They relied heavily upon the agave, or century plant. Evidence for this is the number of mescal pits (agave roasting pits) found in the areas they inhabited.

The Hopi can trace their ancestry to the ancestral Puebloan people who once inhabited Grand Canyon. It is thought that when the ancestral Puebloans abandoned Grand Canyon, they moved east and established the Hopi mesas. The town of Old Oraibi on Third Mesa is the oldest continually inhabited community in the United States. It was established by A.D. 1200.

The Grand Canyon is very important to the Hopi. It is a symbolic place, the place where human beings and animals emerged from the underworld and the place where the dead returned. The *Sipapuni,* or "place of emergence," is located within the Grand Canyon, near the confluence of the Colorado and Little Colorado rivers. According to Hopi belief, the Hopi lived in a number of worlds below this one. They emerged through the Sipapuni into this world.

The Hopi also used the Grand Canyon for salt. Salt deposits are found along the Colorado River near the confluence with the Little Colorado. These salt mines are sacred to the Hopi and have been placed off-limits to non-Hopi by the National Park

Service. The Hopi have been known to make the 100-mile pilgrimage along the Salt Trail into historic times. The last documented trip was made in the 1960s.

The Hopi today are farmers. They practice a type of agriculture known as dry farming. By planting deep in the sandy soil, they have managed to farm desert areas thought by many to be unproductive. They also rely on the tourist trade. Hopi pottery, jewelry, and basketry command an ever-increasing market.

The Navajo are relative newcomers to the Grand Canyon region. Migrating from Canada, the Navajo are an Athapaskan people closely related to the Apache. The Navajo refer to themselves as *Dineh,* which means "the People." Opinions as to when the Navajo migrated vary widely with the earliest dates around A.D. 1000 and later dates around A.D. 1525. The Navajo were established at least by 1680, the time of the Pueblo Revolt that drove the Spanish from the Hopi settlements. The Navajo settled areas surrounding the Hopi lands. Many land disputes have arisen between the two tribes that are still unsettled.

The Navajo Nation is the largest Native American tribe in the United States. More than 200,000 people are considered to be Navajo, and their reservation encompasses more than 2 million acres of land in northern Arizona, New Mexico, and southern Utah. A portion of their reservation has rich deposits of coal, which have been mined by Peabody Coal Company. Revenue from the sale of the minerals is an important part of the Navajo economy, which includes farming, herding, jewelry and rug making, and tourism.

The Zuni, Yavapai, and Western Apache all have complex histories in the Grand Canyon. Although the Pueblo of Zuni is far removed from the Canyon, the Zuni people believe they originated in the Canyon, tracing much of their early history to migrations through the Canyon. Today, Zuni is a thriving community in New Mexico, just east of the Arizona border. For thousands of years, however, Zuni people found their path in the Canyon.

The Yavapai and Western Apache tribes have historic connections to the Canyon, the details of which are still unknown. We do know that all these groups have identified places at Grand Canyon of importance in their own histories. Additional research will shed light on these connections.

None of the tribes living in the Grand Canyon region today is isolated. Each has, in historic times, established trade relations with other groups in the region. Hopi and Havasupai established trade in the 1300s. Navajo and Hopi have traded since the Navajo migrated into the area. Hualapai and Havasupai trade freely and were not recognized as separate groups until 1776 or possibly later. The tribes today co-exist with each other and with the Anglo-Americans who have moved onto their lands.

2 | Natural History

by Lawrence E. Stevens

INTRODUCTION

The first observations on Canyon biology were recorded by Edgar Mearns in 1884, and the first purely biological expedition in the area was mounted by C. Hart Merriam and Vernon Bailey of the U.S. Biological Survey staff in 1889. Merriam studied distinctive zones of vegetation that he encountered from the 2,400-foot floor of Grand Canyon to the 12,633-foot top of the nearby San Francisco Peaks. He formulated his Life Zone Concept (see below), ascribing vegetational zonation to temperature and precipitation norms at different elevations. Biological interest in the Canyon was nominal until 1919, when Grand Canyon became a national park. Ranger-naturalists such as G. E. Sturdevant, E. D. McKee, and Lewis Schellbach observed, collected, and identified the Canyon's biota. A biological expedition to Shiva Temple led by Harold Anthony in 1937 attracted national interest, but yielded no novel animal species on that isolated "sky island." Botanists Elzada Clover and Lois Jotter collected and reported on the vegetation of the Colorado River corridor from the first commercial river trip with Norm Nevills in 1938. By the 1960s river running made access to the inner Canyon easier, and detailed biological research began in earnest. Biological surveys sponsored by the National Park Service in the 1970s and, recently, by the Bureau of Reclamation, have added greatly to our knowledge of Grand Canyon biology.

This chapter discusses the structure and development of biological communities in the Grand Canyon region on a broad scale. The story of vegetation communities in Grand Canyon National Park, Holocene climatic changes, biogeography, and human impacts on Grand Canyon biology are complex and well worth telling. Space does not permit inclusion of exhaustive species lists here, and we have not tried to recount the life histories of individual species; however, checklists of the various taxa present in the park are available from the Grand Canyon Association at the South Rim.

LIFE ZONES AND VEGETATION

The Grand Canyon provides more than 7,000 feet of vertical relief and a diverse climate. From its rims down to the Colorado River, gradients of temperature, precipitation, and exposure regulate the occurrence of plant and animal species. Precipitation, much of it as snow, exceeds 25 inches per year at the highest elevations on the North Rim and may be less than 4 inches per year at Phantom Ranch. Exposure is an important determinant of growing conditions: north-facing slopes are cooler and more moist and harbor different plant species than south-facing slopes. In his Life Zone Concept, Merriam described several zones of boreal vegetation; on the North Rim these include Hudsonian and Canadian forests of spruce, fir, some pine, and aspen interspersed with marshy, open meadows. More notable vertebrates of the North Rim include turkeys, goshawks, various woodpeckers, kinglets, nuthatches, Townsend's solitaires, Kaibab squirrels, chipmunks, deer mice, mule deer, black bear, and bobcats. On the South Rim, the Transition Zone ponderosa pine forest is mixed with stands of aspen, pinyon pine and juniper woodland, and open expanses of grassland, sagebrush, and rabbitbrush. Common South Rim animals include golden eagles, mountain chickadees, pinyon jays, common ravens, robins, mule deer, coyotes, and rock squirrels. At and below the Canyon's rims, deciduous and evergreen shrubs predominate, including serviceberry, skunkbush, New Mexico locust, cliff rose, manzanita, and scrub and Gambel's oak. Douglas fir occupies cooler, north-facing ravines at higher elevations where rufous-sided towhees are likely to be encountered. As one descends to the Tonto Platform, increasing aridity causes tree species to be replaced by low shrubs, such as blackbrush, century plants, barberry, and prickly pear. Here the common vertebrates include collared lizards, side-blotched lizards, and western whiptail lizards, rock and canyon wrens, rock squirrels, mule deer, and desert bighorn sheep. Water courses, such as Garden Creek at Indian Gardens, provide sufficient moisture to support Fremont cottonwood, velvet ash, hop-tree, redbud, and willow. The vegetation of the dry Inner Gorge is comprised of Sonoran desert scrub plants, including prickly pear, hedgehog, tiny fishhook, and barrel cacti; desert sunflowers; century plants; banana and narrow-leaf yucca; other low shrubs; and desert grasses. Western collared lizards, side-blotched lizards, chuckwallas, black-throated sparrows, rock and canyon wrens, rock squirrels, and cactus and canyon mice become increasingly abundant at lower elevations. Riverside vegetation is dominated by tamarisk, mesquite, acacia, coyote willow, brickellia, seepwillow, and more than 1,000 other plant species. And 250 families of insects, 28 species of reptiles and amphibians, and 215 species of birds, as well as mice, beavers, small carnivores, mule deer, and bighorn sheep have been reported from this biologically rich riparian zone.

THREE DESERTS

Three of North America's four desert ecosystems converge in the Grand Canyon region. The rims and higher elevations of the eastern Grand Canyon support the low shrub species characteristic of the cold Great Basin Desert of Nevada and Utah. Bigtooth sage and rabbitbrush occupy open valleys between stands of pine and juniper, and shadscale occurs along the upper Colorado River. The hot Sonoran Desert occupies central and southern Arizona and northwestern Mexico. Honey mesquite, catclaw acacia, and other vegetation characteristic of the Sonoran Desert reach upstream into Marble Canyon in the river corridor. Mohave Desert vegetation in the western Grand Canyon includes creosote bush, chollas, and ocotillo (also found in the Sonoran Desert), and blackbrush at higher elevations.

HOLOCENE CLIMATIC CHANGES

The climate of the Grand Canyon region has changed dramatically since the last ice age. From 23,000 to 15,000 years ago conditions were cooler, more humid, and more moist. Glaciers developed on the San Francisco Peaks 70 miles south of Grand Canyon. At that time the Canyon floor was occupied by junipers and ash trees, and the vegetation zones extended as much as 2,700 feet lower in elevation. Pleistocene mammoths, bison, camels, horses, tapir, and giant ground sloths roamed the Colorado Plateau, and Harrington's mountain goats were common in the Canyon. Condors and Merriam's teratorn (a bird with a wingspan of more than 12 feet) soared the skies and roosted in Grand Canyon caves. With the retreat of the Canadian ice sheets from 15,000 to 10,000 years ago, the climate dried out and these magnificent Pleistocene beasts became extinct. Early humans in the region may have played a role in these extinctions. By 8,500 years ago desertification allowed lower elevation and more southerly plant and animal species to extend their ranges northward and elevationally upward. Likewise, boreal species retreated northward and farther upslope. Today the flora of the North Rim is dominated by vegetation characteristic of northern coniferous forests, while the plant, insect, and animal life on the Canyon floor is derived from desert populations found farther to the south. The Grand Canyon has been a meeting place for diverse groups of species in time as well as in space.

BIOGEOGRAPHY

Biogeography is the study of how and why living things are distributed as they are. Biogeographically, the topography of Grand Canyon exerts a powerful influence on the distribution of species, but this influence depends on a plant or animal's habitat requirements, mobility, and its mode of travel. For several plant and animal species, the Grand Canyon is not an important topographic obstacle: one-seed junipers, common ravens, violet-green swallows, deer mice, rock squirrels, least chipmunks, packrats, bobcats, coyotes, and desert mule deer are relatively ubiquitous throughout the Canyon. But for most species and populations, Grand Canyon serves as either a barrier, a corridor, or a refugium.

The Barrier Effect

As a barrier, Grand Canyon prevents north-south dispersal by terrestrial organisms. The Kaibab squirrel occurs on the North Rim and has been evolutionarily isolated from other races of the tassel-eared squirrel by the erosion of the Canyon and recent climatic changes. Similarly, numerous reptiles such as western skinks, sagebrush lizards, and fence lizards are prevented from spreading southward by the harsh desert conditions of the inner Canyon. Southern plateau lizards and other species are prevented from northward population expansion. In the Canyon itself, rock pocket mice are found almost exclusively on the south side of the Colorado River, while their congeners, long-tailed pocket mice, are found on the north side.

The barrier effect also operates at the end of the Grand Canyon. Steep talus slopes and other habitat differences have prevented Joshua trees, desert iguanas, gopher tortoises, and other Mohave and Sonoran desert species from moving upstream into the Canyon from the region west of the Grand Wash Cliffs. Because of its turbulence and silty waters the Colorado River has also proved to be a barrier to upstream dispersal of Sonoran mud turtles and exotic spiny soft-shelled turtles.

The Corridor Effect

As a corridor, the path of the Colorado River provides a route for low desert species to move from the western Arizona desert into southern Utah. Desert riparian plants such as Gooddings willow, netleaf hackberry, tamarisk, seepwillow, and arrow-weed occupy the banks of the Colorado River throughout Grand Canyon. Desert animal species whose ranges extend through the river corridor include the following species: the migratory monarch butterfly; speckled dace and other fish; red-spotted toads, rocky mountain toads, and canyon treefrogs; yellow-backed spiny lizards, western collared lizards, western whip-tail lizards, side-blotched lizards, and banded geckos; migratory waterfowl, raptorial birds, song birds, and other avifaunae; and mammals such as pocket mice, beavers, mule deer, desert bighorn sheep, ringtail cats, and, formerly, river otters.

This corridor effect is incomplete for many species because habitat availability and climate change gradually with distance downstream. Low desert species from the west, whose ranges extend only partway up through the Canyon, include crucifixion thorn, creosote bush, Herbert's giant water bug, gila monster, and zebra-tailed lizard. The ranges of honey mesquite and catclaw acacia extend upriver into Marble Canyon. Leopard frog, white-tailed antelope, and ground squirrel populations extend southward into the Canyon from the Four Corners region. The corridor effect also operates at intermediate elevations in Grand Canyon. The range of black-brush, a Mohave Desert shrub, has extended into the Four Corners region via a corridor at intermediate elevation through the Canyon that includes the Tonto Platform. Scrub oak is also found at intermediate elevations throughout the national park.

The Grand Canyon as a Refuge

The Grand Canyon serves as a *refugium,* harboring plants and animals that are either *endemic* (occurring only in one locality) or extremely isolated. As an island of habitat, the North Rim's boreal forest supports an endemic population of Kaibab squirrel. The Canyon itself harbors several endemic species. McDougall ragweed occurs only in several small tributaries of the Colorado River in the western Grand Canyon. *Octerus rotundus* is a small, semiaquatic water bug that has been found only in Grand Canyon and in the mountains of central Mexico. The rare and endangered humpback chub is now restricted to the Colorado River in Grand Canyon and apparently only breeds at the mouth of the Little Colorado River. The Grand Canyon rattlesnake, *Crotalus viridis abyssus,* occurs only in the Canyon.

The Grand Canyon provides an abundance of several specific microhabitats that support locally common but highly isolated populations. For example, desert seeps and springs host populations of maidenhair ferns, horsetails, cardinal monkey-flowers, helleborine orchids, and other aquatic and semi-aquatic plants and insects. Cave entrances provide another specific micro-habitat for endemic and isolated arthropods, such as harvest-men and spiders.

Black collared lizard. *Photo © George H. H. Huey*

HUMAN IMPACTS ON GRAND CANYON

Human activity has exerted a profound influence on the biology of Grand Canyon. Although 4 million visitors see the Canyon every year, including nearly 40,000 hikers and 22,000 river runners, impacts from visitation are generally localized and are well managed by the National Park Service. Of greater consequence have been the impacts of animal control and introduction programs and the regulation of the Colorado River.

Predator Control on the North Rim

When Teddy Roosevelt proclaimed the North Rim a National Game Preserve in 1906, he secured protection only for game animals, and an intensive predator elimination program began. One bounty hunter, James T. Owens, killed more than 530 mountain lions on the North Rim. A large pack of wolves and thousands of bobcats and coyotes were also killed. Because of predator control, lumbering, cessation of livestock grazing, and other factors, the North Rim deer herd increased from about 4,000 head in 1906 to more than 30,000 head in 1924. A roundup was attempted that year in which 125 men tried to drive 8,000 deer down the Nankoweap Trail and across the river to the Tanner area. Weather and confusion turned against the men, and the drive failed completely. The deer remained on the North Rim where starvation and a general population collapse soon followed.

Introduced Species

A large number of plant and animal species have been accidentally or intentionally introduced to the Grand Canyon region. Exotic rodents, rock doves, house sparrows, and European starlings have reached inhabited areas, and tamarisk, camel thorn, tumbleweed, sweet clover, and red brome and other

grasses have invaded the Colorado River riparian zone. The
National Park Service unsuccessfully introduced pronghorn
antelope to the Tonto Platform in the late 1920s. Introductions
of Gambel's quail and ring-necked pheasants in the inner
Canyon were unsuccessful, but turkeys and chukar were successfully planted on the North Rim. The Roosevelt elk that
occasionally reach the South Rim were introduced to the
Flagstaff area following extirpation of native Merriam's elk.

Feral Burros

Burros were released in the Canyon by prospectors such as
William Bass around the turn of the century, and over the
years the burro population gradually increased. The National
Park Service unsuccessfully tried to remove the herd in some
areas by shooting in the 1940s. In the mid- and late 1970s
researchers concluded that burros were severely damaging
native vegetation in the central and western portions of the
park, and control measures were undertaken. Cleveland
Amory, president of the Fund for Animals, sponsored a
humane and highly effective removal program. By the end of
1981 he and his staff had rounded up 580 burros, which were
driven out of the Canyon on trails, flown out by helicopter,
and floated out on pontoon rafts. The animals were given to
concerned citizens, and a large portion of the herd was placed
on a ranch in Texas. A few burros still roam the Diamond
Creek drainage on the Hualapai Indian Reservation, but the
burro herd has been eliminated in the park.

Regulation of the Colorado River

Glen Canyon Dam has been man's most significant impact on
the Grand Canyon. Located near the end of Glen Canyon,
15 ½ miles upstream from Lees Ferry, Arizona, this massive

gravity arch dam was completed in 1963. It has influenced the Colorado River corridor in Grand Canyon by preventing floods, by trapping sediments, and by decreasing the river's water temperature.

Glen Canyon Dam largely eliminated annual spring floods that scoured away riparian (streamside) vegetation along the river. By preventing floods, the dam has permitted plant life to invade once-barren riverside beaches. The initial plant invader in the river corridor was tamarisk, a widespread exotic shrub accidentally introduced to the Southwest from the Mideast before the turn of the century. After two decades of flood control, native plants such as coyote willow, honey mesquite, seep-willow, arrowweed, and numerous herbaceous species have also gained a foothold in the riparian zone. This profusion of plant life provides food and habitat for numerous species of insects, amphibians, reptiles, birds, and mammals, and is now an extremely valuable, naturalized habitat.

Another change wrought on the Colorado River by Glen Canyon Dam involves sediment trapping by Lake Powell. Prior to the dam, the Colorado River carried as much as 500 million tons of sediment per year through the Canyon. Now these sediments settle out in Lake Powell and the river runs clear green during much of the year. This clear water has permitted a profuse growth of filamentous green *Cladophora* and other algae in the river channel, and this plant life, in turn, supports aquatic arthropods that serve as food for fish, wildfowl, and other vertebrates.

Glen Canyon Dam has also significantly decreased the river's water temperature. Prior to the dam, the water ranged from near freezing in the winter to more than 80°F in the summer. Eight species of native fish dominated the pre-dam river, including the Colorado squawfish, which grew to 5 feet in length and more than 70 pounds in weight. Now the river's water is released from deep in Lake Powell and ranges between 47°F and 65°F. Cooler, less variable water temperatures have extirpated four of the Canyon's native fish species by preventing them from breeding, and has allowed introduced carp and trout to proliferate.

Has Glen Canyon Dam been beneficial or detrimental to the Colorado River corridor in Grand Canyon? The dam produces much-needed hydroelectric power and has, by accident, allowed a lush growth of valuable riparian vegetation to spring up on formerly bare riverbanks. It has greatly increased the value of the river for white-water recreationists and has produced the best trout fishery in the Southwest. Unfortunately, the dam has eliminated half of the native fish species, endangered another, and may have been responsible for the disappearance of the native river otter. Thus the dam has been a mixed blessing for this system. Heretofore it has been operated without much concern for the newly established ecosystem in Grand Canyon, but the Bureau of Reclamation has recently begun to consider how the dam affects this ecosystem and to consider operational modifications that will rectify some of these detrimental effects.

The Grand Canyon exerts a powerful influence on the organisms that live in and around it. Here, as everywhere, we must try to honor all living things and respect their right to an undisturbed existence. The inner Canyon's plant and animal life are somewhat less conspicuous than at other national parks: desert plants flower rarely and most desert creatures are crepuscular or nocturnal and are not usually observed by humans. This means that seeing the life of the Canyon may take a little more time and attention than elsewhere, but one's patience is rewarded with a deeper appreciation for the ability of living beings to survive and proliferate in this harsh and topographically diverse environment.

3 | Geology

by Michael Young

This discussion of the geology of the Grand Canyon is divided into two sections. The first concerns the evolution of the Grand Canyon region and may be subdivided into four topic areas: (1) age of oldest and youngest rock layers, (2) varieties of sediment, (3) discussion of geologic process as it applies to Canyon rock layers taken in ascending order from the oldest to youngest layers as the hiker will encounter them moving from the bottom of the Canyon to the top, and (4) an introduction to the geologic time scale.

The second section is composed of the descriptions of the individual rock layers. These layers are reviewed in descending order as the hiker will encounter them moving down from the rim. Each layer is described on the basis of five categories: (1) chronologic placement in the geologic time scale, (2) thickness of Grand Canyon exposure, (3) color, (4) character—origin (sedimentary, volcanic, igneous), and (5) prominent features recognizable from the trail.

There is then a brief discussion of recent geologic events.

The mileages refer to river miles measured from Lees Ferry. River guides are available at the South Rim Visitor Center.

You will find it helpful to read this chapter with the *Geological Map of the Grand Canyon National Park* (published by the Grand Canyon Association, P.O. Box 129, Grand Canyon, AZ 86023). And don't forget to put it in your pack when you hike the Grand Canyon. Learning the rock layers of the Canyon is one of the great joys of being there.

EVOLUTION OF THE GRAND CANYON

The rock layers of the Grand Canyon bracket a time period that represents fully one-third of the life of the planet. The most ancient rock in the Grand Canyon, in the Vishnu Group, is 1.7 billion years old; the youngest, the Kaibab Limestone, is 250 million years old.

Varieties of sediment—boulders, breccias, cobbles, gravel, sand, silt, mud, clay, organic chards, chemical precipitates—are found in the stone walls of the Grand Canyon. Examination of these sediments reveals their place of origin, direction of travel, and previous form.

The intensely deformed Vishnu Group, for example, with its mineral migrations, crenulations, and intrusions, was originally a combination of deposited sediments and volcanics. Those sediments were laid down in water and transported by water to Proterozoic seas as, until damming, the Colorado built its delta on our continental margin. From ancestral mountains came the sediment to be left in a subsiding (sinking) catchment offshore. Possibly disinterred, intruded, or covered by volcanics, these sediments were finally reinterred to depths of 60,000 feet at 700 degrees Celsius where, under pressure approaching 75,000 pounds per square inch, these volcanics, sands, shales, and limestone lenses were metamorphosed. This is the initial recognizable geologic event in the Grand Canyon. With the onset of this event came the emplacement of igneous plutons (magma that cooled below the earth's surface), the Zoroaster Granites. The metamorphosis of these intrusive igneous bodies gave birth to the foliated Zoroaster Gneiss.

This event lasted for up to 100 million years and was followed by a second episode of metamorphism—and then a third, where low-grade deformation occurred and zones of intensive shearing developed in this Precambrian complex.

These shear zones (i.e., the major faults) in the Vishnu Group were in place before the deposition of the Bass Formation.

For 450 million years there is no sedimentary record to decipher. The Bass Formation is the next datable rock unit, at 1,250 million years old. That 450-million-year gap, equaling one-tenth of the earth's history, is called the "Early Unconformity." (An unconformity is a block of time when the land was above sea level and therefore under attack by atmospheric agents: heat, cold, water, and wind.)

Somewhere in this unconformity emerged an altered terrain to be attacked and worn smooth by the erosive forces of the planet's surface. From the west came the seas, and from the east, sediments—the Unkar Group: Bass Formation, Hakatai Shale, Shinumo Quartzite, Dox Sandstone, Cardenas Basalts. Deposited from approximately 1,250 million to 1,100 million years ago, the rock types vary from oxidized continental sands, silts, and muds to intertidal dolomites and evaporites.

The Cardenas Basalts, deposits up to 1,200 feet thick, were followed by a separate and distinct suite of intrusive events perforating all Unkar sediments with diabase dikes and sills. The Unkar terrain, exhumed after the Cardenas and exposed to weathering, shows the atmosphere's cumulative effects to a depth of 30 feet. For how long were the lavas naked before the elements? Ten million years? Twenty? Onward rushed the waters with Nankoweap Sandstones— ripple marks, mud cracks—over 300 feet of sediment, and the sea was gone once more.

The Chuar Group—Galeros, Kwagunt, Sixtymile formations, reclining on the mildly undulating weathered surface of the Nankoweap—fully 6,000 feet thick, show shallow-water sedimentation with intermittent desiccation—shales, altered limestones, continental sands. Then the Proterozoic, characterized by fossils of filamentous algae, stromatolites (clump algae), and finally megaplankton (floating plant life), came to a close with a major tectonic event. The more than 13,000 feet of material comprising the Grand Canyon Supergroup, emplaced during a 400-million-year moment in earth history, were exhumed from their subsiding home. Thrust skyward as much as 10,000 feet, the blocks of tortured Vishnu with their layered burden were exposed to the ravages of 250 million years. The "Great Unconformity" is the name of this 250 million years that built a range of north-south-trending fault-block mountains 15,000 feet high, then wore them down to a surface that was regular except for some resistant islands of Shinumo Quartzite. The seas from the west—with animals this time, not just plants—inundated the remnants of Precambrian time, and the Paleozoic was on.

To the west lay the open seaway, and what is now the western Grand Canyon was then the continental margin. In multiple pulses the sea covered the Precambrian landscape with the sandstone, mudstone, limestone sequence of the Cambrian Tapeats, Bright Angel, Muav. Nearshore sands, offshore muds, abyssal limes, these layers all thicker in the west, flick their tongues to the east. "Each of the three Cambrian formations is older to the west than it is to the east. This important discovery clinched the case for a marine transgression. It also illustrates that a formation need not be the same age from place to place. The formation is simply a mapable, recognizable unit indicative of a past environment of sedimentation" (Rahm 1974).

Unconformity—125 to 150 Million Years
The erosional surface of the Muav accepted sediments of the Temple Butte Limestone that represent channel fill in the east and a hypersaline lagoonal environ in the west.

Unconformity—25 or 30 Million Years
Virtually pure carbonate sediments were deposited in shallow Mississippian Redwall Limestone seas during three cycles of marine advance and retreat.

Unconformity—20 Million Years
The redbeds of the Pennsylvanian-Permian were deposited in a warm, humid, tropical clime on top of the Karst topography that had been eroded into the surface of the Redwall during the preceding unconformity. Sediments in the Supai become increasingly limey and dolomitized to the west and south-west—more shale and sand components to the east. Four unconformities are found within the redbed sequence, one marking the boundary of each of the formations of the Supai Group and one at the basal boundary of the Hermit Shale. The change from marine to continental sediments during Supai time is indicated by the decrease of limey sediment.

As the semitropical climate that authored the Hermit redbeds changed to a truly desert environ, a dune field carried by north winds engulfed the northern half of Arizona. The Coconino, thickening from a razor edge near the Utah-Arizona line in the north to 50 feet at the upper end of Marble Canyon and 65 feet in the western part of the Grand Canyon, reached a maximum depth approaching 1,000 feet at the Mogollon Rim, the truncated southern limit of the Colorado Plateau.

Again from the seaway in the cordilleran geosyncline to the west, the Toroweap and the Kaibab formations encroached upon this wedge of dune sand. Both formations represent episodic marine transgression, maximum advance and retreat. However, there is an unconformity separating these two formations—hiatus between Toroweap retreat and Kaibab advance. To the east, Kaibab rests on the surface of the Coconino—Toroweap is absent.

A time-change continuum: land, sea, mountain building, liquid eruptions, metamorphic mobilization of minerals, facies changes; and interspersed within this frame, the unconformities-erosive events. (Any formation may differ substantially from one location to another; e.g., a given formation might be sandy nearshore and limey offshore. These differences in character within a single formation are called facies changes.)

Current data show that, at present rates of deposition, shallow marine environs may produce a meter of sand in 1,500 years, shales in 3,000, and carbonates in 7,500 years. At that rate the entire sequence of Mississippian Redwall could have been emplaced in 1.5 million years. What of the balance of time? From Precambrian through Permian, more than 50 percent of the time cannot be documented—900 million years of unconformity!

GRAND CANYON ROCK FORMATIONS

The Paleozoic

Kaibab Formation—Middle Permian—250 m.y.a. (million years ago)—300 Feet
Cream to tan sands and light gray limestone make up the Kaibab Formation. Three internal divisions of the Kaibab, called members, can be recognized. From top to bottom they are (1) Alpha, (2) Beta, and (3) Gamma. The Alpha member is composed of a mixture of redbeds, thin limestones, and some gypsum ($CaSO_4$) beds. The Beta member is massive and forms the cliff that is the Canyon rim. This layer is well expressed within the park but grades from limestone in the west to sandstone in the east (a facies change). There are abundant chert (a silica precipitate) concretions throughout this member. The basal member (Gamma) is a slope-forming

unit with thin alternating beds of sandy, silty, and limey muds indicative of a mobile shoreline in an equatorial sea. East of the park, the Kaibab rests unconformably on the Coconino Sandstone. Marine invertebrate fossils are abundant throughout this formation and include brachiopods, bryzoans, cephalopods, corals, crinoids, crustaceans, fish, gastropods, and pelecypods.

Toroweap Formation—Middle Permian—
260 m.y.a.—to 200 Feet
Tan sands and light to dark gray limestones form the Toroweap, and three members can be recognized within the formation. They are identified with the nomenclature adopted in the Kaibab Formation—(1) Alpha, (2) Beta, and (3) Gamma—and represent a succession of depositional events very similar to those of the Kaibab. The Toroweap cliff, massive in the west, pinches out to the east in Marble Canyon. The Beta member becomes progressively magnesian or dolomitic in the east, indicating a coastal environ cut off from normal oceanic circulation. The gypsum found in concert with continental sediments may represent evaporite deposits from lagoonal environs.

Coconino Sandstone—Early Permian—
270 m.y.a.—50 to 300 Feet
The cream, tan, and ivory sandstones of the Coconino thin to nearly 50 feet both east and west from its maximum Canyon thickness of 300 feet in the vicinity of Bright Angel Creek. A prominent cliff, the Coconino Formation represents eolian origin—sand dunes blown from the north. This pure quartz sand is composed of well-sorted grains frosted by myriad impacts as they traveled southward. Transverse-type dunes frozen in the rock, some 70 feet long, produce cross-beds that dip as much as 34 degrees in the paleo-windward direction. Laminae in

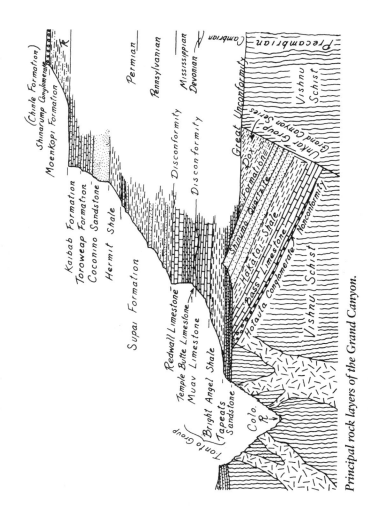

Principal rock layers of the Grand Canyon.

these high-angle beds are graded by wind velocity. Fossil skeletons have yet to be found, though invertebrate tracks and burrows are common.

Hermit Shale—Early Permian—280 m.y.a.—300 Feet
The red shales and siltstones of the Hermit thicken greatly: from 300 feet in the Grand Canyon Village area to more than 1,000 feet in the west. This sequence of redbeds indicates a source in the highlands to the north. Easily eroded, the Hermit forms an almost continuous slope throughout its exposure. In the western Grand Canyon these soft shales have undermined the Coconino cliff, causing its retreat, and have been largely removed from the surface of the underlying sandstone, the Esplanade Formation of the Supai Group. This broad expanse is termed "The Esplanade." The Hermit was deposited in a climate that was at least seasonably wet. Mud cracks and raindrop prints are evident. Fossils from the early Permian flora can be found.

Supai Group—Pennsylvanian—Permian—
300 m.y.a.—600 to 700 Feet
Deep red shaley siltstones and buff sandstones that are stained red on exposed surfaces comprise the Supai Group. The Supai Group has been broken into four formations that represent changes in depositional conditions: from top to bottom, (1) Esplanade Sandstone, (2) Wescogame, (3) Manakacha, and (4) Watahomigi. Both sand facies and shale-siltstone facies become increasingly calcareous to the south and west, indicating that marine conditions existed in those directions. Each formation outlines a cycle of shale-siltstone events capped by a sandstone facies. Continental redbeds diminish to the west and are replaced by more resistant limes that form a more prominent cliff. A dearth of fossils exists in the Supai within the park; however, fern prints and some amphibian tracks

Rock island near the Coconino Overlook on the North Kaibab Trail. Photo © *George H. H. Huey*

attest to a terrestrial origin. A distinctive conglomerate (to 30 feet) at the base of the Esplanade Sandstone is a good marker bed for hikers.

Redwall Limestone—Mississippian—330 m.y.a.—400 to 500 Feet

Light gray limestones with somewhat darker dolomites and white (opaque) lenses of chert form the Redwall Limestone. The Redwall gets its name from the stain of iron oxide on its weathered surface (chert weathers to dark brown). More than any other rock unit, the Redwall is a barrier to hikers in the Canyon. Because it is not weathered to a cliff in any area, ascending or descending the Redwall depends on fault-controlled joints or constructed trails.

Appearing as a single unbroken facade, the Redwall has been divided into four members (top to bottom—Horseshoe Mesa, Mooney Falls, Thunder Springs, Whitmore Wash), each representing a separate depositional cycle. There are six different identifiable sedimentary structures—recrystallized, aphanitic, limestone conglomerate, oolitic, peloidal, and skeletal—which include horizons of both clastic (fragmented) and unbroken fossils, all virtually pure carbonate. Bedding planes are numerous and vary from 2 feet to 20 feet or more. Some beds are highly fossiliferous, while others are void of any fossils, having formed through chemical precipitation of carbonates. Chert lenses are abundant in the Thunder Springs Member and are evident to a lesser degree near the top of the section in the Horseshoe Mesa Member. The Horseshoe Mesa Member, having been exposed to the atmosphere for an extended period prior to deposition of Supai sediment, is honeycombed with solution structures that form a Karst topography (e.g., caves on the west side of Horseshoe Mesa on the Grandview Trail, Vaseys Paradise, Redwall Caverns in Marble Canyon, natural arches, springs, and Cheyava Falls in the Clear Creek drainage). Fossil types to be found in the Redwall are numerous—foraminifers, brachiopods, corals, crinoids, bryzoans, gastropods, pelecypods, cephalopods, fish, trilobites, and algae.

Temple Butte Limestone—Late Devonian—370 m.y.a.—100 to 1,000 Feet

Named for exposures near Temple Butte about 3 miles downstream from the confluence of the Colorado and the Little Colorado rivers, the Temple Butte Limestone represents somewhat of an anomaly. In the eastern Canyon this Devonian interval is represented by freshwater limestone lenses that fill channels eroded into the surface of the underlying Muav Limestone. These channels can be as large as 400 feet wide and 40 to 50 feet deep with a basal pink-to-purple conglomerate layer. Flanking these channels, the Redwall rests directly on the Muav.

Thickening greatly to the west, the limestone becomes dolomitized and is expressed in a well-bedded cliff. These dolomites can run from gray to a distinctive tan-yellow-white combination and thereby constitute a marker bed. A marine fossil assemblage is expressed in the west but to the east there are bony plates identified as belonging to freshwater fish. This Devonian chapter represents the intertonguing of both fresh and saline coastal waters.

TONTO GROUP
Muav Limestone—Middle Cambrian—530 m.y.a.—150 to 800 Feet

The Muav is the youngest of the tripartite Cambrian sequence termed the Tonto Group. These sediments thicken markedly from east to west. The Muav is a series of gray limestone beds separated by greenish gray beds of micaceous shaley mudstones and micaceous siltstones. The upper and lower members of the formation are cliff-forming units, with the basal unit less massive. These are separated by a thinly bedded sequence of calcareous siltstones. Some of these narrow beds are a limestone conglomerate possibly formed by wave action on relatively unconsolidated sediments in shallow seas. Red-brown dolomites in the west trace the marine retreat that left the Muav exposed to Cambrian weather. The erosional surface between the Muav and either Temple Butte or the Redwall exhibits some stream channelization and various solution features. Fossils in the Muav are found primarily in the thin shale-silt beds and include trilobites, brachiopods, algal structures, and ripple marks.

Like the Redwall, the Muav is easily dissolved by flowing groundwater. Waters percolating through the layers above the Muav are halted in their downward movement by the relatively impermeable shales of the Bright Angel which form numerous seeps and several perennial springs, e.g., Thunder River, which flows into Tapeats Creek (Mile 134), and Deer Creek Spring, which flows into Deer Creek (Mile 136).

Bright Angel Shale—Early/Middle Cambrian—
540 m.y.a.—200 to 450 Feet
Composed predominantly of mudstone and fine-grained sandstones, the Bright Angel Shale can be identified readily by its many hues. The mudstones are light green; siltstones are generally gray with brown spots; sandstones range from magenta to pale green to tan; glauconite is bright green; and of course there are gradational changes in color.

The erosion of Bright Angel Shale is the controlling mechanism for the retreat of the Canyon rim. The broad bench eroded into this friable (soft) sediment of the Bright Angel and onto the surface of the underlying Tapeats Sandstone is called the Tonto Platform. Located about 3,000 feet below the

Canyon's South Rim, it is the main east-west trekking route through the eastern Canyon. This terrace thins markedly to the west as the Bright Angel becomes more sandy and less easily eroded and then dips below river level. Representing a mildly active, nearshore coastal environ, the Bright Angel is the central episode in the tripartite advance of Cambrian seas. Fossils to be found are trilobites, brachiopods, casts of worm burrows, and pteropods.

Tapeats Sandstone—Early Cambrian—
550 m.y.a.—100 to 300 Feet
Following the 250-million-year hiatus in deposition termed the Great Unconformity, advancing Cambrian seas covered the existing landscape. The Tapeats sands overlie every Precambrian sedimentary formation and the crystalline metamorphic basement complex. There are several locales where this blanket of sand is pierced (to 800 feet) by islands of Shinumo Quartzite (near Clemente Powell Butte) that were later covered by Bright Angel muds. These islands are surrounded by blocks of quartzite that fell from island cliffs after being undercut by the incessant battering of ocean waves.

The quartzose sands are medium- to coarse-grained and are typically a deep red brown. Weathered surfaces are dark brown, but fresh surfaces are much lighter. The texture becomes finer as the Tapeats grades upward into the Bright Angel. Fossil types include brachiopods, trilobites, and trilobite trails (cruziana). Ripple marks are common in the top of the section where the sands grade into the muds of the Bright Angel. West-dipping cross-bedding in the lower sand units indicates a marine advance from the west on a north-south-trending coast. Tapeats forms the ramparts that guard the shadowed depths of the Inner Gorge and make cross-Canyon travel impossible except through fault-controlled drainages.

The Young Precambrian

Younger Precambrian rock was laid down between 825 and 1,250 m.y.a. Deposits are visible only on the west side of the Butte Fault, named by Charles Walcott "on account of its connection with the origin and development of the six great buttes" that flank the fault on the east from Nankoweap Creek to Tanner Canyon Rapid.

CHUAR GROUP—825 TO 1,000 M.Y.A.—6,400 FEET
Sixtymile Formation—120 Feet
The only exposures of the Sixtymile Formation are in Awatubi and Sixtymile canyons and where it caps Nankoweap Butte. Composed of pebbly sandstones, breccias, and slump structures deposited in a kinetic environ, the Sixtymile joins the balance of the Chuar terrain in filling a drag syncline, a structure associated with movement along the Butte Fault.

Kwagunt Formation—Approximately 2,100 Feet
The Kwagunt is divided into three members: Carbon Butte, Awatubi, and Walcott. The basal layer in the Carbon Butte is a massive red sandstone (an excellent marker bed) on the slopes of Carbon Butte. Resting on this sandstone are red to purple mudstones, which comprise the bulk of this member.

The Awatubi is dominantly shales and mudstones, but again the bottom of the member has a marker unit. This unit consists of a massive biohermal (algal) layer with domelike structures in a dolomitic matrix. A fossiferous layer of black shale is located near the top of this member.

The Walcott Member in ascending order consists of a flaky dolomite, black shales, and thick-bedded dolomites, all exhibiting algal structures.

Galeros Formation—Approximately 4,200 Feet
The Galeros is divided into four members: Tanner, Jupiter,

Carbon Canyon, and Duppa. A dark gray basal marker bed of massive (40–80 feet) dolomite identifies the Tanner Member and therefore the Galeros as a whole. The balance of the member (580 feet) is almost entirely shale. The Jupiter Member repeats the carbonate-shale scenario with thin siltstone-sandstone horizons. The shales are colorful, showing red to purple, blue black, and light green to brown yellow in various layers.

The Carbon Canyon Member exhibits the triplet of limestone, shale, and sandstone throughout the member. Mud cracks and ripple marks are common on the upper surface of the beds. The Duppa Member is primarily argillaceous with scattered limestones and sandstones.

Nankoweap Formation—1,050 m.y.a.—300 to 600 Feet
The Nankoweap is classified separately from both the Chuar and the Unkar groups. Bounded by unconformities, Nankoweap exposures are visible from Basalt Canyon to near the mouth of Carbon Canyon and in Comanche Creek, Tanner Canyon, and neighboring drainages. Ripple marks, cross beds, and mud cracks are evidenced in the white-brown-purple sandstones.

UNKAR GROUP—1,100 TO 1,250 M.Y.A.—
APPROXIMATELY 6,700 FEET
Cardenas Basalts and Intrusives—740 to 1,380 Feet
Due to the 10- to 15-degree NE dip of the fault blocks that they ride, the Cardenas lavas outcrop only in a section from Unkar Creek (Mile 72.5) to Chuar Lava Hill (Mile 65). There is an isolated outcrop at the north end of the trail that follows the Butte Fault 4 kilometers from the Colorado River in the Nankoweap Drainage. To date, fourteen separate flows have been mapped. These are delineated by vesicular zones and thin sandstone layers. The structures found within the flows are described by Breed and Roat (1976): "Scattered throughout

are vesicular horizons, occasional ropy lavas, massive lavas with columnar and fan jointing, and ash layers with bombs. The pillow and sandstone horizons indicate that much of the lava was erupted into shallow water, while the vesicular, ropy, and ash layers suggest temporary emergence." The dark brown to black basalt cliffs of the upper flows grade into a greenish slope at the base of the formation.

Outcrops of the intrusives are more widespread, being visible opposite the mouth of Red Canyon at Hance Rapids, up Clear Creek in Ottoman Amphitheater, along Bright Angel Creek north of Phantom Ranch, up Crystal Creek and along the river in two sections from Bass through Shinumo to Hakatai creeks and from Bedrock through Galloway to Tapeats creeks. The sills range from 60 feet to almost 700 feet in thickness; their composition is primarily medium- to coarse-grained diabase. Perforating all of the Unkar sediments, the sills (horizontal) and dikes (vertical) are predominantly located in the Bass and Hakatai formations. Flanking the sills are zones of contact metamorphism where the surrounding rock was baked following the injection of hot magma. This phenomenon produced local alteration of minerals and accounts for deposits of chrysotile asbestos in the Bass Formation above Hance Rapids and in Hakatai Canyon. William Bass's mine at the contact of the Bass Formation and a diabase sill in Hakatai Canyon (Mile 111) produced asbestos that was shipped to Europe and used in the manufacture of fireproof theater curtains. John Hance's asbestos mine was located in a similar zone of contact metamorphism opposite Red Canyon (Mile 76.5). Hakatai shales were baked to slates in zones up to 15 feet from the contact. These intrusives are fine-grained at their margins due to rapid cooling. Current research indicates that while the intrusives and the lavas are not the same age, they most probably represent successive events with a common parent magma.

Dox Formation—Approximately 1,190 m.y.a.—to 3,100 Feet
The principal exposure of the Dox is in the eastern Canyon
between Seventy-Five Mile and Escalante creeks. This section
illustrates the markedly different responses to weathering and
erosion exhibited by the resistant Paleozoic strata of Marble
Canyon, the extremely resistant metamorphic complex of the
Inner Gorge, and the nonresistant, easily weathered Unkar sediments of the Dox. These gently sloping hills are traversed
south of the river when hiking the Beamer Trail.

The Dox is tentatively divided into four members: Lower,
Lower Middle, Upper Middle, and Upper. The Lower and Upper Middle are arenaceous (derived from sand) while the
Lower Middle and Upper are argillaceous (composed of clays).
The cyclic alternation of sediment types—sands, silts, muds—
indicates a tidal, deltaic, mudflat sequence for deposition. The
Dox consists of oxidized maroon-red-orange mudstones, siltstones, and quartz sandstones, with the exception of a basal
sandstone layer (800 feet) that is light tan to greenish brown.
The formation is overlain by 400 feet of dark brown to green
shales and mudstones. Fossils are restricted to stromatolites,
filamentous algae, and abundant ripple marks, green reduction
spots, mud cracks, and salt casts. Some structures indicative of
deformation prior to lithification include load casts and
slumped bedding. Small-scale cross-beds indicate that sediment
was transported from the west.

Shinumo Quartzite—Approximately 1,200 m.y.a.—
1,100 to 1,350 Feet
Evident only between Papago Creek at the entrance to the Inner
Gorge in the east and Tapeats Creek in the west, the Shinumo is
not a true quartzite, never having been metamorphosed.

The exposures of Shinumo sandstones are not continuous
but are expressed intermittently. The eroded upper surface of

this cliff-forming unit retains resistant "islands" that pierce the Great Unconformity and may continue up-section as far as the Bright Angel Shale. Beds within the Shinumo vary in thickness and character. Well-cemented sands range from poorly sorted to well sorted and coarse to fine. The result of this varied assemblage of sands is an inconsistent cliff with ledgy intervals. Colors found are tan, purple, deep red, rusty brown, and white. The top 400 feet of the formation is a marbled purple and white that can be recognized easily. Load casts and deformed bedding planes (slumped bedding) characterize this upper member. These predominantly quartz sands imply a shallow, high-energy nearshore or shoreline environment for deposition. Cross-beds are abundant throughout; ripple marks, mud cracks, and clay galls are common at specific horizons.

Hakatai Shale—Approximately 1,200 m.y.a.—
550 to 950 Feet
The Spanish Fathers named the river Colorado for the red of its muds; the Havasupai tribe had a name for the Colorado before they came—it was Hakatai. It is most appropriate that the formation with the most exposure of all Unkar Group sediments should be the most brilliantly colored—vibrant orange, red, and purple—and lend its name to the river that carved the Canyon. Similar to the Dox in color and form, the Hakatai is below the Shinumo. Predominantly argillaceous, capped with a thick (200- to 300-foot) bed of poorly consolidated purple sandstone, this formation yields a sloping topography. Whereas the lower contact with the Bass may be difficult to discern because of a transitional environ that interfingers sandstones and conglomerates on top of Bass dolomites, the contact with the overlying Shinumo is sharp and distinct. This basal zone contains interbedded arkosic sand and conglomerates containing metamorphic and volcanic fragments.

The majority of the Hakatai is red (weathered to orange) mudstone and shale, with the color a product of the oxidation of iron-bearing minerals (hematite). The mudstone and shale units are highly fractured. V. Stephen Reed describes this Precambrian time: "The Hakatai Shale was deposited in shallow water with periods of emergence in an arid climate. The mudstones are probably mudflat deposits formed as the sea retreated after deposition of the Bass Formation. The upper sandstones appear to be shallow water deposits laid down shoreward of the mudstones, where energy was sufficient for winnowing."

Bass Formation—Approximately 1,250 m.y.a.—
180 to 330 Feet
Named for William Wallace Bass, the Bass Formation outcrops above Hance Rapids in the east and thence intermittently to the west until Tapeats Creek. The Bass Cliff rests unconformably on the crystalline metamorphic complex of the Vishnu Schist and the Zoroaster complex of intrusives. In the Grand Canyon this break in the record encompasses approximately 450 million years. As the sea encroached upon the stream-cut surface of the Vishnu, waves reworked accumulated gravels and may account for a discontinuous layer of Hotauta Conglomerate, which outcrops primarily in the east and sporadically in the west. The Hotauta Conglomerate (formerly considered a separate formation but now tentatively included in the Bass) consists of a mix of chards from the metamorphics that support it. Thicker in the west, the beds of lime mud, later altered to dolomite by magnesium replacement of calcium, were left by the advancing sea. Marine retreat to the west left shales and muds and possibly some gypsum casts now filled by collapse breccias. Some sands are also seen in the Bass and complete the cycle of depositional environ—from high-energy stream-transported conglomerates, through wave-sorted shore sands and

calm offshore waters precipitating lime muds, to the evaporating brine of stagnant lagoons leaving gypsum. Stromatolites are common in the brown to gray dolomites and typically are preserved as chert. Argillite units vary from red to blue and exhibit mud cracks and ripple marks.

The Old Precambrian

Vishnu Group and Zoroaster Plutonic Complex—
1,700 to 2,000 m.y.a.—to 1,300 Feet

Named for the Hindu god, the Preserver, the Vishnu Group outcrops in Granite Park and in the upper, middle, and lower granite gorges. It is composed of a mix of metamorphosed sediments (sandstone, siltstone, shales, and minor amounts of limestone) with metamorphosed mafic flows (volcanics) and intrusives (dikes and sills). The metamorphic history of these Vishnu metasediments and metavolcanics is extremely complex.

After deposition in a subsiding (sinking) basin these sediments were buried by additional sediment to a depth of approximately 12 miles. At this depth, force was applied from what would now be the west. This directed force may have originated from the collision with or subduction of a wandering plate. Whatever the exact mode for application, these deeply interred sediments were folded tightly, perpendicular to this force. The original clay minerals and quartz sand grains, no longer able to survive in their original form at this depth with temperatures that rise 35 degrees Celsius per kilometer of burial, responded to the intense pressure and were released from their chemical bondage. Mobilized in such manner, the minerals reoriented themselves in parallel planes. This layering of minerals, termed foliation, is characteristic of metamorphic rocks such as schist and gneiss. This erogenic deformation through-prints to the surface with the birth and maturation of mountains. Mountaintops are bent and broken but not metamorphically altered as are the roots. Relict cross-beds from the original sandstones are preserved in these schists. The mafic flows (basalt) and intrusive dikes and sills (diabase) metamorphose to amphibolite and are widely evident in the Vishnu Group as black to dark green bands in an otherwise layered dark gray to gray-green mica-schist with concordant (parallel) white quartz-rich veins.

The Zoroaster Plutonic Complex includes numerous dikes and sills that alternately pinch and swell along their length, plus a series of ten large plutons varying from white to pink in color. These plutons—named for Pluto, Greek god of the underworld—invaded the realm of Vishnu, being emplaced during and after the metamorphosis of the schists. Ranging from quartz-monzonite to quartz-diorite, they are termed "granitic" here. The plutons intruded during the metamorphosis of the Vishnu sediments were further altered to gneiss, while new intrusives remained granitic and nonfoliated. Some of the dikes and sills are pegmatite (coarse-grained), while others are primarily aplite (fine-grained). Large potassium feldspar crystals in the pegmatites are up to 50 centimeters long and indicate a protracted cooling period for the hydrothermal fluids from which they crystallized. These pegmatites may make up from 0 to 100 percent of the total volume of rock, but commonly represent 40 to 50 percent in the zones of most intense metamorphism.

RECENT GEOLOGIC EVENTS

The Grand Canyon continues to enlarge both laterally and vertically. The Colorado Plateau continues to inch skyward, propelled by forces within the planet, aiding the liquid saw of the river in its quest for the base of the Vishnu. But what of the mechanisms that continuously widen the Canyon? "The processes of slab-failure, rock avalanche, rock fall, talus slide, mudflow, landslide, gravity faulting and solution are at present very active in enlarging the Grand Canyon, and there is some evidence that they have at times been even more active in the past" (Ford, Huntoon, Billingsley, and Breed 1974).

Large-scale rotational landslides have been described as "Toreva block" slides by Reiche (1937). There are five within the Canyon; however, only two affect foot travel—these are in Surprise Valley and Tanner Canyon. The Surprise Valley landslide involves approximately 3 to 4 square miles and approximately 1 cubic mile of shattered rock. The trail to Thunder River crosses the slide. This landslide is developed on the Bright Angel Shale at the base of the Muav Limestone. The Muav carries a large volume of water within its boundaries. This water lubricates the shales below and provides a plastic medium that will no longer support the strata above. In this case, approximately 2,000 feet of rock (to the Esplanade Sandstone) broke loose from the supporting cliff. As the blocks slid downhill they rotated backward toward the new cliff face. A similar structure exists adjacent to Tanner Trail.

Due to the profusion of lime deposits in the Canyon and the resultant amount of salts in solution in ground and surface waters, there are many travertine deposits in the Canyon. Numerous examples may be found near the base of the Muav (e.g., near the confluence of the Colorado and the Little Colorado) and throughout the Redwall exposures. Recent river gravels are cemented by these same compounds (e.g., opposite the mouth of Nankoweap Creek).

Keep your eyes open for faults while you walk. They are plentiful in the Canyon and control most of the drainages and certainly all the major geologic features of the plateau surface.

4 | Above the Rim

People come from all over the world to visit the Grand Canyon, and during the peak season of spring, summer, and fall, they come in droves. Each year interpretive rangers at the South Rim's Canyon View Information Plaza and the North Rim's Visitor Center meet with many of the park's 4½ to 5 million visitors.

PLANNING YOUR VISIT

You can make your visit more enjoyable, and the rangers' job a little easier, if you obtain in advance the current edition of *Grand Canyon, The Guide* (call (928) 638-2481, or write Grand Canyon Association, P.O. Box 129, Grand Canyon, AZ 86023). This guide provides a detailed list of visitor services offered at the Grand Canyon, including campground and trailer sites, transportation, service stations and garages, propane dealers, a pharmacy, dental and medical clinics, a U.S. magistrate, a telegraph office, a post office, a bank, a grocery store, showers and laundry, beauty and barber shops, curio and gift shops, kennels, and religious services.

Once there, you can drive around the Grand Canyon, raft through it, hike into it, or just stand and stare at it. But the first thing you should do before planning your trip is decide how much time you can afford to spend at the Canyon and whether you want to spend your time above the rim, below the rim, or a combination of the two.

Maps

There are several maps that will help you prepare for the trip

depart for the Canyon, and help you orient on rim,
trail once you arrive.

d Canyon Map

…e single best map for planning your visit is the 1:100,000
scale U.S. Geological Survey color map called *Grand Canyon*.
It's available free upon your arrival at Grand Canyon National
Park entrance stations, or in advance by contacting Grand
Canyon Association, P.O. Box 129, Grand Canyon, AZ 86023.
Phone (928) 638-7888, or visit www.nps.gov/grca.

Topographical Maps

All of the 7.5-minute and 15-minute quadrangles named at the
end of each trail description can be ordered from the U.S.
Geological Survey by visiting www.usgs.gov.

Geological Map of Grand Canyon National Park

In addition to the topographical maps discussed above, you
would do well to get a copy of the *Geological Map of the Grand
Canyon National Park, Arizona,* and section it into the eight 15-
minute quadrangles that comprise the heart of Grand Canyon
National Park, Arizona: Nankoweap, Vishnu Temple, De Motte
Park, Bright Angel, Powell Plateau, Havasupai Point, Kanab
Point, and Supai. When used with these individual quadrangles
and cross-referenced with each trail or route description, the colorful *Geological Map* is an invaluable reference for the remote,
less-traveled Wilderness Trails and Routes (to order a copy of
the map, visit www.grandcanyon.org or write Grand Canyon
Association, P.O. Box 129, Grand Canyon, AZ 86023).

Heart of the Grand Canyon

If it's not already in your collection, another map worth
acquiring is *The Heart of the Grand Canyon*, compiled by cartographer Bradford Washburn and published by the National
Geographic Society, Washington, DC 20036. This masterpiece

zooms in on the Bright Angel Quadrangle area and colorfully highlights it in great topographical detail.

CAMPING

Camping at the Grand Canyon is permitted only in designated campsites.

At the South Rim, there are three: Mather Campground, located in Grand Canyon Village ($15 per night; call (800) 365-2267); Desert View Campground, located 25 miles east on Desert View Drive ($10 per night; first come, first served); and Trailer Village, located near Mather Campground ($25 per night plus $2 per person; call (888) 297-2757). You can also make reservations in person at either Desert View or Mather campground.

At the North Rim, there is one designated campsite: North Rim Campground near the Transept ($15 to $20 per night; call (800) 365-2267). Group reservations can be made in advance for the summer season, but it is closed in winter.

LATE ARRIVALS: If you've failed to make advance reservations and the campgrounds are full, try your luck at the U.S. Forest Service Ten X Campground, 10 miles south of the South Rim Entrance Station ($10 per night; call (928) 638-2443); the Jacob Lake Campground, at the junction of U.S. 89A and Arizona 67, 32 miles from the North Rim Entrance Station; or the De Motte Campground, 5 miles from the North Rim Entrance Station.

LODGING

At the South Rim, there are six different lodges offering everything from rustic cabins to deluxe accommodations. They are Bright Angel Lodge, El Tovar Hotel, Kachina Lodge, Maswik

Lodge, Thunderbird Lodge, and Yavapai Lodge. Rates vary. For further information and advance reservations, call (888) 297-2757; call (928) 638-2631 for same-day reservations.

Outside the park, five other lodges are located in Tusayan, 2 miles south of the South Rim Entrance Station on Highway 64: Grand Hotel, (928) 638-3333; Grand Canyon Squire Inn, (928) 638-2681; Holiday Inn Express, (928) 638-3000; Quality Inn, (928) 638-2673; and Red Feather Lodge, (928) 638-2414.

At the North Rim, there is the Grand Canyon Lodge. Call (928) 638–2611.

Outside the park, there are four lodges near the North Rim. Starting at the Marble Canyon Bridge on U.S. 89A, they are: Marble Canyon Lodge, (928) 355-2225; Cliff Dwellers Lodge, (800) 433-2543; Jacobs Lake Inn, (602) 643-7232, at the junction of U.S. 89A and Arizona 67; and Kaibab Lodge, (928) 638-2389, 5 miles north of the North Rim Entrance Station. Accommodations outside the park are also available at Kanab, Utah, and at Fredonia and Page in Arizona.

ORIENTATION

One of the first things you'll want to do after arranging for your campsite or other accommodations is to stop at the Canyon View Information Plaza, located 3 miles north of the South Rim Entrance Station. The center's emphasis is on the human history and ecology of the Grand Canyon. Interpretative rangers can answer most of the questions you might have about the Canyon, visitor services, and programs. The center is open from 8 A.M. to 8 P.M. daily in summer. At the North Rim, the Visitor Information Desk is located in the Grand Canyon Lodge at Bright Angel Point. Hours are 7 A.M. to 7 P.M. daily in summer.

MUSEUMS

There are two museums located at the South Rim. The Yavapai Observation Station is located at Yavapai Point, just east of the Canyon View Information Plaza, and features the geological history of the Grand Canyon. It's open from 8 A.M. to 7 P.M. daily in summer. The Tusayan Museum is located 3 miles west of Desert View on Desert View Drive and features the Canyon's archaeological history. Don't miss the Hopi House a few hundred yards east of the El Tovar Hotel, the Fred Harvey History Room in the Bright Angel Lodge, or the Kolb Studio at the Bright Angel trailhead (the studio is open 8 A.M. to 7 P.M. daily).

GUIDED WALKS AND TALKS

The National Park Service offers a series of informative and entertaining programs for the visitor every day. They include the 1 ½-hour-long Sunrise Walk; the Cedar Ridge Hike, a 3 ½-hour hike in and out of the Canyon guided by a park ranger; the Junior Ranger Program, ideal for 9- to 14-year-olds interested in nature; Ask a Ranger; Rim Walks; Nature Walks; and Sunset Walks. (See *Grand Canyon, The Guide* for a list of current walks and talks.) The hour-long Evening Program offers something new each evening. Programs change from season to season. For further details, visit the Canyon View Information Plaza.

READING THE GRAND CANYON

The Grand Canyon Association operates five bookstores on the South Rim: at Canyon View Information Plaza, Yavapai Observation Station, Kolb Studio, Tusayan Museum, and Desert View Bookstore/Park Information. Chartered in 1932, the Grand Canyon Association is dedicated to cultivating knowledge, discovery, and stewardship. Grand Canyon Association bookstores offer a wide variety and enticing selection of nonfiction, photography, and children's books, as well as guides, maps, and postcards. Visit www.grandcanyon.org.

SOUTH RIM SCENIC VISTAS

> If a person does not fear to look into the Canyon and see distance such as he has never seen elsewhere, depth such as he has never dreamt of, and if he becomes lost in shades of gentian and cherry and trout-like silver, watches the unceasing change of hue and form in depth, distance, and color, he will have feelings that do not well go into words and are perhaps more real on that account.
>
> —*Haniel Long*

Once you've gotten your bearings at the Canyon View Information Plaza, you have to take another look at the Canyon—a long one. And take a copy of Hamblin and Murphy's *Grand Canyon Perspectives*.

There are fifteen established panoramic viewpoints on the South Rim, and each offers a different perspective. Watch for the signs identifying each scenic vista.

Park Entrance

Mather Point (7,118 feet)—2 miles from South Rim entrance

Yavapai Point (7,040 feet)—3 miles from South Rim entrance

Desert View Drive

Yaki Point (7,268 feet)—at the head of the South Kaibab Trail

Grandview Point (7,406 feet)—at the head of the Grandview Trail

Moran Point (7,141 feet)—overlooking the New Hance Trail

Lipan Point (7,349 feet)—at the head of the Tanner Trail

Navajo Point (7,498 feet, the highest point in Grand Canyon National Park on the South Rim)—near Desert View

Desert View (7,438 feet)—Desert View Watch Tower

Hermit Road

Powell Point (6,900 feet)

Maricopa Point (6,995 feet)—overlooking the Bright Angel Trail

Hopi Point (7,086 feet)

Mohave Point (6,974 feet)

The Abyss (6,300 feet)

Pima Point (6,796 feet)

Hermits Rest (6,640 feet)—at the head of the Hermit, Dripping Springs, and Boucher trails

Ways to Visit South Rim Scenic Vistas

WALKING: The 9-mile-long Rim Trail between Mather Point and Hermits Rest links each of the scenic vistas. You can hike short stretches of the Rim Trail at various points (see Rim Trail, page 133, for trail distances and shuttle information). The views are exhilarating.

Sneakers or lightweight walking shoes are more than adequate for this trail. If you're not walking off breakfast or dinner, take a snack and a quart of water, and catch the shuttle bus back to the Village Historic District, Canyon View Information Plaza, or other points of interest.

BICYCLING: Bicycles are also an excellent way to visit the scenic vistas along both rims during the summer. But get on the road at daybreak, before the shuttle buses.

SHUTTLE BUSES: Leave the driving to them. Free shuttle buses stop at each of the South Rim's scenic vistas. They depart from the Canyon View Information Plaza and Village Route Transfer every 15 to 30 minutes: the (red) Hermits Rest Shuttle (75 minutes round-trip); the (blue) Village Route Shuttle (60 minutes round-trip); and the (green) Kaibab Trail Shuttle (30 minutes round-trip). See *Grand Canyon, The Guide* for current shuttle schedules and a map.

HIKER'S EXPRESS: The shuttle leaves Bright Angel Lodge and Maswik Lodge during the summer at 5 A.M., 6 A.M., and 7 A.M. and goes directly to the South Kaibab trailhead.

TRANSCANYON SHUTTLE: This shuttle runs round-trip between the North and South rims; call (602) 638-2820.

MULE SUPPORT: If you're not up to lugging a heavy pack down to Phantom Ranch and back, hire a wrangler to load your pack on a mule. Call (928) 638-2631.

NORTH RIM SCENIC VISTAS

Due to the relatively pristine and undeveloped nature of the North Rim, there are only four established panoramic viewpoints there.

Cape Royal (7,685 feet)—22 miles from Grand Canyon Lodge

Vista Encantada (8,543 feet)—on the Cape Royal Road en route to Cape Royal

Point Imperial (8,803 feet)—3 miles off the Cape Royal Road

The view from Lipan Point. Photo © George H. H. Huey

Bright Angel Point (8,255 feet)—a half-mile round-trip by paved footpath from Grand Canyon Lodge

There are also several remote scenic vistas, which are described under "Rim Trails—East" in Chapter 8.

Ways to Visit North Rim Scenic Vistas

HIKING: From the Cape Royal parking lot, you can take the half-mile Cape Royal Trail to both Angels Window and the tip of Cape Royal; or the mile-long Cliff Springs Trail, which starts opposite the Angels Window Overlook and ends at Cliff Springs. The short Bright Angel Point Trail leaves the veranda at Grand Canyon Lodge and ends at the terminus of Bright Angel Point; it makes a fine evening walk.

BUS TOURS: During the summertime, commercial tour buses depart daily from Grand Canyon Lodge to Point Imperial and Cape Royal. Check at the Transportation Desk at Grand Canyon Lodge for fares and schedules.

SCENIC VISTA PHOTO TIPS

Some of the most celebrated color photographs of the Grand Canyon have been taken from its established scenic vistas. By visiting each, you'll be able to get the feel of what photo opportunities are available.

For best results, professional photographers prefer to shoot in the early morning or late afternoon on clear or relatively cloudless days; that's usually when the colors and moods are the most dramatic. If you're shooting just before or after midafternoon, summer thunderstorms can also produce excellent images.

A 35mm (or larger-format) camera, stabilized with a tripod, is best. A polarizing filter is good for reducing or eliminating

Mount Hayden from Point Imperial, North Rim. *Photo © George H. H. Huey*

glare and haze. And you'll want to use a 28mm wide-angle lens if you're trying to capture the breadth of the Canyon.

Don't get so excited about what you're doing that you wander too close to the edge! Grand Canyon rock is dangerously crumbly. Keep an eye on toddlers, and resist the temptation to climb over the guardrails.

Finally, please don't throw your film wrappers on the ground.

AIRCRAFT

Man began flying in the Grand Canyon for the sheer excitement of it in the 1920s. In fact, the first successful landing of any aircraft in the Grand Canyon took place one summer day in 1922 when Commander R. V. Thomas of the British Royal Flying Corps voluntarily landed an airplane on the Tonto Platform near Plateau Point. A. Gaylord writes in *Grand Canyon: Early Impressions:*

> The motor slows down. Thomas waves his hand to the people gathered along the rim high above him. The nose of the plane shoots up. One wing drops. Then the nose topples over and the plane shoots down. The tail wiggles and twists. Down, down, down; five hundred feet, eight hundred feet, one thousand feet—the plane is plunging and whirling to the bottom at a terrifying speed.
>
> Suddenly the motor begins to roar again. The plane has straightened out and now is flying on level course. The most dangerous and yet useful stunt known to aviators has been executed for the first time in the very bowels of the earth! ... stopping about fifty feet from the edge of an 1,800-foot gorge.

What was stomach-in-your-throat excitement for the old barnstormer spelled death over 30 years later for 128 commercial airline passengers, who perished in one of aviation's worst disasters. According to the July 16, 1956, issue of *Life* magazine, "a Trans World Airlines Super Constellation with 70 aboard and a United Airlines DC-7 with 58 aboard had taken off from Los Angeles three minutes apart on June 30. Approaching the Painted Desert, where their scheduled routes were known to cross, they had collided and plummeted over three miles into the Canyon. After both planes had been unreported for several hours, an aerial searcher found two charred and still smouldering smudges high on buff-colored buttes, less than a mile apart near the eastern end of Grand Canyon National Park. It was unlikely that all the victims would ever be found."

Another two decades later, veteran climber and Grand Canyon boatman George Bain was making a remarkable one-day solo ascent of 7,533-foot Vishnu Temple from the river when he discovered—and removed—a .50 caliber copper-jacketed tracer bullet near the bottom of Vishnu's lofty Coconino Sandstone Formation. In the past, pilots from Nevada's Nellis Air Force Base had been reported flying swept-wing jets through the inner Canyon. Bain, who has a degree in mechanical engineering, thinks the shot came from the direction of either 6,406-foot Rama Shrine or 7,349-foot Lipan Point—evidence that at least one of the Canyon's hundred-odd rock temples proved too tempting a target to pass up. Perhaps Department of Defense ballistic experts could shed some additional light on this rare metallic fossil. In the meantime, canyoneers are advised to sport flak jackets before climbing over Vishnu's needle-tipped summit. Flying over the Grand Canyon has literally come a long way from the days of the first barnstormers, and now more than 40 air tour operators carry approximately 300,000 people over and into the Grand Canyon each year. And now it is the rule, rather than the exception, for hikers to see and hear Bell Ranger jet helicopters and twin-engine Cessnas swarming over the inner Canyon's otherwise stone-silent bays and amphitheaters in general, and places like Thunder River, Havasu Creek, and the Corridor Trails in particular. According to writer Dennis Brownridge in an article in *Sierra,* July–August 1986, "An estimated 100,000 tourist planes, helicopters, and military aircraft now fly in and over the canyon each year. In the backcountry their noise is audible 95 percent of the time during the day." What is the bane of the canyoneer, however, has become a boom for air tour operators who, according to Brownridge, haul in an estimated $40 million to $50 million a year. Whatever your own opinion is about this controversial matter, the bottom line is this: 335 people perished in 58 fatal Grand Canyon air crashes between June 30, 1956, and August 10, 2001 (source: *Over the Edge: Death in Grand Canyon*).

How these commercial flights affect the backcountry hiker remains a divisive issue among air tour operators, environmental groups, and park administrators. While air- and rotor-craft have unquestionably played an invaluable role in search-and-rescue operations, as well as contributing to scientific research like helicopter archaeology, what has to be decided is whether commercial airplanes and helicopters are a viable way for visitors to see and experience this natural wonder. The outcome of this debate will set a precedent for future generations and their national parks and wilderness areas. Shall we still use President Theodore Roosevelt's inspired words as guidelines? "Leave it as it is. You cannot improve on it. The ages have been at work on it, and man can only mar it. What you can do is keep it for your children, your children's children, and for all who come after you, as the one great sight every American . . . should see." Or should we administer it as a theme park, so that every man, woman, and child on the planet can go *into* the one and only Grand Canyon—regardless of their age or disposition and the long-term consequences to both this fragile ecosystem and man's atavistic relationship to it? If we do decide every tourist has an inalienable right to visit the inner Canyon, however they do it, perhaps we should salute the intrepid promoter and engineer Robert Brewster Stanton, who proposed building a railroad through the length of the inner Canyon in 1889. If you have an opinion on this controversial issue, write: Superintendent, Grand Canyon National Park, P.O. Box 129, Grand Canyon, AZ 86023.

5 | Below the Rim

What applies above the rim during the peak spring, summer, and fall season generally holds true below the rim when it comes to making reservations for developed or designated campsites, or accommodations at Phantom Ranch. Don't wait until the last minute to make reservations.

CAMPING AND HIKING

Camping below the rim is by permit only; these are obtained through the Backcountry Information Center.

Overnight backpacking fees are $10 per permit plus $5 per person per night. For information, reservations, and a copy of the *Backcountry Trip Planner,* visit www.nps.gov/grca, call (928) 638-7875 (Monday–Friday 1 P.M. to 5 P.M.), or write Backcountry Information Center, P.O. Box 129, Grand Canyon, AZ 86023.

Below the South Rim, Indian Gardens and Bright Angel are two developed campgrounds with staffed NPS ranger stations, privies, emergency phones, and purified water.

Below the North Rim, Cottonwood is the only developed campground.

Designated campsites and at-large camping are listed under each trail and/or route description in this book.

LODGING

Below the North and South rims, Phantom Ranch offers cabin rooms and dormitories for trail-weary dudes and hikers.

Separate men's and women's dormitories include bunk beds, restrooms, and showers. For information, advance reservations, rates, grub, and beer hall hours, call (888) 297-2757.

GUIDED HIKES

Whether it's a brief morning hike down the South Kaibab Trail or a weeklong backpack trip in a seldom-explored area of the park, there are few better ways to see and experience the Grand Canyon than by taking a walk below the rim. Grand Canyon Field Institute offers an exciting schedule of day hiking, backpacking, and river running trips that focus on cultural history, natural history, photography, and wilderness studies. Visit www.grandcanyon.org/fieldinstitute/ for information.

The Sierra Club

The Sierra Club's Outing Department offers weeklong treks into remote areas of Grand Canyon National Park. For information on trip dates, fees, and hiking areas, visit www.sierraclub.org, call (415) 981-8634, or write Sierra Club Outing Department, 85 Second Street, San Francisco, CA 94109.

National Parks Pass

Save money on entrance fees and help the Grand Canyon by purchasing a $50 annual pass; call (888) GO-PARKS or visit www.nationalparks.org.

Grand Canyon National Park Foundation

This nonprofit organization is dedicated to preserving, protecting, and enhancing Grand Canyon National Park; call (928) 774-1760 or visit www.gcnpf.org.

Noncommercial Guided Hiking Groups

Educational institutions, government entities, civic organizations, conservation organizations, and the Boy Scouts and Girl Scouts are generally considered noncommercial groups as long as the leaders' or instructors' salaries are not collected "directly through fees contributed by members of the guided party." If you have any questions regarding the commercial status of your group, contact the Backcountry Information Center (www.nps.gov/grca). Commercial groups need to apply for a one-time Commercial Use License.

RIVER RUNNING

> It has, however, been the good fortune of but a few to be able to journey at the bottom of these canyons, along the only path that is open to man—the raging waters of the river itself—and to look up at the beauties and wonders that nature has formed, piled one upon the other, seemingly to the blue of the sky above; or to live among the stupendous gorges and caverns that have been cut out of the very bowells of the earth, as this mightiest of rivers has carved itself a pathway to the sea.
> —*Robert Brewster Stanton, 1890*

Some 22,000 river runners navigate the Grand Canyon of the Colorado River in whole or part each year. They come from all over the world to experience the wonders and adventures Stanton described and Major John Wesley Powell—some river historians believe it was prospector James White—pioneered. If you have your own river-running gear and the expertise, a private trip through the Grand Canyon is the way to go. But first you must apply to the River Sub-District at Grand Canyon National Park for a permit, and the waiting list for those permits is not a short one. If you have the patience, however, it's worth the wait. (Visit www.nps.gov/grca/crmp for permit information.)

If you're like most folks, however, you probably don't own the expensive gear or have the time to coordinate the food, logistics, and everything else required to put together a successful private river trip—let alone have the patience to wait 5 years or more for a permit—so you might consider booking passage with one of the 17 commercial river-running companies authorized by Grand Canyon National Park to offer trips down the Colorado River. The trip is usually not a difficult one, and has a safety record that's impressive. Outfitters offer an array of different excursions that appeal to nearly everyone, from 3 ½-day trips on bus-sized motorized J-Rigs to 12-day paddle boat adventures and 18-day oar-powered dory expeditions.

Whether oar, paddle, or motorized, these trips are led and navigated by experienced boatmen and -women who wear a variety of different hats in their roles as river guides. A good boatman is part naturalist, historian, geologist, cook, and court jester. And his or her job is to see that you have a safe and rewarding whitewater journey.

The adventuresome should definitely try a paddle trip (see listing). Paddle trips are captained by experienced guides, but passengers actively participate in both propelling and navigating the seven-person raft. Paddle rafts are the one surefire way to experience the power, excitement, and tranquility of the Colorado River.

Whichever type of river trip you choose to take, there is nothing like a two-week-long river trip to engage your soul and rekindle your sense of awe and wonder.

Reserve river trips well in advance.

Grand Canyon National Park Authorized River Outfitters

Key to Trip Types:			
B	Offers both motorized and oar-powered trips	D	Offers dory trips
M	Offers motorized trips only	P	Offers paddle trips
O	Offers oar-powered trips only	K	Offers kayak/canoe support trips
		H	Offers half-canyon multiday trips

ARAMARK/Wilderness River Adventures, Inc.
P.O. Box 717, Page, Arizona 86040
(800) 992-8022; (928) 645-3296; fax (928) 645-6113
www.riveradventures.com
Trip types: B, H, K
Trip lengths: 4, 8, 12, and 14 days

ARIZONA RAFT ADVENTURES, INC.
4050 E. Huntington Drive, Flagstaff, Arizona 86004
(800) 786-7238; (928) 526-8200; fax (928) 526-8246
www.a/raft.com
Trip types: B, P, H
Trip lengths: 6, 8, 9, 13, and 14 days

ARIZONA RIVER RUNNERS, INC.
P.O. Box 47788, Phoenix, Arizona 85068
(800) 477-7238; (602) 867-4866; fax (602) 774-4655
www.raftarizona.com
Trip types: B, H
Trip lengths: 3, 6, 7, 8, and 13 days

CANYON EXPLORATIONS, INC.
P.O. Box 310, Flagstaff, Arizona 86002

Source: Grand Canyon National Park

(800) 654-0723; (928) 774-4559; fax (928) 774-4655
www.canyonexplorations.com
Trip types: O, K, P, H
Trip lengths: 6–9 and 13–16 days

CANYONEERS, INC.
P.O. Box 2997, Flagstaff, Arizona 86003
(800) 525-0924; (928) 526-0924; fax (928) 527-9398
www.canyoneers.com
Trip types: B, K, H
Trip lengths: 3, 5, 7, and 14 days

COLORADO RIVER AND TRAIL EXPEDITIONS, INC.
P.O. Box 57575, Salt Lake City, Utah 84157–0575
(800) 253-7328; (801) 261-1789; fax (801) 268-1193
www.crateinc.com
Trip types: B, P, K, H
Trip lengths: 4, 5, 6, 7, 11, and 12 days

DIAMOND RIVER ADVENTURES, INC.
P.O. Box 1300, Page, Arizona 86040
(800) 343-3121; (928) 645-8866; fax (928) 645-9536
www.diamondriver.com
Trip types: B, H, K
Trip lengths: 4, 5, 7, 8, 10, 12, and 13 days

GRAND CANYON DORIES
P.O. Box 216, Altaville, California 95221
(800) 877-3679; (209) 736-0805; fax (209) 736-2902
www.oars.com/gcdories
Trip types: O, D, K, H
Trip lengths: 5–13 and 15–19 days

GRAND CANYON EXPEDITIONS COMPANY
P.O. Box 0–0509, Kanab, Utah 84741
(800) 544-2691; (435) 644-2691; fax (435) 644-2699
www.gcex.com
Trip types: B, D, K
Trip lengths: 8, 14, and 16 days

HATCH RIVER EXPEDITIONS, INC.
P.O. Box 1200, Vernal, Utah 84078
(800) 433-8966; (435) 789-3813; fax (435) 789-4126
www.hatchriverexpeditions.com
Trip types: M, K, H
Trip lengths: 4, 7, 8, and 10–14 days

HIGH DESERT ADVENTURES
P.O. Box 40, St. George, Utah 84771
(800) 673-1733; (435) 673-1733; fax (435) 673-6696
www.boathda.com
Trip types: B, P, K, H
Trip lengths: 6, 8, 9, and 14 days

MOKI MAC RIVER EXPEDITIONS, INC.
P.O. Box 71242, Salt Lake City, Utah 84171–0242
(800) 284-7280; (801) 268-6667; fax (801) 262-0935
www.mokimac.com
Trip types: B, K, H
Trip lengths: 6, 8, 9, and 14 days

O.A.R.S.
P.O. Box 67, Angels Camp, California 95222
(800) 346-6277; (209) 736-2924; fax (209) 736-2902

www.oars.com
Trip types: O, P, K, H
Trip lengths: 5, 6, 8, 13, 15, and 17 days

OUTDOORS UNLIMITED RIVER TRIPS
6900 Townsend Winona Road, Flagstaff, Arizona 86004
(800) 637-7238; (928) 526-2852; fax (928) 526-6185
www.outdoorsunlimited.com
Trip types: O, P, K, H
Trip lengths: 5, 6, 9, 10, and 13 days

TOUR WEST, INC.
P.O. Box 333. Orem, Utah 84059
(800) 453-9107; (801) 225-0755; fax (801) 225-7979
www.twriver.com
Trip types: B, H, K
Trip lengths: 3, 6, and 12 days

WESTERN RIVER EXPEDITIONS, INC.
7258 Racquet Club Drive, Salt Lake City, Utah 84121
(800) 453-7450; (801) 942-6669; fax (801) 942-8514
www.westernriver.com
Trip types: B, H, K
Trip lengths: 3, 4, 6, and 12 days

WESTERN GRAND CANYON

HUALAPAI RIVER RUNNERS
P.O. Box 246, Peach Springs, Arizona 86434
(800) 622-4409; (928) 769-2219
Trip types: M
Trip lengths: 1 and 2 days

PACK ANIMALS

Horses

The most colorful tale of horseback riding in the Grand Canyon stems from an unconfirmed account in a National Park Service memorandum dated January 11, 1944. About a hundred years ago, the story goes, a ragtag bunch of horse thieves rode from the slickrock canyons of Utah, across sprawling Houserock Valley, to Saddle Mountain near the head of Nankoweap Canyon. They peered into the depths of the Canyon, then spurred their mounts on a daring ride across the fluted terrain of the eastern Grand Canyon to the Colorado River. Swimming their steeds across the wild river, they followed an old Indian route up Tanner Canyon to the South Rim, then headed across the pinyon-juniper country to Flagstaff, 60 miles distant. There they'd raid some unsuspecting pilgrim, then ride hell-for-leather with their stolen stock all the way back across the Grand Canyon to the Utah badlands before turning around and doing it again. Onetime Colorado miner Peter D. Berry claimed that after the gang had shot it out with the sheriff, one wounded man had reached his place at Grand Canyon. Before the man died he confided that a copper kettle at the foot of the Tanner Trail contained the gold collected for the horses.

Whether or not this tale can be verified, both horses and mules played an integral part in the early exploration and history of the Grand Canyon area. Major John Wesley Powell favored the back of a horse when not sitting in the captain's chair of the Emma Dean. So did government bounty hunter Jim Owens, who shot 530 mountain lions on the North Rim at the turn of the century—compromising the tenuous ecological balance between the North Kaibab deer population and mountain lions. Likewise, geologist Charles Doolittle Walcott, who spent the fierce winter of 1882 studying Grand Canyon rock layers.

Horses were also favored by several prospectors-turned-dude-ranchers who guided many of the Canyon's first tourists into the inner Canyon on the backs of these sure-footed animals.

If you prefer saddle leather to Vibram, you can ride your horse into the Grand Canyon, but private stock use is permitted only in a handful of designated areas and requires a Backcountry Permit for both day and overnight trips. Contact the Backcountry Information Center (www.nps.gov/grca) for permit guidelines, written regulations, and a pretrip oral briefing before you put the cart before the horse. The Saddle Mountain, Butte Fault, Colorado River crossing, and Tanner Trail would make one helluva ride!

Mules

> We are the first, and will doubtless be the last, party of whites to visit this profitless locality.
>
> —*Lieutenant Joseph C. Ives, 1858*

More than 100 million people have visited the Canyon since Ives's proclamation, and each year thousands of them experience the Canyon the way Ives did, from the back of a mule.

Below the South Rim, one-day trips go to Plateau Point and back, and two-day overnight trips go to Phantom Ranch and back. Both trips are physically demanding but generally safe and rewarding. The one-day trip includes a box lunch. The two-day trip includes overnight accommodations at Phantom Ranch and a box lunch, hearty dinner, and cowboy breakfast. For further information, schedules, and rates, call (928) 638-2631 or visit the Bright Angel Lodge transportation desk.

Below the North Rim, Grand Canyon trail guides lead dudes and packstrings down the North Kaibab Trail to Roaring Springs, 9 miles round-trip. For further information and reservations call (435) 679-8665.

CLIMBING

> Many of the buttes have never, so far is known, been climbed . . .
>
> —*Joseph Wood Krutch*

An early edition of the Grand Canyon National Park brochure read: "*Climbing in the Canyon is dangerous;* technical experts won't attempt it, so unskilled climbers shouldn't either." Nevertheless, people have been climbing in the Grand Canyon since prehistoric times, and the little-known history of Grand Canyon climbing is as exciting and colorful as that of Yosemite Valley's. To inner-Canyon hikers and trekkers this history is important whether they do any technical climbing in the Grand Canyon or not. The 107 named temples, spires, towers, castles, crests, and buttes—and the 20 to 30 unnamed ones—offer reliable landmarks and orientation points for inner-Canyon travel. They also add dimension and perspective to the Canyon's stunning scale.

Many remote inner-Canyon routes were pioneered by pre-historic, historic, and modern climbers, and this history merits an overview. Archaeological evidence indicates that climbing in the Grand Canyon began approximately a thousand years ago; that's about the time ancestral Pueblo peoples negotiated the descent across the bay from 7,762-foot Tiyo Point on the North Rim and succeeded in climbing to the mesa-top summit of 7,646-foot Shiva Temple. The Pueblo people climbed Shiva Temple, it is believed, for the flint embedded in the Kaibab Limestone that caps many of the Canyon's "islands in the sky." This fact was later confirmed by the American Museum of Natural History's expedition to Shiva Temple in 1937. Led by the museum's curator of animals, Dr. Harold Anthony, and accompanied by American Geographic Society mountaineers, the expedition discovered atop Shiva Temple pottery, crude hand tools, and *yanta* ovens over a thousand years old. They also couldn't help noticing rock cairns left by the late Emery Kolb, onetime Canyon explorer, lecturer, and photographer, who made both the first and second non-Indian ascents of Shiva Temple several weeks prior to the American Museum's ballyhooed "first" ascent. The American Museum had rebuffed Kolb's offer to guide the expedition.

But Dr. Anthony and crew weren't out looking for arrowheads or pot shards, nor were they primarily out to bag a summit. Expedition scientists theorized Shiva Temple's Kaibab squirrel population evolved differently from those on the North Rim because they believed Shiva Temple was cut off from the North Rim by 30,000 years of erosion. Scientists also wondered if perhaps "sidetracked descendants, somewhat different from the mammals living today" didn't exist on Shiva Temple as well. Their scientific findings produced no evidence to support this theory, but in the search they did make the first non-Indian ascent of 7,721-foot Wotans Throne.

In addition to Shiva Temple and Wotans Throne, evidence was discovered by canyoneers Harvey Butchart and Donald Davis that ancestral Pueblo peoples also succeeded in climbing 7,431-foot Elaine Castle and 7,281-foot Guinevere Castle, two Coconino Sandstone temples overlooking the North Rim's Modred Abyss. Who's to say how many other temples the Pueblos or the ancestral Puebloans climbed, whether in search of flint or to harvest yucca, make a spiritual rite of passage, or escape marauding enemies?

Certainly not the scores of prospectors who arrived at the South Rim during the 1800s. Responsible for constructing at least 84 trails that once probed the inner Canyon and many of the accompanying gloryholes, these argonauts were too busy poking around the Canyon in search of the mother lode in the form of gold, silver, copper, asbestos—*some* kind of pay dirt.

Once the asbestos mines played out, it was generally thought that the Grand Canyon was devoid of any significant mineral wealth. Miners like Captain John Hance and William Wallace Bass then took up the more profitable profession of guest ranching and guiding tourists down their hand-forged trails. With the influx of the Canyon's first tourists came the first recorded ascents of Canyon temples. Bass and an unidentified tourist climbed 6,281-foot Mount Huethawli, near the junction of the South Bass and Apache trails, sometime before 1900; an unnamed Hance guest scaled 7,162-foot Coronado Butte, situated between the New and Old Hance trails, in the late 1890s. Several other temples were climbed about the same time by both prospectors and tourists. These are believed to be 6,252-foot Apollo Temple, overlooking Basalt Creek in the trailless eastern Grand Canyon; 4,528-foot Cope Butte, at the junction of the Hermit and Tonto trails; 5,031-foot Dana Butte, above the Tonto Trail at Horn Creek, a few miles west from the Bright Angel Trail; 5,126-foot Sumner Butte, near where climbers sometimes cache water above the Redwall on the Zoroaster Temple approach; 7,344-foot Sinking Ship, overlooking the Old Hance (or "Red Canyon") Trail; and the twin summits of 6,536-foot Escalante and 6,281-foot Cardenas buttes above the Esplanade Formation a few miles down the Tanner Trail. (The Hopi or ancestral Puebloans, however, should probably be credited with the first ascents of both Cardenas and Escalante. There's a prehistoric-Indian route Harvey Butchart discovered that goes over the pass between the two buttes; and it is no more than a half-hour scramble up the east side of either Escalante or Cardenas Butte for the excellent vantage that both provide.)

No matter how you look at it, though, the first postmortem ascent of a Canyon temple goes to W. W. Bass. After his death in 1933, his ashes were scattered from an airplane over 6,711-foot

Holy Grail Temple; sometimes called Bass's Tomb, Holy Grail Temple is perched high above the Shinumo, or North Bass, Trail.

Climbing in the Grand Canyon, however, didn't really get serious until a math professor from Northern Arizona University came along in the fall of 1945 and took his first hike into the Canyon. Little did he know at the time that a lifetime of adventure stood before him. His name, and it's one you shouldn't forget, was J. Harvey Butchart. He was the father of canyoneering. In the more than five decades between Butchart's first hike down the South Kaibab Trail and his death at age 95 on May 29, 2002, he trekked 12,000 miles in the Grand Canyon, much of it off trail; discovered 116 rim-to-river routes (in 1882, geologist Clarence E. Dutton erroneously claimed there were only four, each within a day's journey of the next); and climbed 83 temples and buttes (35 recorded as first ascents).

Butchart had a predecessor, though: Merrell Clubb, a former professor of Old English (specializing in *Beowulf*) at the University of Kansas. Before Butchart climbed Shiva Temple in 1957, his first, Clubb had already climbed 10 temples and was laying the groundwork for first ascents, like 5,401-foot Cheops Pyramid, 7,344-foot King Arthur Castle, and others. The most important of these was probably 7,533-foot Vishnu Temple, the largest and highest detached mountain in the Grand Canyon.

But these were what some modern Grand Canyon rock climbers sometimes call "dirt piles." Nobody really got into ropes and ironmongery until September 1959. Enter Dave Ganci, a onetime adventurer who'd worked his way on a tuna boat all the way to Valparaiso to climb Peru's 20,000-foot Nevada Laredo. When the giants of Yosemite rock climbing like Warren Harding, Royal Robbins, and Yvon Chouinard were putting up the Valley's first multiday routes on the glacier-polished granite walls of El Capitan, Half Dome, and Sentinel Rock, Ganci was exploring the Grand Canyon. He thought if he could adapt the rock-climbing techniques he learned in Yosemite to sandstone climbing, and use the Alpine-style climbing tactics he'd used to climb peaks in Peru's Cordillera Blanca, it might be possible to do the Canyon's "first real rock climb." His objective was the one temple that's greeted everyone who's ever peered over the tip of the South Rim, the then-unclimbed 7,123-foot Zoroaster Temple.

The actual rock climb would present only half the challenge. At the time, not even Butchart had discovered the key to getting through the formidable Redwall barrier. Ganci and his partner, Rick Tidrick, did much probing, backtracking, and reascending, and used most of their precious water supply pioneering what is now the standard 4th Class approach through the Redwall Formation. It was a remarkable accomplishment, especially considering the loads they were carrying and the season. Even during September, the climb up to the base of Zoroaster Temple is not considered one of the more pleasant Canyon treks. Sunrise to sunset, the entire route burns under a relentless sun; in the Zoroaster Amphitheater late summer, that means 100°F+.

Once atop the Redwall, Ganci and Tidrick were faced with vertical and overhanging sections of Supai Sandstone to pick their way through—eventually arriving exhausted at Zoroaster's base at the end of day two. The following morning, still suffering from the approach march, they quickly picked out what they thought to be Zoroaster Temple's weakest line, on its north side. With marginal climbing gear and a quart of water apiece, Ganci and Tidrick climbed through the heat of the day and into the late afternoon of day three. Still three full pitches below the summit, the dynamic duo came to grips with the Big Decision: to retreat, or to bivouac where they were and try to finish the climb the next morning. They were out of water and possibly, just possibly, the quart of water each of them had remaining in their packs several hundred feet below would get them all the way back down to Phantom Ranch, where they could drown themselves in the beer hall that evening.

Knowing others were "standing in line to do Zoro," Ganci and Tidrick burned their bridges.

Their summer of skulking around Phoenix's Sonoran Desert in training paid off. At 11:05 A.M. on September 11, 1959, Dave Ganci and Rick Tidrick completed the first ascent of what is now regarded as *the* classic Grand Canyon climb.

Once Butchart and Clubb had pioneered many of the Redwall breaks and 3rd and 4th Class temples, and Ganci and Tidrick had demonstrated technical climbing techniques in the Grand Canyon, the temples started to fall. One by one, more than 40 temples, both technical and nontechnical, were climbed for the "first" time by the likes of Clubb, Donald Davis, Butchart, Allyn Cureton (who set the record for running the 20.6 miles from the North Rim to the South Rim in 3 hours and 56 minutes), and others. Butchart established yet another climbing record by topping out on five different temples in six days during July 1965: 3,945-foot Chuar Lava Hill, 6,200-foot Espejo Butte, 4,242-foot Lava Butte, 6,252-foot Apollo Temple, and 6,281-foot Venus Temple on the Canyon's east end.

During the same period, Ganci and Hughes Airwest pilot Jerry Robertson were making plans for yet another technical first ascent; this time it was 5,411-foot Mount Sinyella, which looms over heavily traveled Havasu Creek on the Canyon's west end (now a part of the Havasupai Indians' Traditional Use Area and off-limits to non-Indians because it is revered by traditional Havasupai as a sacred mountain). After three separate attempts over a period of five months during the first half of 1969, Ganci and Robertson finally reached the summit of this truly majestic temple, only to discover a 4-foot-high cairn and a note: "UCLA 1958." They were not amused.

Nor was it the last time temple climbers discovered summit cairns while pulling down a "first ascent." As late as 1977, climbers have found human artifacts atop several other Canyon temples. After several prior attempts by experienced Flagstaff climbers, Jim Ohlman and his party eventually succeeded in climbing 5,031-foot Dana Butte, a grungy Redwall Limestone temple situated 2,000 feet below the South Rim's 7,086-foot Hopi Point. Once on the summit of Dana, the Ohlman party discovered large pieces of weathered hemp rope. Butchart wrote, "In 1919, one of the Canyon's more ambitious entrepreneurs wanted to build a scenic tramway across the Canyon . . . from Hopi Point down to Dana, across the river to the Tower of Set, and back up to Tiyo Point." A cross-Canyon Tyrolean traverse!

Led by Larry Trieber, one of Arizona's most prolific rock climbers, the 1970s in the Grand Canyon turned into a mad scramble for anything that hadn't already been climbed. Close to 50 temples were climbed for the first time, with Trieber and crew doing high-standard 5th Class first ascents of 5,584-foot Malgosa Crest, 8,121-foot Brady Peak, 6,711-foot Holy Grail Temple, and 7,200-foot Wolf Pinnacle—all at the 5.8 level or above; Butchart claiming nine 4th Class ascents; and Ohlman, the latest tornado on the scene, pulling down nine 4th and 5th Class temples for a total of 61 temples during this period.

Ganci, accompanied by fellow Phoenix climber Chuck Graff, displayed his usual tenacity and inherent reptilian qualities by doing the first ascent of the difficult-to-reach-from-either-rim 6,761-foot Angels Gate on March 30, 1972.

During the 1970s few climbers from outside the immediate Southwest had actually climbed in the Grand Canyon—the known exceptions being a group of British Columbia climbers who did the first ascent of 6,071-foot O'Neill Butte, at the end of Cedar Ridge on the South Kaibab Trail, and Brits Pat Littlejohn and John Mothersele, who put up the difficult (5.10) Book of Genesis, also immediately off the South Rim.

Larry Trieber best encapsulated why a growing number of rock climbers sought out the Grand Canyon during the heyday of first ascents. "The problems of climbing temples in the Grand Canyon are as complex as those found in remote mountain ranges. Only the climbs are located in a vast canyon, and are on desert mountains." When doing the first ascent of Holy Grail Temple with Bruce Grubbs in 1977, Trieber came *this* close to causing Bass Tomb to be christened the official North Rim boneyard. While leading Holy Grail's final pitch, Trieber pulled on a large rock that happened to be the keystone for the tons of loose rock behind it. Straddling the funnel (5.8) with a hand and foot on each wall, Trieber watched in horror as an avalanche of sandstone debris and rubble cascaded between his legs—expecting at any moment to be swept to his death.

Trieber survived his close brush to complete the last major first ascent, up 6,377-foot Kwagunt Butte (overlooking Horsethief Trail) with Dennis Abbink, Jim Haggert, and Bruce Grubbs on March 24, 1979.

With first ascents of all but a handful of temples having been recorded, climbers began doing new routes on Canyon temples, primarily on Coconino Sandstone plums like 8,362-foot Mount Hayden, the southwest face of Zoroaster Temple, 7,212-foot Buddha Temple, and others. An exception to these Coconino temples was the first ascent of 6,800-foot Comanche Point Pinnacle, the Lost Arrow Spire of the Grand Canyon, done by Trieber and Grubbs. These climbs, along with George Bain's lightly equipped, one-day solo ascents of equally remote temples like Mount Sinyella and 5,248-foot Mount Akaba, set the tone and style for climbing in the Grand Canyon during the 1980s.

Access and Resources

Because the North Rim has eroded back from the river three to four times farther than the South Rim, most temples are situated on the north side of the Colorado River; the majority are located within the Vishnu and Bright Angel quadrangles. Many temples are best approached from the South Rim, while others can only be approached from the North Rim. All demand careful logistical planning; preplanned water sources and caches; great competence in finding inner-Canyon routes; and grace under pressure when it comes to moving over exposed ground and trailless terrain with a heavy pack.

Be prepared for long and difficult approaches. What looks like a feasible route on your map is often barred by at least one of the Big Five formations, and frequently more: Kaibab Limestone, Coconino Sandstone, Supai Sandstone, Hermit Shale, Redwall, Temple Butte, and Muav limestones, and the Grand Canyon Series (Tapeats and Archaen). Lastly, be careful not to burn your bridges: The inner Canyon can be as unforgiving as any high-altitude objective.

It is worth noting that the North Rim is usually buried under a half-dozen feet of snow from December through April. So unless your objective can be reached from the South Rim—necessitating a river hitchhike or tenuous mattress float through dangerous currents and breath-stopping 48°F water if your route doesn't cross the Kaibab Suspension Bridge—be prepared to wait until the snow melts or to make a 40-mile ski tour one way from Jacob Lake.

Permits are no longer required for climbing in the Grand Canyon; however, you must still get a Backcountry Use Permit for overnight trips (www.nps.gov/grca).

In the back of this book, "Climbers of Temples and Buttes in the Grand Canyon Region" includes each temple's name, quadrangle maps it's located on, the predominant kind of rock it's composed of, its elevation, and the name and (when known) date of the first-known ascent party. An excellent way to familiarize yourself with these key features of Grand Canyon topography for backcountry travel is to get a copy of Hamblin and Murphy's *Grand Canyon Perspectives: A Guide to the Canyon Scenery by Means of Interpretive Panoramas* and the appropriate topographical map, which will make the terrain and the Canyon's scale more comprehensible once you're in the field.

CAVING

A necklace of Grand Canyon caves, swallowed by sheer cliffs, have kept a secret about 12,000 years old: These were the dining nooks of carrion-eating condors.

—*Carle Hodge, Arizona Republic.*

In 1984 the National Geographic Society funded a scientific expedition into the Grand Canyon. The party was led by zoologist Steve Emslie, who believed caves in the Redwall Limestone might have been Pleistocene nesting areas for prehistoric condors. Emslie's scientific hunch was right. According to Carle Hodge, the expedition spent 35 days in the Canyon, climbing up to and rappelling into dozens of caves—discovering in no less than seven of them remains of condors that Emslie believed may be related to modern California condors.

The fact that Emslie and his crew were able to discover and collect well-preserved remnants of this ancient bird can be attributed not only to his scientific skills, but also to the remoteness and aridity of these caves, as well as to the undisturbed nature of their interiors. It's one of the primary reasons caving, or spelunking, in the Grand Canyon requires special permission from the Resources Management Division and a Backcountry Use Permit. For further information, write: Chief, Resources Management Division, P.O. Box 129, Grand Canyon National Park, AZ 86023.

6 | Hiking the Grand Canyon

From the standpoint of biogeography, hiking a Corridor Trail out of the Grand Canyon is the equivalent of traveling from northern Mexico to central Canada. More often than not it's a journey that's done in a single day: first through the Lower Sonoran Life Zone at the Colorado River up to the Tonto Plateau; then, as you climb higher, the Upper Sonoran Life Zone, which generally includes that area from the Tonto Plateau up to both North and South rims; the Transition Life Zone atop both rims, comprising ponderosa pine forests; and the Canadian and Hudsonian Life Zones beginning at around 8,000 feet atop the North Rim.

What was it like for the Canyon's ancient inhabitants to make that journey, the rim-to-river-and-back hikes most people do in the Grand Canyon today? Nobody knows for sure. But one thing is certain: the days of the ancestral Puebloans are over, and with them has gone the mode of traveling simply, efficiently, and in harmony with the natural rhythms of the Canyon. And no one is more disheartened by that fact than myself, but the signs are everywhere, from the trampled shallows of Elves Chasm in the western Grand Canyon to the high-altitude garbage dumps on 29,035-foot Mount Everest.

We expand our horizons and seek out that one spot where no one else has stood before. But someone *has* been there and left archaeological remnants: toilet paper hanging on trees and shrubbery, a fire ring the size of an ancestral Puebloan granary, space-age Mylar soup packages, #10 institutional food cans, dead trout in a stream awash with fecal coli and biodegradable soap . . .

The list of affronts against Mother Nature is endless because many backcountry users think the canyon is a garbage disposal capable of digesting the swill and artifacts of modern humanity. It is not. Gone are the days when you could pitch camp with little regard for the environment or those who follow in your footsteps. Our once-vast planet has become a global village, and this fact is nowhere more evident than in our nation's wilderness areas and national park backcountry areas. In a recent year, nearly 30,000 backpackers hiked Corridor Trails to overnight at Phantom Ranch and nearby Bright Angel Campground. Unfortunately, we are part of the problem, and unless we exercise more care the pristine oases dotting the inner Canyon will become further inundated by a tumultuous avalanche of litter and noise.

But nobody wants to flee the harness of civilization only to have their wilderness experience restricted by government regulations: not you, and certainly not me. But we are, as boatman and conservationist Rod Nash wrote in the July 1978 issue of *National Geographic*, "loving the Grand Canyon to death. We must protect it from its friends." His sentiment was echoed by W. E. Garrett in the same issue when he wrote "the children's children for whom [Theodore] Roosevelt wanted to save the canyon are here. We're hiking and boating through the park with a Malthusian vigor that Roosevelt couldn't have anticipated. We wear heavily on the trails, the ecology, and each other's tempers."

As a result, several patient and prescient rangers and administrators at Grand Canyon National Park were forced to establish and enforce a list of Backcountry Use Regulations to both lessen and redistribute our impact on the inner Canyon's fragile ecosystem.

A WORD ABOUT BACKCOUNTRY RANGERS

Of all the National Park Service jobs at the Grand Canyon, few are as stressful as the backcountry ranger's. Many people think these chosen few get paid to hike all over the Grand Canyon, trumpeting the call of the wild. Their responsibility, however, is twofold: to protect both the Canyon's nonrenewable resources and your well-being, while maintaining the wilderness experience you seek.

Unfortunately for these rangers, most of their hiking time is spent in an overcrowded trailer called the Backcountry Information Center (BIC). Sitting there listening to the phone ringing off the hook, the squawking of the NPS radio, and the questions of hikers lined up 20-deep reminds one of frantic air-traffic controllers trying to land jumbo jets on a foggy runway, or waiting at the local travel agency while booking transportation and lodging the week before the Super Bowl. During the peak spring hiking season, the pace inside the BIC is no less frantic, because the Grand Canyon *is* the Super Bowl of America's national parks.

Of the 4½ million people who visited the Grand Canyon in 2003, millions walked into the Canyon View Information Plaza. Who knows how many of them walked up to the Backcountry Information Center to ask about "taking the mulies down the stairs" or to find out where they could get a trailer hookup or camping space. The job of the Backcountry Information Center is to orient you about the hazards, peculiarities, and rewards of hiking in the Grand Canyon, and to issue permits. But the sheer number of hikers the backcountry rangers are forced to deal with would make most people cave in from the pressure.

On any given day, these patient rangers—and there are real

human beings inside those Smokey the Bear outfits—will field hundreds of questions in German, Japanese, French, and English. Many are the same tired old questions because people didn't take the time to visit the website or to read the information that was mailed or handed out to them. Rangers answer hundreds of letters, emails, and phone calls each day, and they issue hundreds of permits for overnight camping. If they had a presidential-sized staff, that'd be one thing. But this work has to be done by a handful of rangers who, like you and me, would rather be hiking in the Canyon than dealing with an arrogant 20-year-old who thinks he can hike to Phantom Ranch and back with five hours of daylight left.

Why would someone choose so stressful a job? Fortunately, there are people dedicated to protecting this incomparable resource and to seeing that hikers don't get in over their heads. And when their pace slows down to a modest hum, this glamorous job always affords rangers the opportunity to patrol the backcountry to pack out other people's trash, clean the toilet-paper streamers out of the brush, or zip somebody up in a body bag.

So next time you walk into the Backcountry Information Center burning a short fuse because *you* didn't believe the rangers when they tried to explain how difficult hiking in and *out* of the Grand Canyon is, or because you've been waiting since sunup with 55 other backpackers who didn't make advance reservations, try to smile. These fine people deserve that much. It's because of them that your hike in the Grand Canyon is still a rewarding wilderness experience.

The Backcountry Information Center is temporarily located in a parking lot near Maswik Lodge. It is open seven days a week, 8 A.M. to noon and 1 P.M. to 5 P.M.

BACKCOUNTRY PERMITS

A BACKCOUNTRY USE PERMIT IS REQUIRED FOR ALL OVERNIGHT BACK-
COUNTRY USE. YOUR PERMIT *MUST* BE IN YOUR POSSESSION WHILE IN
THE BACKCOUNTRY. 36 CFR 2.10(B)8

"Why do I have to get a permit, when the Canyon's so
big?" is a frequently asked question.

In the words of Grand Canyon boatman and climber
George Bain: "Before the Park Service enforced regulations for
river running, beaches were being trashed out from garbage
and porta-potties [20 tons of human feces a year!]. Before the
Park Service enforced hiking permits, people were climbing
trees for firewood and shitting next to creeks. So, many of
their regulations were a response to overuse and abuse—born
more out of people's ignorance than anything else. What
would you do if trail-head limitations were lifted and you went
for a hike down the South Bass expecting solitude, only to discover 45 other hikers down there with you?"

There are three ways to obtain a Backcountry Use Permit:
by email, by mail, or in person at the Backcountry Information
Center on the North or South rim. Visit www.nps.gov/grca,
call (928) 638-7875 (Monday through Friday 1 P.M. to 5 P.M.),
or write Backcountry Information Center, P.O. Box 129,
Grand Canyon, AZ 86023.

PLANNING YOUR TRIP

Before you request a Backcountry Use Permit, there are a number of things you should consider—not the least of which is
where and when to go. To help you determine where to go, you
should familiarize yourself with the Backcountry Zoning and
Use Areas, Use Area Limits and Length of Stay, and Area Clo-
sures detailed in the *Backcountry Trip Planner* (see page 62).

When planning your hike into the Grand Canyon, you should also take into account backcountry visitation figures, which will give you some indication as to the availability of permits for specific trails and routes and what kind of solitude you can expect, and, of course, you should consider the weather.

Weather

Ask any farmer or rancher who's knee-deep in bills—and that's most of them, unfortunately—what he thinks of weather predictions. Or ask a Bureau of Reclamation hydrologist why, with all the scientific weather data beamed out of orbiting satellites, no one was prepared for the record precipitation of 1982–83—precipitation that nearly spilled over the top of Glen Canyon Dam.

There may be recognizable weather patterns and cycles the Grand Canyon hiker can use as guidelines, but the weather itself is always subject to change. Trying to predict the weather in the Grand Canyon is no easy matter. In hiking down any rim-to-river trail or route, you're dealing with the climatic equivalent of hiking from a Canadian forest to a Mexican desert in a day.

Mid-February on the Bright Angel Trail can mean postholing through snowdrifts or slipping on ice near the top of the switchbacks; rain at Indian Gardens in the early afternoon; and maybe shirtsleeve weather by the time you reach Phantom Ranch. What happens if you reverse the scenario? You're lying on a picnic table at Bright Angel Campground, basking in the warm winter sun, reading the rocks, and it's getting about time to hike out. Assuming the weather holds—something you really can't predict from the bottom of the inner Canyon (so check the bulletin board at Phantom Ranch Ranger Station)—

you'll be hiking from this oasis to the top of a 7,000 foot mountain in winter conditions. If the weather closes in on the inner Canyon, which it does every few years, the snowline can drop all the way down to Phantom Ranch. Now let's hike down the same trail in late July and early August. You can be wearing a jacket at the top of the Bright Angel Trail; be drenched by a summer rain or have your hair stand on end from St. Elmo's fire a few hundred yards out from Indian Gardens; and be stripped to your skivvies, burning your way through a heat-induced mirage, by the time you drag yourself through the sand to the Phantom Ranch beer hall. Going out the same trail the next day (it's imperative you start hiking no later than 5 A.M.!), you might be doused by violent monsoons at Phantom Ranch, walking across the Tonto in your swimsuit trying to catch a few rays, and pelted by hail or drilled by lightning by the time you reach the top of the South Rim. Weatherwise, the best rule of thumb is to hope for the best but be prepared for the worst.

For up-to-date weather information call the National Weather Service, (602) 774-3301, or the Backcountry Information Center, (928) 638-7888.

Visit Grand Canyon National Park's real-time weather cam at www.nps.gov/grca. For winter road conditions and high-profile-vehicle wind warnings, call the Arizona Department of Public Safety at (602) 779-2711.

The following table and synopsis are taken from averages at GCNP and should be used only as guidelines.

Weather Synopsis

SOUTH RIM: March can be cold and windy. April, especially late April and early May, seems to be the most fickle time of year for Canyon weather, no matter where you're hiking in the park. (I've been snowed on, sunburned, and snowed on

TEMPERATURES AND PRECIPITATION (FAHRENHEIT AND INCHES)

Average:	South Rim			North Rim			Inner Gorge		
	Max.	Min.	Precip.	Max.	Min.	Precip.	Max.	Min.	Precip.
January	41	18	1.32	37	16	3.17	56	36	0.68
February	45	21	1.55	39	18	3.22	62	42	0.75
March	51	25	1.38	44	21	2.63	71	48	0.79
April	60	32	0.93	53	29	1.73	82	56	0.47
May	70	39	0.66	62	34	1.17	92	63	0.36
June	81	47	0.42	73	40	0.86	101	72	0.30
July	84	54	1.81	77	46	1.93	106	78	0.84
August	82	53	2.25	75	45	2.85	103	75	1.40
September	76	47	1.56	69	39	1.99	97	69	0.97
October	65	36	1.10	59	31	1.38	84	58	0.65
November	52	27	0.94	46	24	1.48	68	46	0.43
December	43	20	1.62	40	20	2.83	57	37	0.87

again all in the same week.) June is normally dry, hot, clear, and breezeless. Sudden, frequently violent thunderstorms are not uncommon during July and August. Autumn is short and, like spring, can be fickle: warm and sunny one day, cool and cloudy with a breeze blowing the next. The first snowflakes usually start falling atop both rims about the end of October, but snowfalls don't normally become a serious factor until Thanksgiving. Winter days are clear and crisp during stable weather, and cold and stormy during unsettled conditions.

INNER CANYON: The inner Canyon is a desert. Summertime temperatures range from 100°F to 110°F during the day, accompanied by hot upstream winds blowing midafternoon. The 4 to 15 inches of precipitation annually recorded at Phantom Ranch generally fall in the form of rain during July and August monsoons and January rains. However, storms on the rims can unexpectedly slop over into the inner Canyon at any time of the year.

NORTH RIM: The Kaibab Plateau receives up to 30 inches of precipitation annually, most of it falling in the form of about 100 inches of snow. Consequently, the North Rim's paved access roads are closed from late October to early May. The North Rim is approximately 1,500 feet higher than the South, and its weather is generally cooler and wetter. Summer days on the North Rim are usually clear and crisp, with periodic thunderstorms during July and August. Even in direct sunlight the days can be cool, and the nights are biting. There's nothing like the warm days of an Indian summer on the North Rim during the more stable weather of late September and early October. Whatever happens on the South Rim during late fall, winter, and early spring happens about twice as hard on the North Rim.

TRAINING

Admission into the incomparable land below the rim does not come easy, nor is it without its own hazards. But if you prepare yourself physically, spiritually, and intellectually, you'll come out of the Canyon under your own power with unforgettable experiences.

Whether you're a veteran backpacker with thousands of miles under your Vibrams, a dedicated long-distance runner, or a rank beginner, you'll find hiking in the Grand Canyon unique. It is the reverse of mountain climbing.

First you breeze into the Canyon (probably carrying a duffel-bag-sized pack), get tired, and camp. Then you try to crawl out, your legs screaming with each step, the air growing thinner with each switchback. Don't overestimate your own abilities, and don't underestimate the arduous nature of inner-Canyon foot travel, or canyoneering. Far too many hikers still make these mistakes: Grand Canyon park rangers report an average 400 search-and-rescue incidents every year, most involving people on their first hike in the canyon (see Deadly Hazards, page 115).

Get in shape before you come to the Grand Canyon.

Physical Training

At the turn of the nineteenth century, the Havasupai elder Sinyella was quoted on his training methods. "When I was about six years old my father said, 'Do not sleep after sunrise; wake as soon as daylight appears. Run toward dawn. You should do this every day. Run out as far as you can. Do not walk; run. Do this always when you are a young man too. Then you will be able to run fast, and when you race with someone you will win. If you do not, you will be beaten.'"

That kind of advice may have worked for generations of Havasupai, Hualapai, Hopi, Navajo, and Paiute who lived in and around the Grand Canyon because, for most, running, travel, trade, hunting, religion, and spiritual quests were part of the fabric of their lives. But the vast majority of us—even those holed up in the remote outposts of the United States—are inextricably linked to city life. And while there is no question that a regular program of running and cycling will improve our general condition for canyoneering, increase our red blood cell mass for aerobic activities such as hiking uphill, and strengthen our legs for the demands of inner-Canyon foot travel, there's probably no better general training advice to follow than that of the preeminent Everester, Sir Edmund Hillary: "The only way to get in shape to climb mountains is to climb mountains." And the same holds true for canyoneering. However, most of us do not live near enough to the Grand Canyon or canyon country to use canyoneering as a viable form of training for our first big Grand Canyon hike. Whether you train by mountain biking, trail running, or backpacking, you need to simulate the following in your training:

- The *total distance* you plan on hiking in the Grand Canyon over the same—or shorter—period of time, carrying an equal amount of weight.

- The *total elevation gain and loss* of your proposed hike. For most rim-to-river trails and routes, figure a vertical mile down and up; double that for the popular rim-to-rim-to-rim Bright Angel, North Kaibab trek. Hike up a mountain that has a similar elevation gain and loss; if it has only a 2,500-foot vertical elevation gain, hike it twice.

- The *environmental conditions* of your proposed hike. You wouldn't want to train for a hike down the Hermit Trail in May by limiting all of your training to cycling or jogging through the local city park near sea level during cool spring weather. By the same token, you wouldn't want to train for a multiday trek on the Tonto Trail (a desert) in the still-warm month of October by limiting all of your training to the boggy Sasquatch forests of the Northwest or the hickory-stippled slopes of Wisconsin's Kickapoo Valley. So plan your first Grand Canyon hike or two in an environment and season your body is already physiologically adapted to, and one you're psychologically prepared for.

"Expect nothing, be prepared for everything," a sage Japanese master once said. If you apply that concept to the rest of your physical training for canyoneering, you should cover all the bases. In addition to simulating distance, total elevation loss and gain, environmental conditions, and hiking pace, your training should be well rounded enough so that you can comfortably deal with those unexpected situations that always rear their little heads while hiking a Grand Canyon Wilderness Trail or Route. You may have planned a comfortable hike down one of the nonmaintained miner trails, but Mother Nature usually has a way of rearranging the topography, so you should be physically trained to climb under and over fallen trees and scramble over boulders with a pack on. You can supplement your regular aerobic base of exercise such as cycling, running, or hiking with those kinds of activities that will condition your abdomen (where the movement of uphill hiking begins) and upper body. You may prefer calisthenics or swimming, as many triathletes do; ballet, modern dance, or aerobics, as did Bjorg Austrheim-Smith (four-time women's champion of the Western States 100-miler run across California's Sierra Nevada); or yoga and martial arts as others do. Add a thrice-weekly routine of bent-knee sit-ups, plus push-ups and/or pull-ups, and you still won't be too well trained for the physical demands of Grand Canyon hiking.

Psychological Training

Many backpackers are outdoor enthusiasts and adventurers—independent, strong-willed, right-brained performers who have their own ideas about breaking through the barriers of physical discomfort—that nonetheless maintain a firm footing in the cerebral wildland of endurance activity. But there are a few psychic techniques we can take from the spoonbenders and firewalkers if we learn how to apply them to both our training and canyoneering. Perhaps the best known of these is the *power of positive thinking*—the notion that you can set your mind to the goal of hiking in and out of the Grand Canyon, and enjoy it. Another technique is *disassociation*, which many long-distance runners use to remove themselves from the physical elements of running in order to enjoy the aesthetic qualities of their journey. Try looking at the scenery and daydreaming the same way you do on a long automobile drive. *Concentration* is the flip side of disassociation. Use it when you're hiking a trail so narrow and precipitous—like the Boucher Trail along the Hermit Formation in winter, or the Beamer Trail after a good rain—that even momentarily taking your focus off the trail or the physical act of hiking could cause you to fall. If you practice concentrating on lifting, moving, and simply placing your feet, it will prepare you for the precipitous and exposed nature of canyoneering. Buddhist practitioners call it *mindfulness*. *Previsualization* of your proposed hike before you go will also help stretch your psychic muscles, so once you're in the Grand Canyon you'll be psychologically equipped to deal with whatever emotions arise.

Another important psychic technique to use when canyoneering is what I call *segmenting*. When American rock climber Bev Johnson became the first woman to climb El Capitan's imposing 3,000-foot-high Salathe Wall solo, she said, "The only way to eat an elephant is one bite at a time." And I've found that this holds true for running end-to-end through the Grand Canyon or inner Canyon. If you gaze up at the South Rim from Phantom Ranch and say, "I've got to make it all the way up *that* today!" the big picture may overwhelm you. But if you look at hiking little pieces of it, the climb out is more manageable. For instance, first concentrate on making it up to the Tonto Formation. Then, after you've taken a reasonable break, focus on the next leg or series of switchbacks, and so on and so forth until you've finally topped out on the South Rim.

GEAR FOR THE PACK

Most hikers have their own system or way of doing things when it comes to food and gear. Still, there are several specific items that will make your Grand Canyon hike safer and more enjoyable. An internal-frame or soft pack is generally preferred for hiking nonmaintained Wilderness Trails and trans-Canyon Routes, primarily because it rides lower and fits your body better and thus makes negotiating precipitous ledges and rugged sections of trail easier and safer. Antiquated external-frame packs have a tendency to catch wind, or act as a kite, and they frequently bang against rock overhangs—and the last thing you need on an exposed Canyon trail or route is to be thrown off-balance.

Know your fluid requirements. If you prehydrate by drinking several quarts of water, you can probably make it to Phantom Ranch in the wintertime on one gallon of water. During the summertime, if you prehydrate with three or four quarts of water the evening before (so your urine is clear the morning of your hike), it'll still take you two gallons of water (more if you're not acclimated) to reach the South Rim from

Phantom. You have to either carry that water or cache some of it on the hike down. Many hikers and runners add electrolyte replacement drink powder to their water to replace precious minerals lost through profuse sweating. You'll also find this helpful for canyoneering, particularly in the warmer months. Always carry and cache more water than you think you'll need.

The following equipment list was compiled by GCNP backcountry rangers. For further information, see the *Backcountry Trip Planner* (page 62). For last-minute gear and equipment needs and rentals, visit the Canyon Village Marketplace general store on the South Rim.

Suggested Equipment for Grand Canyon Overnight Hiking

THE ESSENTIALS: Water; purification tablets: iodine, chlorine, or water purification pump; extra food; hat; sunscreen; sunglasses; topographic map; compass; flashlight; signal mirror and whistle; pocket knife; first aid kit: bandages, tape and surgical adhesive, moleskin, antiseptic, Ace bandage; nylon cord; safety pins.

CLOTHING: Appropriate for season. Remember—guard against wind, wetness, and cold. Dress in layers! Bring only what you actually need, but keep the weight down! Shirts: heavy and light; pants: heavy and light; socks: 2 pairs heavy, 2 pairs light; boots or hiking shoes—broken in; underwear.

FOOD: Meal items: well balanced, high in carbohydrates; snack items; vegetables and fruits (can be dried); drink mixes (e.g., ERG, Gatorade).

KITCHEN/COOKING: Stove; fuel; cooking pot(s); plate, bowl, cup, knife, fork, spoon; can opener; matches (strike anywhere); salt, pepper, and other spices; plastic food containers; plastic bags.

SHELTER: Poncho or rainsuit; lightweight tent; sleeping bag or bedroll and foam pad; ground cloth.

SANITATION ITEMS: Toilet paper and trowel; biodegradable soap; trash bags to carry out your paper.

PERSONAL ITEMS: Toothbrush and paste; comb; washcloth; lip balm; foot powder; insect repellant; needle and thread; camera and film.

Suggested Substitutions for Winter

CLOTHING: Wool, polypro, or pile caps, sweater; pants, socks, underwear, gloves or mittens; shirt and wind/rain parka; rainsuit; waterproofed boots; gaiters and instep crampons; light, waterproof tent; winter sleeping bag; space blanket.

HIKING BELOW THE RIM

Caches

If you plan to hike down the Tanner Trail or one of the other rim-to-river trails, spend a day at the river, then hike out the same trail, consider using a water cache. Unless you enjoy carrying the additional 16 pounds (2 gallons) of water as a workout, there's really no practical reason to carry everything you're going to need for the hike out all the way down to the river. So select one or two spots along your descent route—say one-third and two-thirds of the way down—where you can cache food, water, and other essentials for the return hike. Make sure your food is animal-proofed, and keep your water in the shade.

Method of Travel

During the summertime—absolutely the worst time of the year to hike into the Grand Canyon—it is imperative you leave the

TRAIL DESIGNATIONS

The Grand Canyon's 14 established rim-to-river trails and routes and its principle trans-Canyon trails and routes total more than 330 miles. Most have been officially designated as either a Corridor Trail, Wilderness Trail, or Route. Corridor Trails are maintained, clearly marked, rugged but easy to follow, and patrolled by backcountry rangers. Wilderness Trails are non-maintained, less clearly marked, rugged and more difficult to follow, and patrolled less frequently. Routes often follow the lay of the land such as a geological fault or terrace, are sometimes marked by cairns, are more rugged, exposed, dangerous, and difficult to follow, and are seldom patrolled.

South Rim Trail	Designation	Mileage to Colorado River
	Rim-to-River	
Bright Angel Trail	Corridor Trail	9.3
South Kaibab Trail	Corridor Trail	7.3
Hermit Trail	Wilderness Trail	9.3
Grandview Trail	Wilderness Trail	8.0 (Horseshoe Mesa Loop)
South Bass Trail	Wilderness Trail	7.8
Tanner Trail	Wilderness Trail	10.0
Boucher Trail	Wilderness Trail	10.5
New Hance Trail	Wilderness Trail	8.0
Old Hance Trail	Route	9.0

Trail	Designation		Mileage
	Trans-Canyon		*End-to-End*
Tonto Trail	Wilderness Trail & Route		95.0
Beamer Trail	Wilderness Trail & Route		9.0
Escalante Route	Route		10.0
Apache Trail	Route		20.0 (approximately)
	Havasupai Land		*Mileage to Colorado River*
Hualapai Trail	Wilderness Trail & Route		18.0
North Rim			
Trail	*Designation*		*Mileage to Colorado River*
		Rim-to-River	
North Kaibab Trail	Corridor Trail		14.2
Bill Hall Trail	Wilderness Trail		12.0
Thunder River Trail	Wilderness Trail		15.0
Nankoweap Trail	Wilderness Trail & Route		14.5
North Bass Trail	Wilderness Trail & Route		14.0
	Trans-Canyon		*End-to-End*
Clear Creek Trail	Wilderness Trail		8.7
Butte Fault ("Horse Thief Trail")	Route		20.0 (approximately)

river or Phantom Ranch no later than 5 A.M. in order to beat the heat to the Tonto Formation. So eat hearty and pack everything except your sleeping gear the night before. If you sleep in and get caught on the Tonto in the heat of the day, wait until noon passes before you start walking again. In wintertime you might want to sleep in a bit, but you should be on the trail by daybreak so you're hiking during the warmest part of the day. The last mile or two out, most South Rim trails tend to be icy and treacherous during winter months due to their shaded northern exposures.

Hiking Techniques

Most Grand Canyon pilgrims have a tendency to walk very guardedly when descending into the Canyon, mainly because the awesome breadth and exposure can be so unnerving. This tendency leads to locking the knee at each and every step. Knee and hip joints just can't take that kind of repeated stress—especially when you're carrying a pack. So before you get to the Canyon, try the *shuffle* when hiking downhill on one of your training hikes. Relax your body and legs and waddle from side to side, so the downhill torque and stress are absorbed in your calves and quadriceps instead of your ankle, knee, and hip joints. If you fall while hiking downhill, which happens to the best of us, fall uphill onto your buttocks. There are many places in the Grand Canyon where a simple fall can prove fatal.

Almost the opposite holds true for hiking uphill out of the Canyon. Going up, use the *rest step*: take a short- or moderate-length step, then lock your knee so your body is resting on the skeletal structure of your leg while the opposite leg is taking the next step. Lock, rest, step, and so on until you're all the way out. Otherwise, if you have a tendency to just march on out without locking your knees, the constant churning of the leg muscles can be exhausting.

WATER

> We have run out of food and water. God help us. We're trying to get to water.
>
> —*Incident report, Grand Canyon National Park*

They never made it, and the note those two hikers left before they fell to their deaths is a cry that's been echoed around the world for as long as humans have tried to cross the Earth's great deserts on foot. But the Grand Canyon isn't merely a desert; it's an inverted desert mountain range, and its relatively few reliable water sources can be far more difficult, precipitous, and dangerous for the uninitiated to reach than those cool, deep wells and fly-infested seeps that sustain life in the comparatively flat deserts of the Gobi, the Sahara, and the more forgiving arid reaches of the Southwest.

Historically, Native American runners and traders like the Mojave, Hualapai, Havasupai, and Hopi traveled long distances across northern Arizona, frequently under dire conditions, to trade bighorn sheepskins or red ochre paint for seashells, turquoise, pottery, and other precious, easily transportable goods. They were able to endure their arduous trading forays to one another's distant villages not only because they were well conditioned and had a photographic knowledge of the terrain, but also because they planned their journeys to link one perennial or seasonal water source to the next. You would do well to emulate the practice by planning your own inner-Canyon trek so it links one known water source with the next.

Water Treatment

A study completed in 1980 by the University of Arizona's School of Renewable Resources concluded that all side streams in the Grand Canyon, as well as the main stem of the Colorado River, need to be treated before drinking because of high fecal-coli counts. Of the numerous methods backpackers use to treat drinking water, the most widely practiced now is the use of a water purification pump. If you suspect your water source may be home to the intestinal amoeba Giardia—a safe bet in the Canyon—you may opt to pack a chlorine or iodine crystal kit. That's assuming you're not sensitive to iodine and have not been treated for hyperthyroidism; if you have any doubts, it'd be safer to boil your water—but that requires time and fuel. Investigate the best method of water purification for yourself before your hike.

Water Sources

Colorado River
For canyoneers using rim-to-river trails and routes that have no reliable springs or seeps, the Colorado River is the only water source to replenish depleted reserves. Use the water treatment methods described above. If Paria Canyon or the Little Colorado Gorge is flooding, the Colorado River will become heavily laden with sediment. If you need to use this water because it's your only, or best, water source, and you're not dying of thirst, let the water stand until the sediment has had time to settle before pouring it into another container for treatment.

Perennial Water Sources
According to the Cooperative National Park Services Resources Studies Unit, "Sources are classified as perennial on the basis of detailed historic records indicating the source has not gone dry within historic times or on the presence of maidenhair fern." The list on pages 104–107 has been compiled from their study "An Inventory and Classification of Surface Water Resources in Grand Canyon National Park, Arizona," the Western Speleological Institute's "Technical Note #36," the Backcountry Information Center's "Water Sources in Grand Canyon National Park," and the author's field research, maps, and notes.

Seasonal Water Sources

If you are planning an inner-Canyon trek that does not link together a sufficient number of reliable perennial water sources to ensure a safe and rewarding outing, I strongly advise you to plan your trek so it coincides with the late-winter and early-spring runoff, when a larger number of tributary drainages may be running with water. If you're looking to do a high-country trek near the North or South Rim, July and August monsoons can generally be relied upon to supply some marginal water sources in the form of water pockets before they succumb to evaporation. However, lightning, flash floods, and the smothering heat present their own hazards during the summer. The tributary drainages listed on pages 108–109 have been recorded as having seasonal water, but this list should be used only as a planning aid. It's imperative that you check these water sources with the Backcountry Information Center.

Emergency Water

If you're running low on water (although you should never allow yourself to get into that situation), and you're prevented—by either distance or some geological barrier—from reaching either the Colorado River, a perennial or seasonal water source the BIC has confirmed in advance is reliable, or a developed water source on either of the rims, you have several alternatives *during the wet seasons*. Rain frequently collects for short periods of time in wide, but shallow, rain pockets on broader sections of the Tapeats Sandstone, Esplanade Sandstone, and Hermit Shale. Zip-locking bags are best for removing water from these shallow "kiss tanks." If you're not in the vicinity of any of these formations, you can pretty well surmise from the list of perennial water sources that your best bet is to look for indicator plants (like maidenhair fern) in the Muav Limestone, Bright Angel

(continues on page 110)

PERENNIAL WATER SOURCES

Warning: Conditions in the backcountry continue to change. Check first with the BIC on the latest status of these water sources and others before betting your life on them. The BIC maintains up-to-date files on backcountry water sources based on ranger patrols and hiker reports.

Below the South Rim

From the Little Colorado River in the east end of the Grand Canyon at River Mile 61.5, proceeding west to Havasu Canyon at River Mile 156.5.

Name	Location	Source
1. Little Colorado River	River Mile 61.5, east end of Beamer Trail	Blue Springs
	(Warning: High radioactive spill in Rio Puerco tributary. Also, due to high concentration of carbonates, water is difficult to stomach. Do not use long term.)	
2. JT Spring	Hance Canyon, east arm of Grandview Trail	Muav Limestone
3. Grandview Spring	Hance Canyon, east arm of Grandview Trail	Muav Limestone
4. Grapevine Creek	East fork of Grapevine Canyon, off Tonto Trail	
5. Burro Spring	Pipe Creek, on Tonto Trail west of S. Kaibab	Bright Angel Shale
6. Pipe Spring	Pipe Creek, Tonto Trail west of S. Kaibab	Bright Angel Shale
7. Garden Creek	Bright Angel Trail	Muav Limestone
	(Don't drink! High fecal coli. Use developed water sources.)	
8. Monument Creek	Tonto Trail, 10½ miles west of Indian Gardens	

9. Hermit Creek	Tonto Trail, 2½ miles west of Monument Creek	
(Don't drink! High fecal coli. Use Colorado River.)		Esplanade Sandstone
10. Santa Maria Springs	Hermit Trail, below junction of Dripping Springs Trail	Coconino Sandstone
11. Dripping Springs	Boucher Trail, mile west of Hermit Trail junction	
12. Boucher Creek	Boucher Trail, upstream of Boucher Creek camp	
13. Slate Creek	Tonto Trail, 5 miles west of Boucher Creek camp	Muav Limestone
14. Turquoise Canyon	Tonto Trail, 11½ miles west of Slate Creek	Bright Angel Shale
15. Copper Canyon	Tonto Trail, 4½ miles west of Bass Canyon	
16. Royal Arch Creek	Below Apache Trail	Elves Chasm
(Don't drink! High fecal coli from lower and middle Elves.)		
17. Forster Canyon	River Mile 123, river left (facing downstream)	Bright Angel Shale
18. Hundred and Fortymile	River Mile 140, river left	Bright Angel Shale
19. Olo Canyon	River Mile 145.5, river left	
20. Matkatamiba Canyon	River Mile 148	
21. Havasu Creek	Havasupai Indian Reservation	Havasu Springs
(Don't drink! Semi-treated sewage pumped into creek below Supai.)		
22. Havasu Springs	Havasupai Indian Reservation	Supai Group

(continues on next page)

PERENNIAL WATER SOURCES (continued)

Warning: Conditions in the backcountry continue to change. Check first with the BIC on the latest status of these water sources and others before betting your life on them. The BIC maintains up-to-date files on backcountry water sources based on ranger patrols and hiker reports.

Below the North Rim

From Little Nankoweap Creek in the east end of the Canyon at River Mile 52, proceeding west to Kanab Creek at River Mile 143.5.

Name	Location	Source
1. Vaseys Paradise	River Mile 32, river right (facing downstream)	Redwall Limestone
2. Buckfarm Creek	River Mile 41, river right	Muav Limestone
3. Nankoweap Creek	Nankoweap Trail along Nankoweap Creek	Muav Limestone
4. Cliff Spring Formation	Cliff Spring Trail below Cape Royal	Toroweap
5. Clear Creek	Clear Creek Trail, east end	North Rim
6. Bright Angel Creek	Bright Angel Campground *(Don't drink!* High fecal coli. Use developed water sources.)	
7. Phantom Creek	N. Kaibab Trail, 2 miles north of Phantom Ranch	Muav Limestone
8. Ribbon Springs	N. Kaibab Trail, 5½ miles north of Phantom Ranch	Muav Limestone
9. Transept Spring	Transept Canyon, north of Cottonwood Campground	Muav Limestone

10. Roaring Springs	N. Kaibab Trail, 10 miles north of Phantom Ranch	Muav Limestone
11. Crystal Creek	North Rim trans-Canyon route, Crystal Creek	Tapeats Sandstone
12. South Big Springs	West of Big Springs Canyon at head of Shinumo Creek	
13. Shinumo Creek	River Mile 108.5, river right	Muav Limestone
14. White Creek	Below east side of Muav Saddle	
15. Hundred and Twentymile Creek	River Mile 120, Blacktail Canyon, river right	
16. Bedrock Canyon Creek	River Mile 130.5, river right	
17. Galloway Canyon Creek	River Mile 131.5, river right	
18. Stone Creek	River Mile 132, river right	
19. Tapeats Creek	River Mile 133.5, river right	
20. Tapeats Spring	Tapeats Cave above Thunder River confluence	Muav Limestone
21. Thunder River	Thunder River Trail at Tapeats Creek confluence	Muav Limestone
22. Thunder Spring	Thunder River Trail, below Redwall	Muav Limestone
23. Deer Creek	River Mile 136, river right	
24. Deer Spring	Surprise Valley Trail, below Redwall	Muav Limestone
25. Unnamed seep	River Mile 138, river right	Tapeats Sandstone
26. Kanab Creek	River Mile 143, river right	

SEASONAL WATER SOURCES

The following tributary drainages have been recorded as having seasonal water. However, this list is to be used only as a planning aid. Never trust this information without first checking with the Backcountry Information Center. The BIC maintains up-to-date files on backcountry water sources based on ranger patrols and hiker reports. (*Tinajas* are rock cavities that collect rainwater.)

Below the South Rim (East to West)

Name	Location	Comments
1. Tanner Canyon	Fork below Desert View	Marginal, off trail
2. Seventyfive Mile Canyon	West fork	Difficult to reach
3. Red Canyon	Below point trail descends Redwall	
4. Cottonwood Creek	Middle fork	In reeds (not O'Neill Springs)
5. Boulder Creek	Marked by spring	Marginal
6. Lonetree Canyon	Marked by spring	Marginal
7. Cremation Canyon	East wall	Marginal
8. Horn Creek		More reliable
9. Salt Creek		Marginal
10. Ruby Canyon	Above Tonto Trail	*Tinajas*
11. Serpentine Canyon	Above Tonto Trail	*Tinajas*
12. Bass Canyon	Bedrock tanks	
13. Garnet Canyon		*Tinajas*

14. Chemehuevi Point   Seep west of point above Apache Trail
15. Fossil Bay, main arm   Seeps below Coconino
16. Keyhole Natural Bridge   Spring to west

Below the North Rim (East to West)

Name	Location	Comments
1. Kwagunt Creek		More reliable
2. Sixtymile Creek	Near Butte Fault	Marginal
3. East fork of Carbon Creek		Avoid seep; may be toxic
4. Lava Canyon	Runoff	
5. Basalt Creek	North of where map says "Basalt"	
6. Unkar Creek	Runoff	
7. Asbestos Canyon	Below Tonto Formation in main arm	
8. Vishnu Creek	Near Tonto Formation	Runoff and *tinajas*
9. Trinity Creek	Near Tonto Formation	Stomach-wrenching
10. Dragon and Crystal creeks	Runoff	
11. Tuna Creek	Runoff	
12. Powell Spring		Marginal
13. Saddle Canyon	Below Muav Saddle	Runoff and *tinajas*
14. Tuckup		May be difficult to reach from river
15. Cottonwood Spring	In upper Tuckup	

Shale, Redwall Limestone, or whichever formation is in the closest proximity to your location.

Again, don't plan extended hikes away from perennial water sources at any time of the year unless you know *exactly* what you're getting yourself into. Assuming you can find any barrel cactus, you will not be able to stomach eating all the pulp it takes to replenish massive fluid depletion.

WATER REQUIREMENT CHARTS

A. Number of days of expected survival in the desert, no walking at all

Max. daily shade temp., in °F	Available water per person, in U.S. quarts					
	0	1	2	4	10	20
120	2	2	2	2.5	3	4.5
110	3	3	3.5	4	5	7
100	5	5.5	6	7	9.5	13.5
90	7	8	9	10.5	15	23
80	9	10	11	13	19	29
70	10	11	12	14	20.5	32
60	10	11	12	14	21	32
50	10	11	12	14.5	21	32

The importance of temperature reduction to the survivor is highlighted by the following in Chart A: Temperature 120°, water available 2 quarts, days of expected survival 2; reduce the temperature to 100°, and 2 quarts of water will extend your life expectancy THREE TIMES. This importance to a potential "survivor" cannot be overemphasized. Night travel, or better, NO TRAVEL, is stressed.

At equal temperatures, the body requires two to three times as much water to maintain water balance in the desert as it requires in the jungle with its high humidity.

Dehydration: An increase in body temperature of 6 to 8 degrees above normal (98.6) for any extended period causes death (from *The Physiology of Man in the Desert*, by Adolph & Associates).

B. Number of days of expected survival in the desert, walking at night until exhausted and resting thereafter

Max. daily shade temp., in °F	Available water per person, in U.S. quarts				
	0	1	2	4	10
120	1	2	2	2.5	3
110	2	2	2.5	3	3.5
100	3	3.5	3.5	4.5	5.5
90	5	5.5	5.5	6.5	8
80	7	7.5	8	9.5	11.5
70	7.5	8	9	10.5	13.5
60	8	8.5	9	11	14
50	8	8.5	9	11	14

EFFECTS OF LOSS OF BODY FLUID

Loss	Effect
2½%	Dehydration commences
5%	Nausea
6–10%	Giddiness, headaches, limbs itch
15%	Death imminent in 90-degree weather
25%	Death even in cool climates

The preceding water requirement charts should be used as a guideline for your fluid requirements, with the qualification that section B was based on walking at night over relatively flat desert. (Don't walk at night in the Grand Canyon unless you know what you're doing and where you're going.)

Water Requirements

If you look at the big picture of hiking in the Grand Canyon, you'll see that the greatest number of potential hazards that can befall both the unwary and experienced backpackers are water-related, and they may involve either too much of it (in the form of a flash flood), or not enough.

By far the highest number of unfortunate hiker-related incidents have to do with *not enough water,* primarily because too many hikers choose to do their inner-Canyon hiking during the hottest and driest months of the year. But even those hikers who plan their outings for the relatively cool months of April and May are still faced with the prospect of heat cramps, heat exhaustion, and frequently deadly heat stroke. Why? Because their bodies simply aren't prepared for the sudden heat that claims those environmentally adapted to hiking during the cold winter and cool spring months.

That leaves the hiker coming to the Grand Canyon during heat spells of April and May two alternatives: overdress during your training, to simulate a warm desert environment, and/or prehydrate before your most strenuous hiking days—and continually replenish your lost fluids by drinking enough water. Thirst is a poor indicator of your fluid requirements. It's far better to use the color of your urine as an indicator of your fluid requirements. If it's clear, you're doing great. But once your urine starts turning yellow, you're either slipping into fluid deprivation and need to fill up the tank, or you're taking too many vitamins (B-complex and A, which have a tendency to turn your urine yellow), or both. Once your urine turns dark yellow, you're getting into serious trouble.

If you're walking during daylight hours and carrying a pack, figure on doubling or trebling these fluid requirements—depending on your fitness and acclimatization, the air and ground temperature, the humidity, the terrain, the elevation gain, and the weight you're carrying.

The best treatment for dehydration is prevention, and the best practical indicator is your urine color, so consider leaving your A and B-complex vitamins (or multivitamins that include these) in the car until you return. Remember, you lose water three ways: perspiration, urination, and breathing. If you're sitting on the hot ground (midsummer in the Inner Gorge, it's 140–160°F), the heat will accelerate these losses.

My personal experience has been that it takes a minimum of 1 gallon of water to trek or run 8 to 10 miles along a relatively flat course through the Sonoran Desert midday during 100°F+ temperatures. For peak ascents, this basic requirement increases by an additional 1 to 2 quarts of water for each and every 1,000 vertical feet climbed. Depending on your pack weight, for example, in climbing 5,000 vertical feet out of the Grand Canyon from the Colorado River via one of its 8- to 12-mile-long rim-to-river trails midday during the summertime, you'll need a minimum of 1 to 1 ½ gallons of water for the linear distance you're going to travel, plus an additional 1 to 2 quarts of water for every 1,000 vertical feet you're going to climb. That's a minimum of 2 ½ to 4 gallons of water (20 to 34 pounds!) to climb out of the Grand Canyon during the unforgiving summer heat, when thousands of American and foreign backpackers embark on inner-Canyon death marches (source: John Annerino, *Desert Survivor: An Explorer's Guide to the Great American Desert;* visit www.4w8w.com).

Warning: Drinking too much plain water on an empty stomach, however, has caused a dangerous sodium deficiency in the bloodstream of heat-stressed Grand Canyon hikers called *hyponatremia.* To prevent it, eat something (salty snacks, for example) before you rehydrate, and replenish lost minerals by drinking powdered electrolyte drinks such as Gookinaid and Gatorade.

Mile for mile, hiking out of the Grand Canyon during the summertime is more difficult and dangerous than trekking the *Camino del Diablo,* "Devil's Road." During a 130-mile-long midsummer journey, I wanted to see and experience what prospectors endured during their deadly 1850s-era treks. My companions and I each drank 3 to 5 gallons of water a day (See "El Camino del Diablo, Notes on Trekking," in *Adventuring in Arizona;* visit www.uapress.arizona.edu or call (800) 426-3797). Common sense dictates you should only hike the inner Canyon during the coolest months of the year, but if you choose to hike the Grand Canyon during the summer, for whatever reason, it's imperative you leave the Colorado River for the South or North rim no later than 5 A.M.!

For a detailed discussion of the treatment of heat cramps, heat exhaustion, and heat stroke, send for the excellent booklet *Desert Awareness* (write DARES, P.O. Box 39340, Phoenix, AZ 85069).

HAZARDS

SUNBURN: Prevent by using sunblock and wearing long-sleeved white cotton shirts and a white cotton hat.

SUN GLARE: Choose sunglasses that are polarized, to block glare and reduce visual light transmission (VLT), and that provide 100% UV protection to block harmful ultraviolet rays.

FLASH FLOODS: These occur suddenly, often during summer monsoons when several inches of precipitation can hammer the higher elevations in a short period of time. This peak runoff has only one way to go, *downhill,* and if you happen to be hiking along the bottom of one of the tributary creeks or canyons that frequently act as funnels for this tremendous runoff, chances are you may not be able—or may not have time—to climb to higher ground. Consequently, you may suddenly find yourself bodysurfing to the Colorado River—and your death. If you doubt the power and danger of a Grand Canyon flash flood,

DEADLY HAZARDS OF GRAND CANYON NATIONAL PARK*

Activity, Location, or Cause	No. of Fatalities	Date
Hiking	161	April 10, 1872, to October 3, 2001
Cardiac Arrest 38		June 6, 1956, to October 16, 2000
(heat related) (12)		
Dehydration and Heat 21		August 7, 1903, to June 2, 2000
Falls 53		January 20, 1880, to October 3, 2001
Flash Flood 14		January 2, 1910, to August 10, 2001
Hypothermia 6		March 1900 to February 14, 1994
Lightning 3		July 25, 1895, to May 13, 1993
River Crossings 20		April 10, 1872, to May 26, 1955
Rock Fall 6		January 18, 1901, to February 26, 1996
Walking (Rim Trail/South Rim)	5	April 8, 1979, to November 28, 1992
Drowning	36	May 17, 1919, to January 29, 2000
River Running	29	August 29, 1867, to November 15, 1994
Scenic Vistas	39	March 22, 1925, to November 23, 2001
Air Crashes	355	June 30, 1956, to August 10, 2001

*Does not include murder, suicide, and traffic fatalities.
Source: Michael P. Ghiglieri and Thomas M. Myers, *Over the Edge: Death in Grand Canyon*, www.grandcanyontreks.org/tom.htm.

ask any boatman who's rafted Crystal Rapid before and after the awesome flash flood of 1966 created one of the most treacherous rapids in North America; or ask any of the boat-men and passengers who were driving out Diamond Creek dur-ing the summer of 1984 and scrambled for their lives when a flash flood came thundering down Diamond Creek and swept the stake-side truck containing all their boats and gear into the Colorado River! So stay out of tributary canyons, creeks, and drainages during the July and August monsoons.

LIGHTNING: Lightning will present problems during rains and thunderstorms if you're in an open area or shallow cave, standing on a point or ridgetop, or hunkered down beneath a tree. Stay out of these areas during lightning storms, and head for the boulder fields and protected areas such as forests, or any other site you feel will offer you some protection.

ROCKFALL: Rockfall is caused many ways: sonic booms, storms, a freeze or thaw, hikers, and even the wind. When hik-ing trails or cross-country, make sure you're out of the fall line of rocks that could be knocked down by other parties or mem-bers of your own party. And exercise care as to where you place your hands and feet. As far as storms are concerned, the most predictable areas for rockfall are those water streaks that adorn so many canyon walls; they turn to waterfalls during heavy rains and carry debris and rubble with them. Stay out of their fall line.

SPRAINS: Storms, erosion, mules, and hikers are constantly changing the conditions of Grand Canyon trails and routes. So make sure your footwear can meet the demands of the terrain and provide you with adequate ankle support.

RIVER CROSSINGS: There have been numerous drownings of experienced canyoneers who've been ill-prepared for crossing the Colorado River. Unless you've practiced river crossings elsewhere, with a pack on, don't attempt your first on the Colorado River. Historic pre-dam records indicate that the Colorado River at Diamond Creek sometimes reached a surface temperature near 80°F during the hottest part of summer, but the post-dam river temperature is closer to 48°F on the east end of the Grand Canyon, where many river crossings are attempted. Even if you're wearing a full-length wetsuit, your body may not tolerate cold-water immersion for more than a few *active* minutes without succumbing to hypothermia—and death, even in the calm stretches of the Colorado River, where your crossing should be made.

If your cross-river trek is planned for April through September, you have a better chance of hitching a ride with a commercial river outfitter to take you across the river, but the National Park Service now discourages the practice. If you *must* cross the river, consider these two types of inflatable rafts:

An inflatable raft or canoe, with a minimum size of 3 ½' x 6' x 12" tubes (approximate weight, 10–15 pounds), commonly referred to as a two-man raft, is a reasonably stable craft. The seams should be sealed so that there is a rounded surface, not a "trim," on the outside perimeter of the tube. No more than two people with packs should use such a craft at any one time (shuttle if necessary). Life preservers, either Type II or Type III, must be worn while crossing.

An air mattress is lighter to carry, but very dangerous to use. It's easy to upset even in seemingly flat water, which has dangerous currents in the form of eddies, whirlpools, and boils. The Colorado is far too cold to swim across most times of the year, even if you don't have a pack on. Contact the Backcountry Information Center for a river-crossing permit and recommendations on techniques, gear, and the best crossing sites (www.nps.gov/grca).

CREEK CROSSINGS: Several hikes described in this guide require creek crossings. But there are certain times of the year, during heavy spring runoff, when you just *can't* ford creeks like Shinumo, Tapeats, Saddle Canyon (below Muav Saddle), and others without endangering your life. So plan your treks into these areas well before or after heavy spring runoff and summer rains. (Check with the BIC for the latest conditions.) During the years of particularly heavy precipitation and runoff, these seasons may be extended on either end.

If for some reason your route or situation requires you to ford a creek before or after spring runoff, and you feel the crossing will be a marginal one for you, select the area you feel is safest, e.g., not at the top of Deer Creek Falls, Thunder River, Lower Tapeats Narrows. Heave your pack across to the other side. Then put on your Sterns or inflatable U.S. Divers' life vest and make your crossing as carefully as possible. If you get knocked off your feet, float on your back, arms paddling at your sides, knees bent, and legs pointed downstream, and hope like hell you can grab a limb or tree root before you're swept over Never Never Falls. Unless you're an experienced climber who's set up Tyrolean traverse river crossings elsewhere, *don't use a rope*. It'll drag you to the bottom like an anchor, and the more your pard heave-hos on the other end, the more stonelike you'll become.

HYPOTHERMIA: "Killer of the unprepared." Commonly referred to as "exposure" in your local newspaper headlines, hypothermia is simply the cooling of your body's inner core. While the inner Canyon should be considered desert, the Tonto Plateau up to both rims can be considered a mountain environment. There are certain times of the year, however, when you can fall victim to hypothermia in either of these environments or on the Colorado River.

WIND SPEED: COOLING POWER OF WIND

mph	Temperature (°F)											
Calm	40	30	20	10	5	0	−10	−20	−30	−40	−50	−60
	Equivalent Chill Temperature											
5	35	25	15	5	0	−5	−15	−25	−35	−45	−55	−70
10	30	15	5	−10	−15	−20	−35	−45	−60	−70	−80	−95
15	25	10	5	−20	−25	−30	−45	−60	−70	−85	−100	−110
20	20	5	−10	−25	−30	−35	−50	−65	−80	−95	−110	−120
25	15	0	−15	−30	−35	−45	−60	−75	−90	−105	−120	−135
30	10	0	−20	−30	−40	−50	−65	−80	−95	−110	−125	−140
35	10	−5	−20	−35	−40	−50	−65	−80	−100	−115	−130	−145
40	10	−5	−20	−35	−45	−55	−70	−85	−100	−115	−130	−150

Danger	Increasing Danger (Flesh may freeze within 1 minute)	Great Danger (Flesh may freeze within 30 seconds)

Example: At 10°F, a 25 mph wind speed produces a −30°F chill temperature.

Mark Twain purportedly wrote, "The coldest winter I ever spent was a summer in San Francisco." The coldest I ever remember being at the Grand Canyon was *not* on the snow-covered, eight-thousand-foot Kaibab Plateau, but during a damp, bitter night on the Tonto Plateau in Sumner Wash on the Clear Creek Trail. So be prepared no matter where you will be.

To prevent hypothermia you must, in all circumstances, be able to keep yourself warm. This is no easy task if you are wet and/or if the wind is blowing and/or if you are immersed in the

Colorado River. Think about this carefully when you select clothing and gear for your pack.

For a detailed discussion of the cause, treatment, and prevention of hypothermia, read *Medicine for Mountaineering & Other Wilderness Activities* (www.mountaineersbooks.org). This excellent source also addresses *frostbite,* which several experienced canyoneers have also fallen victim to here.

POISONOUS BITES AND STINGS: Of the three species of rattlesnake that inhabit the Grand Canyon, the most common is the timid Grand Canyon "pink." Don't put your hands or feet where you can't see and you've got nothing to worry about. However, if you *do* get bitten, there are no fewer than five methods of treatment. All are controversial. Snake bite treatments include:

The Extractor®, a lightweight vacuum pump venom extractor, (800) 940-4464, Sawyer Products. I carry this.

Horse serum antivenin injection kit, (800) 666-7248, Wyeth-Ayers. This should be physician-administered, because horse serum can cause anaphylactic shock.

Physician-administered hydrocortisone injections. A Texas doctor has been successful with this treatment.

CroFab, a physician-administered Australian sheep serum antivenin, developed by Protherics PLC (www.protherics.com) in 2001 and now distributed by Fougera, has been successfully used to treat several thousand snakebites in the U.S.

Once-popular yet controversial and dangerous methods: cut and suck, ligature-cryotherapy.

Do nothing, sit still, don't panic, send your pard for help, and statistics prove you'll survive.

Source: John Annerino, *Desert Survivor: An Adventurer's Guide to Exploring the Great American Desert,* www.4w8w.com

If you get up and start walking, and you have been envenomated (which happens only 50–75 percent of the time, and you'll *know* if you have been), complications arise in minutes.

Scorpions like to cling to dark, damp places, such as the bottom of your ground cloth, so shake out your boots and sleeping bag every morning. If you get stung, you'll get pretty nauseous, and maybe even cramp up, but you'll probably survive to make the climb out. (For children, however, the sting can be lethal.) Some river runners carry a small black light to look for scorpions before rolling out their sleeping mat.

One far more common type of sting you might encounter is that of a red ant. Treat stings with an ammonia stick applicator (After Bite®, The Itch Eraser®; visit www.tendercorp.com), and clean up your food scraps and crumbs or they'll beat a path straight to your hands and ankles.

For further information on treatment of poisonous bites and stings, as well as practical applications of desert survival, see Venomous Animals of Arizona (to order, visit http://cals .arizona.edu/pubs, or call (877) 763-5315).

EMERGENCY EVACUATION

All right, you did all your homework—your training, your reading—you bought all the right gear, you achieved the proper mental attitude, the whole nine yards. But somehow you still managed to get in trouble. What are you going to do now that you (or your companion) have broken a leg or met one of the other Grand Canyon dragons face to face? After you've administered first aid, you have to decide whether one of you is going to go for help, or whether you're both going to sit where you are and wait for help to come. Only *you* can make that judgment. If you've got adequate water, food, shelter, and clothing—and you should have—and you're too far from either rim or the Colorado River, your best bet may be to sit tight; use your signal mirror to flash signs to one of the air-tour operators or commercial airliners. If they've seen your flash, they'll notify park authorities, so don't quit flashing until you hear the sound of their voices or the *whup-whup-whup* of the mothership. If they bring in a helicopter, stay clear of the rotors. *Let them come to you.*

Don't rely on getting a signal for your cell phone in the inner Canyon or atop the North Rim in the Western Grand Canyon. You're off the grid. If you have any doubts, you may be better off carrying a satellite phone. However, in obstructed or narrow canyon areas you may only be able to triangulate satellite signals every 10 to 15 minutes. (For Globalstar satellite phone "trip insurance," call toll free (877) 977-6305, or visit www.PHILeasing.com).

When you're too far away from the developed sites or highways on either of the rims or you're just plain closer to the river, if you know a sure way down to the Colorado, that may be your best bet during the commercial river season. River outfitters have their own passengers to take care of and schedules to follow, so it had better be an *emergency*. If it is, they'll take care of you. They carry major first-aid kits, are trained in advanced first aid or are EMTs, and they carry airnet radios, which can send messages out at 122.9 mc and/or 123.05 mc. Stay out of their way and let them do what they know how to do. The message they'll broadcast will probably be: "Emergency, emergency, require helicopter, require helicopter, Mile-_____, Colorado River. Notify NPS, Grand Canyon."

Before you leave your injured partner and head for the Colorado River, write down the time of trauma, condition, medication administered (if any), location of victim, and any other pertinent information you think a successful treatment and evacuation might require. Keep a cool head, and take something bright or reflective—a red or yellow shirt or jacket or a mirror, for example—down to the river, something a boatman will be able to see when you try flagging him or her down. And don't try flagging someone down in the middle of a rapid or immediately below it. Pick a calm stretch of water where they have ample time to pull over, or a spot where they've pulled over for lunch or camp or to scout a rapid.

Note that there is no scheduled air traffic over some parts of the Colorado River. Among these are Marble Canyon between Rider Canyon (Mile 17) and 60 Mile Canyon; Stephen and Conquistador isles (Miles 117–122); and Deer Creek to Vulcans Anvil (Miles 138–178). It may be advisable to move to an area where more air traffic occurs, if possible. Or try flashing any of the scenic vistas.

WILDERNESS ETHICS

> The richest values of wilderness lie not in the days of Daniel Boone, nor even in the present, but rather in the future.
>
> —Aldo Leopold

As hikers and canyoneers we have the desire and, in many cases, the ability to reach remote areas of the Grand Canyon that most of its 4 ½ million annual visitors will see only in a scenic photograph. And that's the primary reason we have the potential to inflict the most—sometimes irreversible—physical damage upon its fragile ecosystems. More damage than the mule-riding concessions, which use only the maintained South Kaibab, Bright Angel, North Kaibab, and Condor trails; and more than the heavily regulated, closely monitored commercial river concessionaires, whose boatmen guide most of the riverside day hikes. So that leaves us with the responsibility to clean up our own act, and that of others, so that future generations of canyoneers can enjoy the wilderness qualities of Grand Canyon

National Park. Failing this, national park rangers will have no recourse but to enforce backcountry regulations more severely.

Note these rules:

1. *Don't use firearms.* 36 CFR 2.4(a). This includes bows and arrows. The Grand Canyon is not an armed camp. Nor is it a hunting preserve. Unless you'd enjoy taking lunch with the U.S. magistrate, complete with an armed escort, go ahead, make *everybody's* day, and leave your weapons at home.

2. *Don't use motorized vehicles or wheeled vehicles on trails.* 36 CFR 4.10(a). The trails were not constructed for motorcycles, baby buggies, mountain bikes, and similar vehicles, which create a hazard for you as well as other hikers.

    The classic incident involving this regulation was the citation Colorado River boatman Gary Kuchel reportedly received for rolling 10 cases of beer down the Bright Angel Trail on a hand dolly in order to resupply a thirsty river party. He was not only cited under this law, but he had to push his still-loaded hand dolly back up to the South Rim!

3. *Don't take dogs or other pets below the rim.* 36 CFR 2.15(a)1. As much as little Bowser may look like White Fang sitting next to the fireplace, he is an exotic species when it comes to the inner Canyon. And most exotic species, including modern man, have a difficult enough time trying to adapt to the peculiarities and hazards of canyoneering—not to mention avoiding disturbing wildlife and other hikers. You can arrange for his personal lodging at the South Rim kennels. (Call (928) 638-0534 for further information.)

4. *Do not cut switchbacks or take shortcuts.* 36 CFR 2.1(b). If you're hiking either a maintained or nonmaintained trail, stay *on* the trail. Cutting switchbacks isn't going to get you there any faster, but it does cause erosion, contributes to the damaging and confusing braiding of trails, and poses a dangerous risk to people hiking below in the fall line of rocks. If you're doing a cross-country or trans-Canyon route, use some common sense with regard to disturbing and trampling fragile plants and delicate surface areas covered with cryptobiotic soil; a single footprint in this erosion-controlling soil will remain for a hundred years.

5. *Do not throw or roll rocks into the Canyon.* 36 CFR 2.1(a)3. Everybody's had the urge to throw a rock or push a boulder off a cliff to watch and listen to it explode far below, including no less than early Alpine mountaineer Sir Martin Conway, who wrote in *The Alps from End to End,* "We amused ourselves by throwing stones down the slope we had come up and watching them vanish in the fog." But serious injuries and at least one fatality have occurred in the Grand Canyon from boulder trundling. Resist the temptation.

6. *Set up camp away from water holes.* Arizona state law prohibits camping within a quarter mile of any water source. With the paucity of water sources in the Grand Canyon, that general rule becomes especially critical. When camping in developed zones and undeveloped areas with preexisting campsites, use them whenever possible. When camping in areas without preexisting campsites, try to pick an area that doesn't require gardening (clearing away vegetation, leveling a tent site,

delimbing trees, etc.) and that's far removed from archaeological and historical sites.

7. *Don't set wood or charcoal fires.* 36 CFR 2.13(a)1. For many wilderness enthusiasts, the opportunity to sit around a warm campfire at night howling at the moon is often the high point of a backpacking trip. Unfortunately, fires scar rocks and trees, and charcoal lasts thousands of years. Due to the shortage of wood and the dangers of wildfire, open fires are not permitted in Grand Canyon National Park unless it's a life-threatening emergency.

8. *Dig privies away from the nearest water source.* Before commercial river outfitters were required to carry human waste out of the Grand Canyon, over 20 tons of feces per year were being deposited on the dissipating beaches of the Colorado River. The backcountry is undergoing a similar, if more widely dispersed, threat from slowly decomposing human waste. And that problem has the potential to be a greater threat to this fragile ecosystem and the health of other hikers and wildlife. So select an area at least 300 feet from the nearest water source and your neighbor's camp when privies are not available, and dig a cat hole 6 to 8 inches deep with your plastic trowel. After use, fill the hole up completely, then compact the soil. Burning toilet paper has caused numerous wildfires in the Grand Canyon; pack it out in zip-locking bags. The Canyon's soft sandstones make excellent toilet paper substitutes. Grand Canyon climber and boatman George Bain is an expert on such matters and further advises, "Dry, rounded streambed cobblestones are the best; collect a few as you walk well away from the stream or wash. Dust the rocks off well. If they

have sharp edges, go slow. If the rocks are black and hot from lying in the sun, go fast. If they're both sharp and hot, be *very* careful."

9. *Don't fish without a license.* 36 CFR 2.3(a). Many of the tributary canyons and creeks along the Colorado River, such as South Canyon, Bright Angel, and Tapeats Creek, to name a few, have excellent trout fishing near their confluence with the Colorado River. However, fishing by anyone 14 years or older requires a valid Arizona fishing license or a nonresident permit. These can be purchased at the Canyon Village Market General Store on the South Rim, or at nearby Arizona sporting-goods stores. Several river outfitters offer special river trips keyed specifically to the needs of fishermen (see Authorized River Outfitters, page 66).

10. *Do not dig up, collect, or otherwise remove plants, rocks, animals, or other natural or cultural features.* 36 CFR 2.1(a)1. After 20 years of research and an estimated 1,000 hours of helicopter flight time, Dr. Robert C. Euler and his staff of researchers discovered more than a thousand historic and prehistoric sites in the Grand Canyon. Not all of them were ancestral Puebloan sites, which comprise the majority of the Canyon's 4,300 recorded archaeological sites. Some were those of the "ancient hunters known as the Pinto Basin Culture," who may have been responsible for constructing delicate split-twig figurines of deer and bighorn sheep, archaeologists believe, as effigies to ensure a successful hunt. Other sites were those of the Southern Paiute Indians, "ancestors of the Walapai and Havasupai. They settled along the South Rim and utilized portions of the inner Canyon south of the Colorado River." Still others were

those of prospectors who came to the Canyon during the late 1800s looking to strike pay dirt.

If you visit any historic or prehistoric sites while camping or hiking, leave them alone. Don't camp in them or climb around them; they're a nonrenewable resource. That includes potsherds, arrowheads, and the like; leave them for the next visitor to enjoy. Besides, they're protected by federal laws such as the Archaeological Resources Act of 1979 and the Antiquities Act of 1906, which carry stiff federal sentences for first offenses.

11. *Don't write on, scratch, or otherwise deface natural features, signs, buildings, or other objects.* 36 CFR 2.31(a) and 36 CFR 2.1(a)1. This includes carving your name on rocks.

12. *Do not feed wild animals.* 36 CFR 2.2(a)2. "But the squirrels will eat it." Maybe. But animals accustomed to surviving on handouts frequently face population collapse off-season when forced to revert to their natural diet.

13. *Carry out your own trash.* 36 CFR 2.14(b). And your neighbors' too.

    Name it—aluminum packages, cigarette butts, grease, food scraps, etc.—and it probably will take years to decompose, if it decomposes at all in the arid desert environment of the inner Canyon. So bring along freezer-strength zip-locking bags, and seal all of your trash before packing it out.

14. *If you see someone in trouble, give him or her a helping hand.*

15. *If you make a positive identification of a rare sighting,* such as a mountain lion in the inner Canyon, a desert bighorn on either of the rims, or a feral burro anywhere,

or if you stumble across what looks like undiscovered historic or prehistoric artifacts, fill out a Natural History Observation Card, which is available at the Backcountry Information Center.

16. *If you discover a water source outside heavily used areas, fill out a report form at the BIC.*

part II

TRAILS OF THE GRAND CANYON

7 | South Rim

RIM TRAILS

If you're short on time, just getting in shape, or have arrived at the Grand Canyon in the searing heat of midsummer—as most visitors do—the Canyon's rim trails make an excellent alternative to *inner*-Canyon hiking. For all practical purposes there are only two rim trails located on the South Rim: the South Rim Nature Trail and the Comanche Point Trail.

Comanche Point Trail

The first leg of the Comanche Point Trail is a nonmaintained jeep road once used primarily by Navajo families who live and graze sheep on the reservation lands adjoining the eastern boundary of Grand Canyon National Park. According to John C. Van Dyke, who wrote of his extended visit to the Grand Canyon in 1919 in *The Grand Canyon of the Colorado,* the trail out to Comanche Point is "an old Mormon wagon-road." (Vehicle traffic is prohibited in what's now a backcountry wilderness area.)

As far as backcountry foot travel is concerned, this trail is of primary interest to those rock climbers skilled enough to climb 6,800-foot Comanche Point Pinnacle, the Lost Arrow Spire of the Grand Canyon, located several confusing rappels below 7,073-foot Comanche Point; to canyoneers interested in scrambling up 6,200-foot Espejo Butte, located several trailless miles north of Comanche Point along the rim of the Palisades of the Desert; and to those hikers who'd like to explore the

THE RIM TRAIL

Starting at 7,120-foot Mather Point, the self-guiding 9-mile-long Rim Trail ends at 6,640-foot Hermits Rest. If you don't want to complete the entire hike, you can hike shorter legs of the Rim Trail between scenic vistas, then catch the shuttle back to your starting point. It's an excellent way to stretch your legs, see the view, and acclimate to the altitude.

Length	Scenic Vistas, East to West	Shuttles from Canyon View Information Plaza
0.7 mile	Mather Point to Yavapai Observation Station	(walk ¼ mile to Mather Point)
1.0 mile	Yavapai Observation Station to Village Transfer	Village Route Shuttle (Blue)
0.7 mile	Village Transfer to Trailview Overlook	Hermits Rest Shuttle (Red)
0.7 mile	Trailview Overlook to Maricopa Point	Hermits Rest Shuttle (Red)
0.5 mile	Maricopa Point to Powell Point	Hermits Rest Shuttle (Red)
0.3 mile	Powell Point to Hopi Point	Hermits Rest Shuttle (Red)
0.8 mile	Hopi Point to Mohave Point	Hermits Rest Shuttle (Red)
1.1 miles	Mohave Point to The Abyss	Hermits Rest Shuttle (Red)
2.9 miles	The Abyss to Pima Point	Hermits Rest Shuttle (Red)
1.1 Miles	Pima Point to Hermits Rest	Hermits Rest Shuttle (Red)

Returning to Village Transfer, the Hermits Rest Shuttle stops only at Mohave Point and Hopi Point. For a map of the shuttle routes, see *The Guide*, available free throughout the park.

cooler pinyon-juniper country of the South Rim during the summer while taking in a breath-stopping view of the Painted Desert and eastern Grand Canyon.

To reach Comanche Point, park your vehicle at the East Entrance Ranger Station a half mile east of Desert View. Follow this rock-strewn dirt track approximately 2 ½ miles downhill around the east arm of Tanner Canyon. Turn left (north) and descend into and climb out of Straight Canyon, covering another 2 ½ to 3 miles before reaching a T junction designated on your Desert View Quadrangle (7.5 minute) map by Peak 6684. Turn left again, this time striking out cross-country through the pinyon-juniper in a N/NE direction for half to three-quarters of a mile until you're overlooking the drainage immediately below (east of) the word *the* on your quadrangle. Pick your way into this drainage and follow it north for approximately 1 mile to the base, or southeast slope, of Comanche Point. (Seasonal water is sometimes found in this drainage.) The first summit you see is a false one, tallying up to an 800 foot vertical climb in about three-quarters of a mile to reach the apex of Comanche Point. The afternoon winds sweeping up out of the inner Canyon are normally strong, so you may want to place your camp on the leeside of Comanche Point on one of several suitable flat areas between its summit and the drainage.

Once on top you'll no doubt see, as George Wharton James noted in 1910, that "the walls are precipitous to three thousand five hundred feet below, and the outlook afforded is about seventy miles in either direction, up and down the Canyon." During a trip to Comanche Point, I watched in awe as a bald eagle rode a canyon thermal up over the rim. Experienced canyoneers have descended to the Colorado River via Comanche Creek using the saddle between Comanche Point and BM 6841, but this exposed and precarious route is

3rd and 4th Class and is best reconned and approached from below before considering a descent.

ELEVATION:	7,400 feet to 6,300 feet to 7,073 feet.
MILEAGE:	Approximately 7 miles one way.
VEGETATION:	Pinyon-juniper.
WATER:	Seasonal *only* (see description).
CACHE POINTS:	At T junction, below Peak 6684.
SEASONS:	Spring through fall. Wintertime may require a good mountain tent, cross-country skis, and other winter camping gear.
MAPS:	Desert View Quadrangle (7.5 minute) and South Kaibab National Forest Map (visit www.fs.fed.us/R3/kai/).
NEAREST SUPPLY POINTS (for all South Rim trails & routes):	G. C. Village, Cameron, Flagstaff, and Williams.

RIM-TO-RIVER—MAINTAINED CORRIDOR TRAILS

At present two rim-to-river trails located on the South Rim are maintained by National Park Service trail crews and are designated Corridor Trails. These two, the South Kaibab and Bright Angel trails, are the most heavily used trails in Grand Canyon National Park. They are perhaps the easiest rim-to-river trails, offering inexperienced canyoneers a challenging introduction to inner-Canyon hiking while providing them with a base of experience to draw upon for more difficult Canyon treks later on. (Harvey Butchart took his first hike down the South Kaibab in 1945.) If you haven't hiked into the Canyon before, you should consider hiking one or both of these trails—either one way, or tying both of them together in a loop hike—before striking out for the Great Unknown.

The South Kaibab and Bright Angel trails are also used by mule trains to ferry dudes and supplies to and from Phantom Ranch, as well as to "drag out" hikers. If you're hiking either of these trails, chances are you'll encounter a mule train; if you do, the wrangler will ask you to step to the high side of the trail until he moves his pack string past. If you hear a pack string coming your way, you'll be safer and make the wrangler's job easier if you take the high ground at a wide spot on the trail before they reach you.

PLEASE NOTE: The maintained rim-to-river Corridor Trails, the South Kaibab and Bright Angel, as well as the seven nonmaintained rim-to-river Wilderness Trails provide the major avenues of ingress and egress for those canyoneers hiking any, or all, of the South Rim's trans-Canyon Wilderness Trails and Routes. Because trans-Canyon Trails and Routes are described east to west, both the Corridor and Wilderness Trails will also be listed in a geographical order of east to west, rather than according to difficulty. (The approximate difficulty of each of the rim-to-river trails is listed at the end of the South Kaibab Trail description.)

South Kaibab Trail

Most of the Grand Canyon's rim-to-river trails were Native American routes developed by prospectors during the late 1800s. The South Kaibab, however, was constructed by the National Park Service in 1924 as an alternative to the Bright Angel Trail because hosteler Ralph Cameron had a franchise to charge a $1 toll to anyone riding or hiking down it. It was down the South Kaibab's steep, thigh-pummeling 6.3 miles that 42 Havasupai Indians carried eight steel cables, one at a time, in order to help construct the new Kaibab Suspension Bridge across the Colorado River. According to former ranger-naturalist J. Donald Hughes's *The Story of Man at Grand Canyon,* each of those cables was "550 feet long, 1 ½ inches in diameter and weighed 2,320 pounds." The procession looked like "some giant squirming centipede."

To reach the South Kaibab trailhead, take the green shuttle bus from Canyon View Information Plaza to 7,268-foot Yaki Point. The trail is well marked all the way to the Colorado River, with aluminum placards identifying each of the major geological formations you'll descend en route to the Colorado River. In the 2.2 miles to Cedar Ridge you'll hike through first the Kaibab Limestone, Toroweap Formation, and Coconino Sandstone before reaching the Hermit Shale that comprises Cedar Ridge; the hike to Cedar Ridge and back is a good introductory day hike. There are privies there, and a bird's-eye view of 6,071-foot O'Neill Butte, named after Rough Rider William Owen "Bucky" O'Neill, who fought in Cuba during the Spanish-American War.

The trail angles off the east side of Cedar Ridge through the Supai Formation, then corkscrews through the Redwall Formation, covering 3 miles from Cedar Ridge to the Tonto Trail junction. (The Grandview Trail is 21.3 miles east, and the Bright Angel Trail is 4.5 miles west.) (For trail descriptions of the Tonto east and west of the South Kaibab, see "Tonto Trail," p. 169.)

Going in, the Tonto Formation makes an excellent rest or lunch stop, and you can usually find some shade in the Tapeats Sandstone immediately below the Tipoff, a quarter mile farther. From the Tipoff, it's less than 2 miles to the Kaibab

Suspension Bridge, and another quarter mile to the Bright Angel Campground and ranger station.

ADDITIONAL CONSIDERATIONS: Many first-time canyoneers use the South Kaibab Trail as the first leg of the popular 14.6-mile loop hike via the South Kaibab, Tonto, and Bright Angel trails; the 16.6-mile rim-to-river hike via the South Kaibab and Bright Angel trails; and the 21.5-mile rim-to-rim hike via the South Kaibab and North Kaibab trails (see North Kaibab Trail, page 203). *Wilderness Trail Loop Hike:* If you're in great shape and have the canyoneering experience necessary to complete a long wilderness hike, you can loop hike 27 miles via the Grandview, Tonto, and South Kaibab trails (see Cottonwood Creek to South Kaibab Trail, page 174).

WARNING:	Don't attempt hiking out the South Kaibab during the hot summer months or the warm, dry months of spring and fall.
ELEVATION:	7,260 feet to 2,450 feet.
TOTAL ELEVATION LOSS & GAIN:	9,620 feet (4,810 vertical feet each way).
MILEAGE:	6.7 one way to Bright Angel Campground.
VEGETATION:	Mountain Transition Zone to Lower Sonoran Desert.
WATER:	Colorado River and Bright Angel Campground only!
CACHE POINTS:	Cedar Ridge and the Tipoff.
SEASONS:	Fall through spring. Summer has proven deadly.
MAP:	Phantom Ranch Quadrangle (7.5 minute).

The view from Yaki Point. Photo © *George H. H. Huey*

DIFFICULTY: The following list has been compiled
               in sequential order—from easiest to
               most difficult—and has been
               included as a planning aid for those
               who want to increase their back-
               country experience in increments
               rather than in leaps and bounds:
               1. Bright Angel Trail, Corridor Trail
               2. South Kaibab Trail, Corridor
                  Trail
               3. Hermit Trail, Wilderness Trail
               4. Grandview Trail (Horse Shoe
                  Mesa loop), Wilderness Trail
               5. South Bass Trail, Wilderness Trail
               6. Tanner Trail, Wilderness Trail
               7. Boucher Trail, Wilderness Trail
               8. New Hance Trail, Wilderness
                  Trail

Bright Angel Trail

Most rim-to-river trails fall into one of two major categories: ridge trail or drainage trail. The South Kaibab is a ridge trail because it crests or parallels Cedar Ridge most of the way into the Canyon. It offers exposed hiking and spectacular views en route. The Bright Angel Trail, on the other hand, is a drainage trail because it follows and crisscrosses Garden Creek most of the way to its confluence with Pipe Creek near the Colorado River in the Vishnu Schist. As a result, the hiking isn't as airy nor are the views as spectacular as are those from the ridge trails.

The Bright Angel was originally a footpath used by the Havasupai to reach their gardens at present-day Indian Gardens. The route—unlike many of the miner trails that had to be blasted through different formations—utilized a natural break through that upper geological barrier known as the Bright Angel Fault. Prospectors developed the Havasupai trail in the 1890s and pegged it the Cameron Trail. The name stuck until Coconino County finally wrested control of the trail from Ralph Cameron in 1928. It was officially named the Bright Angel Trail by the U.S. Board of Geographic Names in 1937.

To reach the Bright Angel trailhead, take the (blue) Village Route Shuttle to Bright Angel Lodge; stroll a few minutes west of the Bright Angel Lodge and you're there. Like the South Kaibab, the Bright Angel Trail is well marked for all of its 9 ½ miles to Bright Angel Campground on the north side of the Colorado River. At 1 ½ and 3 miles down the trail there are rest houses built in the 1930s by the Civilian Conservation Corps. At a switchback called Two Mile Corner, there are pictographs dating back to A.D. 1300. Any of these three points will make an invigorating round-trip morning saunter.

Indian Gardens is 4.7 miles down the trail, and if you're used to remote backcountry travel you might not be prepared for the developments that have taken place since the prospectors first arrived in the 1890s. There is a ranger station, developed campground, corral, toilets, water, and shade from cottonwood trees. Indian Gardens is a good turnaround point for a day hike, as is the well-marked 1 ½-mile-long trail out to 3,740-foot Plateau Point; that's pretty near where the first airplane landed in the Grand Canyon and where you'll get your best views of the Inner Gorge from this trail.

To reach the Colorado River, continue beyond the Tonto Trail junction and descend into Tapeats Narrows before tackling the Devils Corkscrew; the latter switchbacks through the Vishnu Schist and will take you to the Pipe Creek rest house near the Colorado River. This is where you pick up the River Trail and follow it east for 1.7 miles to Bright Angel

Suspension Bridge. If you make a left and cross this bridge, Bright Angel Campground (and water) is not more than a half mile beyond; if you continue a mile east, you'll reach the foot of the South Kaibab Trail and the historic Kaibab Suspension Bridge a mile farther.

ADDITIONAL CONSIDERATIONS: If you're planning a rim-to-rim hike from the North Rim to the South Rim, consider coming out the Bright Angel Trail; it's 2 miles longer than the South Kaibab but it's not as steep, so your legs will have some respite on the long haul out, and there's water en route.

Corridor Trail Loop Hike. The most popular Corridor Trail loop hike is 14.6 miles via the South Kaibab, Tonto, and Bright Angel trails (see South Kaibab Trail to Bright Angel Trail, page 177).

Wilderness Trail Loop Hike. A favorite Wilderness Trail loop hike is the 24.4-mile Bright Angel, Tonto, and Hermit Trail loop (see Bright Angel Trail to Hermit Trail, page 178).

ELEVATION:	6,860 feet to 2,480 feet.
TOTAL ELEVATION LOSS & GAIN:	8,760 feet (4,380 vertical feet each way).
MILEAGE:	4.7 one way to Indian Gardens Campground; 9.5 one way to Bright Angel Campground.
WATER:	Indian Gardens, Colorado River, and Bright Angel Campground.
CACHE POINTS:	Immediately below the Tonto Formation in the shade and seclusion of Tapeats Narrows.
SEASONS:	Fall through spring. Summer's hot.
MAPS:	Grand Canyon and Phantom Ranch quadrangles (7.5 minute).

Footbridge over Bright Angel Creek at Phantom Ranch.
Photo © George H. H. Huey

Phantom Ranch

When Major John Wesley Powell and his crew first navigated the Colorado River in 1869, they stopped near a little creek they named Bright Angel for its beauty; they were looking for timbers to replace the oars they'd destroyed upstream. Perhaps the most enlightening discovery Powell made during that layover was the small group of prehistoric ruins he described in his river log, adding perhaps as an afterthought: "It is ever a source of wonder to us why these ancient people sought such inaccessible places for their homes."

Not far from where Powell first discovered those ancient dwellings, David Rust established a tent camp in 1903 for hunters and tourists. The Fred Harvey Company thought it was an equally enchanting area, bought it in 1921, and hired architect Mary Jane Colter to design what today is a renowned destination for Grand Canyon hikers, tourists, and mule riders. One can't help but wonder what Powell would think about that today.

RIM-TO-RIVER TRAILS—NONMAINTAINED

During the Grand Canyon's gold and mineral rush from the mid- to late 1800s, 84 rim-to-river trails were chiseled and dynamited along prehistoric Indian routes and paths to diggings, prospects, mines, and gloryholes in the heart of the Canyon. Only a few of these hand-forged miner trails are still used today—and they exist primarily in the form of nonmaintained rim-to-river Wilderness Trails. These trails are not currently maintained by NPS trail crews. Their conditions vary from the cobblestone Yellow Brick Road stairway of the Hermit Trail to the steep and rugged Old Hance Trail. Whether you call these historic pathways *trails* or *routes* is not important because each will present its own distinct characteristics, challenges, and rewards.

Tanner Trail

Somewhere to the west of Tanner Canyon—no one has pinpointed the exact spot—a soldier of fortune by the name of García López de Cárdenas first "discovered" the Grand Canyon in 1535 with the help of the Hopi. At the time, most Spaniards ventured into the Southwest in what they called *Nueva España,* "New Spain," in quest of gold or souls or both. Cárdenas was no different. Under orders from conquistador Francisco Vásquez de Coronado, Cárdenas was sent to look for the legendary Seven Cities of Cibola. What the tough mercenary and his men found instead were insurmountable odds in their unsuccessful three-day attempt to reach the Colorado River on foot somewhere near Tanner Canyon. "What appeared to be easy from above was not so, but instead very hard and difficult." And that has been the case for Grand Canyon explorers, adventurers, and hikers ever since.

If Cárdenas's men tried to descend Tanner Canyon, they no doubt missed—or lost—the old Hopi route that once descended the east arm of Tanner Canyon. Mormon pioneer and prospector Seth B. Tanner rebuilt the upper third of this trail circa 1884, beginning near Lipan Point, to reach his copper diggings near the Colorado River. This same trail, one leg of the Horsethief Trail, was used during Prohibition by moonshiners who transported their redeye from stills near the Colorado River to the thirsty revelers at the South Rim village.

To reach this historic spoiler's route, take Desert View Drive out to 7,349-foot Lipan Point. The trailhead is just east of the parking lot.

During the late 1970s, hiking the Tanner, Boucher, Thunder River, and several other miner trails required real route-finding skills—not necessarily to keep from getting lost, but to stay on the trail. Today, however, the Tanner Trail is so popular that you can follow it with one eye closed all the way to the Colorado River. At a moderate pace, it takes about an hour to descend the first series of switchbacks to 5,600-foot Seventyfive Mile Saddle; that's the first major saddle you'll come to, and the trail stays just to the east (right, going down) of its Supai Sandstone crest. From here the trail contours around the base of 6,529-foot Escalante Butte and 6,269-foot Cardenas Butte across a broad section of Supai Sandstone; if you're not deadheading to meet a river trip, the area below the 5,800-foot Escalante/Cardenas saddle is a great place to camp. If you use care, the summits of these buttes are enjoyable half-hour scrambles from their saddle, offering the best panoramic views on the Tanner Trail.

Back to the trail. Once you've contoured the base of Cardenas Butte, this ridge trail begins its enchanting little descent of the Redwall, and going down or climbing out these steep, rocky switchbacks is the toughest stretch on the Tanner Trail.

Once the trail finally breaks out of the Bright Angel Shale, it heads almost due north along a ridgetop of Tapeats Sandstone before sliding off its east side through a standing wave of Dox Sandstone all the way to the *Río Colorado*. Going down, this section of the Tanner is the most enjoyable, because you feel like you're flying.

If you reach the river during white water rafting season, you may find a group of river runners camped near the mouth of Tanner Creek, but the area is such a large one, there's no reason to feel crowded. Just head west along the sand dunes and you'll have the solitude you came to enjoy.

ADDITIONAL CONSIDERATIONS: From the foot of the Tanner Trail, you can follow the Beamer Trail 8 ½ miles east to the mouth of the Little Colorado River Gorge (see Beamer Trail, page 163), or you can follow the Escalante Route 10 miles west to the foot of the Hance Trail (see Tanner Canyon to Red Canyon, page 166).

Wilderness Trail and Route Loop Trek. The challenging, multiday 28-mile Tanner Trail, Escalante Route, and Hance Trail loop has become popular among outdoor education programs.

ELEVATION:	7,360 feet to 2,700 feet.
TOTAL ELEVATION LOSS & GAIN:	9,320 feet (4,660 vertical feet each way).
MILEAGE:	10.4 miles.
WATER:	Colorado River only.
CACHE POINTS:	Seventyfive Mile Saddle, and top of the Redwall.
SEASONS:	Fall through spring. Summers are hot and can be deadly. No water, and virtually no shade.
MAP:	Desert View Quadrangle (7.5 minute).

New Hance Trail

One of the most famous quotes concerning Grand Canyon trails was written by Rough Rider Bucky O'Neill in the guest book "Captain" John Hance kept at his ranch on the South Rim. It read: "God made the cañon, John Hance the trails. Without the other, neither would be complete." According to geologist Edwin McKee, who described the Canyon's historic trails in the classic *Inverted Mountains,* the "Old Trail" that Hance forged down Hance Canyon in 1883 to reach his asbestos mines on the north side of the Colorado River was a refurbished Indian trail used for hundreds of years by the Havasupai. But remnants of this famous trailblazer's original

The view from Moran Point overlooking the New Hance Trail.
Photo © George H. H. Huey

rim-to-river route continue to elude the footsteps of most canyoneers today. Even during its prime in the 1880s, the Old Trail was such a steep and precipitous route that Hance had to use ropes to lower tourists and guests down one particularly nasty section of cliff. Those guests included Mrs. Edward Ayres, who in 1882 reputedly became the first woman to reach the bottom of the Grand Canyon. By 1900 the trail had washed out and had become practically inaccessible, so Hance built the Red Canyon (or New Hance) Trail to reach his inner Canyon mine and to accommodate the growing number of tourists who had responded to his 1886 newspaper ad, published in the *Arizona Champion*: "Being thoroughly conversant with all the trails leading to the Grand Canyon of the Colorado, I am prepared to conduct parties thereto at any time. I have a fine spring of water near my house on the rim of the Canyon, and can furnish accommodations for tourists and their animals."

To reach the New Hance trailhead, drive east on Desert View Drive to 7,160-foot Moran Point. Walk 1 mile south of Moran Point to the signed trailhead and follow the cairned trail into the head of the Red Canyon drainage immediately east of 7,162-foot Coronado Butte. You shouldn't have any problem picking up the start of the trail in either the Kaibab Limestone or Toroweap Formation. The descent of these top two formations, as well as the Coconino Sandstone, is short, steep, and rocky, so make sure you're on the trail before you go plunging off into the abyss and get rimrocked. Except during heavy snows—which have a tendency to bury this first stretch of trail all the way down to the Coconino saddle between the rim and Coronado Butte—and immediately after heavy spring runoff, the route is clearly defined if you scout the way.

Once you've reached the 6,000-foot Coronado Butte saddle, the trail veers generally northeast as it snakes its way through the Hermit Shale, Esplanade Sandstone, and lower Supai. You may encounter rockslides, depending on what's eroded, and the footing can be loose. So take your time and exercise care in negotiating this section and locating the beginning of the Redwall descent, which *should* be marked by a totem-sized cairn. The Redwall descent won't be any easier than what you've just done, but your legs will be more tired and the rock more crumbly, so use your best judgment regarding your pace and foot placement.

Below the Redwall the trail tracks across the Tonto Plateau, which until recently was crisscrossed by a confusing series of feral burro trails. Since this exotic species has been removed from the Canyon, this section across the Tonto Plateau is now much easier to follow. Just about where you want to tip off the Tonto Plateau, there should be a drainage on your left and one on your right. Make sure you descend into the eastern drainage (right-hand side, going down); this is the one that will get you down to the creekbed below and to Hance Rapids at the mouth of Red Canyon a few boulder-strewn miles farther.

ADDITIONAL CONSIDERATIONS: *Wilderness Trail Loop Trek.* If you tackle the 22.7-mile New Hance, Tonto, and Grandview trail loop, you should find it safer and less confusing to descend the New Hance Trail and ascend the Grandview Trail via Cottonwood Creek, where there is seasonal water (see Hance Creek to Cottonwood Creek, page 172).

ELEVATION:	6,982 feet to 2,600 feet.
TOTAL ELEVATION LOSS & GAIN:	8,764 feet (4,382 vertical feet each way).
MILEAGE:	8 miles.
WATER:	Colorado River only.

CACHE POINTS:	Coronado Butte saddle and top of the Redwall.
SEASONS:	Fall and spring. Upper sections can be treacherous in winter snow. Summertime can be unforgiving.
MAPS:	Grandview Point and Cape Royal quadrangles (7.5 minute).

Grandview Trail

During the 1800s, hundreds of prospectors followed their wanderlust and dreams of gold throughout the unexplored reaches of the inner Canyon. Peter D. Berry was perhaps the most successful, but the mother lode Berry struck was in the form of high-grade copper ore he discovered 3 miles below 7,399-foot Grandview Point atop 5,246-foot Horse Shoe Mesa. He called it the "Last Chance Mine," and according to J. Donald Hughes, "8 or 10 mules, each carrying 200 pounds" were used to carry out Berry's prizewinning ore to a stamp mill located on the South Rim above. Berry was prescient, because he invested some of his pay dirt and built the Grandview Hotel in 1895; it proved to be the leading tourist hotel at the Canyon until the Santa Fe Railroad ran a track from Williams up to the South Rim a dozen miles west of the Grandview Hotel. That pretty well took care of Berry's dude ranching profits. When the bottom dropped out of the copper market in 1907, Berry sold his mining operation to newspaper magnate William Randolph Hearst.

Of Grand Canyon National Park's dozen remaining rim-to-river trails, the Grandview is one of the least practical for reaching the Colorado River. Most people who hike the Grandview Trail use it primarily to hike down to and around Horse Shoe Mesa.

To reach the Grandview Trail, drive east on Desert View Drive to Grandview Point and pick up the trailhead there. The trail is obvious and straightforward enough all the way down to Horse Shoe Mesa, but some of the upper switchbacks are still riprapped with iron rods and logs from the heyday of the Last Chance Mine. There are also several exposed sections in the Toroweap Formation that are slippery and dangerous during icy winter conditions—and spectacular most other times of the year. Once you reach the Hermit Formation, the trail skirts the west side of a Coconino Sandstone fin before continuing through the Esplanade Sandstone and lower Supai Group to the neck of Horse Shoe Mesa.

Once atop Horse Shoe Mesa, you have numerous options. You can camp and explore the mining relics that still litter the area. You can take the eastern spur trail into Hance Canyon and take the Tonto Trail down to the Colorado River; or, from Hance Canyon, you can take the Tonto Trail west around the base of Horse Shoe Mesa and come up either the spur trail that ascends the northwest arm of Horse Shoe Mesa past the Cave of the Domes, or hike the spur trail that continues west around the base of Horse Shoe Mesa and ascends Cottonwood Creek. Without a pack, you can day hike all the way around the base of Horse Shoe Mesa and have enough time to reach camp before nightfall.

ADDITIONAL CONSIDERATIONS: *Wilderness Trail Loop Trek.* The 31.4-mile Grandview, Tonto, and South Kaibab trail loop is a thorough multiday introduction to the rigors and rewards of trans-canyoneering.

| ELEVATION: | A—7,406 feet to 4,932 feet on Horse Shoe Mesa. |
| | B—4,932 feet to 4,000 feet on Tonto Trail. |

TOTAL ELEVATION LOSS & GAIN:	A—4,948 feet (2,474 vertical feet each way). B—1,864 feet (932 vertical feet each way).
MILEAGE:	3 miles to Horse Shoe Mesa. 4–5 miles around base of Horse Shoe Mesa.
WATER:	Grandview and J. T. springs, east arm of Grandview Trail below Redwall Formation.
CACHE POINTS:	Coconino saddle approximately 1 mile below Grandview Point and Horse Shoe Mesa—depending on the hike planned.
SEASONS:	Spring and fall. Early morning summertime, the hike to Horse Shoe Mesa and back is a good day hike. In wintertime you might need instep crampons for the upper switchbacks.
MAPS:	Grandview Point and Cape Royal quadrangles (7.5 minute).

Hermit Trail

The first leg of the original Hermit Trail was constructed in 1896 by a New York prospector named Daniel Hogan. The trail was improved with inlaid cobblestones and extended by the Santa Fe Railroad around 1913 as the first of two Canyon trails that sought to bypass the tolls Ralph Cameron charged to use his Bright Angel Trail. The Sante Fe Railroad folks ran a way station at the end of the trail, called Hermits Camp, which provided an overnight stop for saddle-weary dudes until the 1930s.

The area this Wilderness Trail descends is called the Hermit Basin Natural Area; it comprises 1,280 acres and "was established to exemplify the geological strata and phenomena of the Grand Canyon" (Hermit Basin Natural Area Abstract). Two trails descend into this remarkable basin: the Hermit Trail descends the east wall below 6,640-foot Hermits Rest, and the Dripping Springs / Boucher Trail descends the west wall of 6,400-foot Eremita Mesa. The Hermit is the easiest and safest of these two trails because there's water en route and because it's well worn. It's also a popular introductory hike for those hikers who've already done the Bright Angel and South Kaibab and are looking to extend their horizons without getting in over their heads on one of the more difficult rim-to-river Wilderness Trails.

To reach the Hermit trailhead, take the (blue) Village Route Shuttle to the Village Route Transfer, then the (red) Hermits Rest Shuttle to Hermits Rest. The Hermit Trail drops an abrupt 1,300 vertical feet in the 1.3 miles it takes to reach the Waldron Trail junction and is clearly marked. The Waldron Trail, which comes in from the left (south), was the original section of the Hermit constructed by Hogan from Horsethief Tank into Hermit Basin. (The Waldron trailhead can be reached by taking the Rowes Well Road from Grand Canyon Village to Horsethief Tank.) From the Waldron Trail junction, turn right (north) and proceed another .3 mile to the Dripping Springs / Hermit Trail junction.

To continue down the Hermit Trail, turn right (north) and follow this cobblestone stairway through the Supai Sandstone Formation past Santa Maria Spring. The hike down to this spring makes an excellent morning walk and provides some of the best views of this awesome tributary canyon formed by Hermit Creek. Just beyond Santa Maria Spring, the trail descends through the Supai Formation and stays atop the

Redwall Limestone past Four Mile Spring to Cathedral Stairs; the round-trip hikes to Four Mile Spring (dry) and the top of Cathedral Stairs are both also good day hikes. The latter provides a raptor's view of 4,528-foot Cope Butte, used by the Santa Fe Railroad when it ran its aerial tramway from 6,796-foot Pima Point all the way down to Hermits Camp.

To reach Hermits Camp, continue down Cathedral Stairs to its junction with the Tonto Trail; the camp is another mile to the south atop the Tonto Plateau. Hermit Rapids can be reached by following the bed of Hermit Creek another 1.5 miles. During the river-running season, you can enjoy the vicarious thrill of whitewater rafting by watching boatmen run one of the most fun stretches of river in the Canyon—the wavetrain of Hermit Rapids.

ADDITIONAL CONSIDERATIONS: The Hermit Trail is frequently used for the Bright Angel, Tonto, and Hermit trail loop, one of the most popular multiday loop hikes in the park.

Wilderness Trail Loop Hike. The 24.4-mile Bright Angel, Tonto, and Hermit trail loop (see page 178) can also be hiked west to east using the Hermit Trail as the first leg. If you're thinking of looping the Hermit and Boucher Trails (see page 179), you'll probably find it easier and safer to descend the Boucher Trail and climb out the Hermit Trail.

ELEVATION:	6,640 feet to 2,400 feet.
TOTAL ELEVATION LOSS & GAIN:	8,480 feet (4,240 vertical feet each way).
MILEAGE:	8.5 miles one way to the Colorado River.
WATER:	Santa Maria Spring and Colorado River. High fecal coli count in Hermit Creek.

CACHE POINTS:	In seclusion of Dripping Springs Trail junction, top of Cathedral Stairs, and Hermits Camp—depending on hike planned.
SEASONS:	Fall through spring. Summer's hot.
Map:	Grand Canyon Quadrangle (7.5 minute).

Boucher Trail

If there is one trail in Grand Canyon National Park I'm reluctant to describe, it's the Boucher Trail. It's one of the most spectacular trails, and also one of the more difficult. If you continue to tread lightly, it will remain one of the most pristine.

The Boucher Trail was constructed by French Canadian prospector Louis D. Boucher before 1893. He called it the Silver Bell Trail and started the first leg a few miles west of the Waldron trailhead near 6,400-foot Eremita Mesa to reach his camp and oasis at Drippings Springs. He continued the Silver Bell Trail down to Boucher Creek, where he prospected for graphite, planted a fine little orchard, and delighted tourists until about 1910. It's been said of Boucher that "he wore a white beard, rode a white mule and told only white lies," a claim the tall-speaking John Hance couldn't make—not with his yarns of snowshoeing across the Grand Canyon on a cloud-hopping journey to the North Rim.

The most commonly used access to the Boucher Trail is from Hermits Rest. To reach the Hermit trailhead, take the (blue) Village Route Shuttle to the Village Route Transfer, then the (red) Hermits Rest Shuttle to Hermits Rest. Hike 1.6 miles down the Hermit Trail to the Hermit Trail junction. The road out to the Eremita Mesa trailhead can be more difficult to follow than the trail itself and is frequently impassable during summer rains, winter snows, and spring thaws.

From the Dripping Springs/Hermit Trail junction, turn left (west) and follow the Dripping Springs Trail 1.1 miles along the very rim of the Supai Formation to its junction with the Boucher Trail, which can be followed after crossing the Dripping Springs drainage. If you walk up the bed of this little drainage, you'll reach Dripping Springs. The 2.7-mile walk from Hermits Rest down to Dripping Springs is a good day hike, even during the relatively hot summer months, if done early enough in the morning. The Boucher Trail continues north from the Dripping Springs drainage and skirts the very rim of the Supai Formation for approximately 2 ½ miles to 6,440-foot Yuma Point. This leg, from the Hermit Trail junction to Yuma Point, offers some of the most exposed and exciting hiking in the Grand Canyon. But it can be quite dangerous if you attempt to hike it during icy winter conditions because there are sections where you're walking on the *very* edge of the Supai Formation. The abyss yawns below your footsteps.

The Boucher Trail contours around the base of Yuma Point for another half-mile before it begins its descent through the Supai Formation; there are several sections along this line of descent that require the use of hands and feet, as well as keeping an eye open for the actual line the Boucher Trail takes to the head of Travertine Canyon. Once you're in Travertine Canyon, the Boucher Trail follows the west side of this drainage to the saddle immediately below 4,860-foot Whites Butte. The trail through the Redwall is picked up just west of the 4,533-foot Whites Butte saddle and runs basically due north 1.3 miles to its junction with the Tonto Trail. This is the most grungy and difficult section of the Boucher Trail, primarily because the trail descends abruptly through the Redwall and Muav limestones.

It's a clearly marked half-mile from the Tonto Trail to Boucher Creek. From Boucher Creek, you have the option of camping in the vicinity or boulder-hopping another 1 ½ miles down Boucher Creek to the Colorado River.

ADDITIONAL CONSIDERATIONS: The Boucher Trail is frequently used as the first leg of the increasingly popular Boucher, Tonto, and Hermit trail loop hike or to start the trek across the Tonto to the head of the South Bass Trail.

Wilderness Trail Loop Hike and Trek. The 21-mile Boucher, Tonto, and Hermit trail loop is the shortest and most exciting South Rim and Tonto loop (see Hermit Trail to Boucher Trail, page 179). The 45-mile Boucher, Tonto, and South Bass trail loop is long, remote, and intimidating for many. Do some of the shorter South Rim–Tonto loops before embarking on this one (see Boucher Trail to South Bass Trail, page 180).

ELEVATION:	6,640 feet (Hermits Rest) to 2,325 feet at the Colorado River.
TOTAL ELEVATION LOSS & GAIN:	8,630 feet (4,315 vertical feet each way).
MILEAGE:	10.8 miles one way to the Colorado River.
WATER:	Dripping Springs, Boucher Creek, Colorado River.
CACHE POINTS:	Dripping Springs drainage, Yuma Point, and Whites Butte Saddle.
SEASONS:	Spring and fall. Winter can be treacherous along the exposed sections of Supai, and summers can be unkind.
MAP:	Grand Canyon Quadrangle (7.5 minute).

South Bass Trail

Few other prospectors who came to the Grand Canyon had a greater effect on the development of the area than William Wallace Bass. He came to the Canyon for his health in 1884, married Ada Diefendorf eleven years later, raised four children—the first family on the South Rim—and didn't succumb to ill health until he was 84. During his 40-odd years at the Canyon, the tireless Bass built a 70-mile road for tourists from Ashfork, Arizona, to Bass's Camp on the South Rim, delivered mail from the Grand Canyon Village to Havasupai, went to Washington, D.C., to drum up financial support to build the first school in Havasupai, led the first cross-Canyon treks for tourists, built trails, and prospected.

The first leg of the Bass Trail was originally the Mystic Springs Trail, which the Havasupai used for years before the spring reportedly vanished after an earthquake. Bass improved this trail and extended it down to the Colorado River in order to take tourists up to the North Rim, as well as to haul out asbestos and tend to his garden along Shinumo Creek on the north side of the river.

To reach the South Bass Trail requires more effort than any other rim-to-river trail on the South Rim. The trailhead is located approximately 4 miles north of the Pasture Wash Ranger Station at the end of the Pasture Wash Road. (See South Kaibab National Forest Map for directions to Pasture Wash Ranger Station.) The entire road, from the Rowes Well Road turnoff to the trailhead, is frequently impassable during summer rains, winter snows, and spring thaws. But if you've done the navigation necessary to reach this remote trailhead, you shouldn't have any problem following the South Bass Trail 7 miles down to the Colorado River.

The trail drops 1,400 vertical feet in the 1 ½ miles it takes to reach the broad sweep of the Esplanade Sandstone that comprises Darwin Plateau, Spencer Terrace, and Huxley Terrace. You can pick up the Apache Trail on the Esplanade, but you'll have to start looking for the junction not long after you break away from the Hermit Shale, especially if you're the first one on it during the spring; this junction has been wheeled at 1.45 miles from the trailhead. It's just under a mile across the Esplanade to where you begin your descent through that formation. Mystic Springs (dry) makes a good day hike from the rim, and you can reach it by following the edge of the Esplanade west and then north along the rim of the Darwin Plateau until you reach the neck of Spencer Terrace on the northwest side of 6,281-foot Mount Huethawli.

To continue down the South Bass, it's another mile from the top of the Esplanade due east of Mount Huethawli to the top of the Redwall Formation. From here it's 2 miles along this sometimes brush-covered trail to the Tonto Trail junction, and another mile down Bass Canyon to Bass Rapids. You'll have to look for the cairn before beginning this last pitch because the creekbed drops off abruptly just short of the Colorado River.

ADDITIONAL CONSIDERATIONS: The South Bass Trail is used by climbers to climb 6,281-foot Mount Huethawli, river runners joining or leaving a Colorado River trip at Bass Rapids, and canyoneers headed across the Tonto Plateau for points east.

Wilderness Trail Loop and Trek. The 45-mile Boucher, Tonto, and South Bass trail loop (see page 180) can also be hiked west-to-east, using the South Bass Trail as the first leg. Because of the South Bass trailhead's remote location and unpredictable road conditions, you may find it safer to descend the South Bass Trail, cross the Tonto Plateau, then hike out the more accessible Boucher Trail or Hermits Trail to Hermits Rest.

ELEVATION:	6,646 feet to 2,200 feet.
TOTAL ELEVATION LOSS & GAIN:	8,892 feet (4,446 vertical feet each way).
MILEAGE:	7.8 miles.
WATER:	Colorado River.
CACHE POINTS:	Esplanade Formation and Tonto Plateau.
SEASONS:	Spring and fall. Access road impassable most of winter without cross-country skis. Summer's hot.
MAPS:	Havasupai Point and Explorers Monument quadrangles (7.5 minute).

TRANS-CANYON TRAILS AND ROUTES— NONMAINTAINED

You've hiked most or all of the South Rim's rim-to-river trails, and now you're looking to do something other than hike to the Colorado River and back. What are your options? You can link two rim-to-river trails on the South Rim with those on the North Rim via Corridor Trails such as the South Kaibab and Bright Angel Trails with the North Kaibab Trail, or the Wilderness Trails of the South Bass and North Bass Trails (see related sections for trail descriptions). Or you can tackle either multiday or multiweek trans-Canyon trails and routes that traverse the heart of the Grand Canyon east to west, or vice versa. If you're interested in starting off your canyoneering career with one of the more popular multiday treks, it's possible to descend any of the previously described rim-to-river trails, follow one of the major geological benches or other natural lines of weakness east- or westward, then exit any of the other rim-to-river trails. The loops you decide to embark on will depend on your own canyoneering experience and how many days you want to be in the backcountry. However, if you're interested in undertaking a multiweek trek, it's possible to hike all the way from Cameron on the Navajo Indian Reservation, down the Little Colorado River Gorge, through the heart of the Grand Canyon (resupplying at Phantom Ranch or Grand Canyon Village) to Supai on the Havasupai Indian Reservation—and beyond.

The following section will describe the major routes from the confluence of the Little Colorado and Colorado rivers leading westward to 6,322-foot Apache Point near the eastern border of the Havasupai Traditional Use Area. (See page 249 for a description of the Little Colorado River Gorge from Cameron to its confluence with the Colorado River.) Taken individually, it's possible to combine sections of the trans-Canyon trails and routes with rim-to-river trails for multiday loop hikes or a multiweek trek from one end of the Grand Canyon to the other.

Note that each of the trans-Canyon trails and routes is described east-to-west and each links one individual section with the next.

Beamer Trail

Ben Beamer was another prospector who came to the Grand Canyon in the late 1800s to find the mother lode. He built a 4-mile section of trail from Palisades Creek to the mouth of the Little Colorado River that no doubt was used earlier by the Hopi to reach their sacred salt mines in the eastern Grand Canyon. This section of trail gave Beamer the access he needed to link together the old Tanner Canyon Trail with his stone house at the mouth of the Little Colorado River. This ancient dwelling was actually a ruin—built into the convoluted walls of the Tapeats Sandstone—that Beamer refurbished and lived in for the two years he prospected and farmed in the area.

The Beamer Trail begins—or ends, depending on which direction you're coming from—near the mouth of the Little Colorado River by the last sand spit on the left (south) bank. It climbs no more than several hundred feet through the Tapeats Sandstone, and is marked by both cairns and hiker use. Once you've topped out on this Tapeats Sandstone bench, the trail stays atop it all the way to Palisades Creek. Like the Tonto Trail, the Beamer is neither flat nor straight. It curves in and out of drainages cut by headward erosion, frequently descending 50 to 100 vertical feet into each drainage before climbing out the opposite side. Just make sure you see the trail or cairns on the opposite sides of each of these minor drainages before descending into them and you'll save yourself time and unnecessary scrambling.

About the time you reach the last major drainage opposite (or across the river from) the mouth of Carbon Creek, the Beamer Trail braids off on three different and distinct levels. Like the Boucher Trail, the Beamer Trail has certain sections that can be dangerous to negotiate if you're carrying an external-frame pack and encounter strong upstream winds. In this section, taking the highest trail, which is marked by cairns, might be safer for you than traversing the outer rim 200 feet above the Colorado River. The Beamer Trail continues contouring the Tapeats Sandstone until you're overlooking Palisades Creek. This is where the Beamer Trail makes an abrupt and well-marked descent through the Dox Sandstone to the mouth of Palisades Creek.

From Palisades Creek, the trail is straightforward enough through the sand, boulders, and tammies—passing the McCormick Mine en route—until you encounter the first of two sections of Dox Sandstone that have to be negotiated before you reach the mouth of Tanner Canyon. This first section of Dox Sandstone begins just opposite the north end of the exposed sandbar on the left side (facing downstream) of the Colorado River, at River Mile 66.5. If high water has covered up this sandbar, you can tell you're at your first section of Dox Sandstone because there's no longer any beach to walk on. Two faint trails traverse their way through the Dox to the next beach, less than a half mile downstream. The lower route can be followed at low water, though there are a couple of boulder moves you might find awkward to do with a pack on; or you can take the upper route, which is marked by cairns.

Once you're through this section of Dox, the trail links up with the next section of beach and remains on it until you've crossed the mouth of Comanche Creek and reached the next major unnamed drainage to the west. Here you'll encounter the second section of Dox Sandstone. Two routes traverse this section. The upper route may require a little more walking because it climbs to the top of the Dox, but it's more clearly marked and safer than the lower route. There are several exposed boulder moves near the west end of the low route where a fall would necessitate a dangerous cold-water swim—assuming you can swim with a heavy, waterlogged pack.

Once you're through this section of Dox, it's a few minutes' stroll to the expanse of the Tanner Canyon delta and the foot of the Tanner Trail.

ADDITIONAL CONSIDERATIONS: The Beamer Trail is most frequently done as an out-and-back hike from the top of the Tanner Trail simply because it's far easier to drive to the Tanner trailhead than to negotiate the maze of unmarked roads leading to the head of Salt Trail Canyon (the main access route into the Little Colorado River Gorge) or to trek the length of the 57-mile-long Little Colorado River Gorge from Cameron to the east end of the Beamer Trail.

PRIMARY ACCESS TRAILS & ROUTES:	Tanner Trail, Salt Trail Canyon, Little Colorado River.
ELEVATION:	2,725 feet to 2,720 feet, at river level.
TOTAL ELEVATION LOSS & GAIN:	Approximately 500 vertical feet each way.
MILEAGE:	Approximately 8 to 9 miles one way.
WATER:	Colorado River.
CACHE POINTS (if hiked out-and-back from Tanner trailhead):	Mouth of Tanner Canyon and Palisades Creek.
SEASONS:	Fall through spring. Summer's hot, and upstream winds can be unusually strong.
MAPS:	Desert View and Cape Solitude quadrangles (7.5 minute).

Tanner Canyon to Red Canyon, a.k.a. the Escalante Route

At one time the 2 ½-mile stretch between the mouth of Tanner Canyon and Cardenas Creek was a faint path. But so many river runners have hiked it over the years that there is now a distinct trail.

From Tanner Canyon the trail heads west along the contact point of Dox Sandstone and the south end of Tanner Beach. If you're unsure which braided trail to take, head south across the beach until it merges with the Dox and you'll pick up the trail to Cardenas Creek; for the most part it follows this contact line all the way.

Once at Cardenas Creek you'll be following another river-runner trail, which climbs abruptly to Hilltop Ruin and Unkar

Overlook. If you lie on your stomach you'll get an incredible view of Unkar Rapids several hundred feet below. When Welshman Colin Fletcher first backpacked this route in 1966, the Colorado River was a veritable trickle at 1,260 cfs (cubic feet per second); that was low enough for him to walk along the south bank of Unkar Rapids at river level. But chances are the Colorado River won't be that low when you do this section, so from the Unkar Overlook you'll have to follow an increasingly faint trail up a ridge of Dox Sandstone until you find the next cairn, or until you can eyeball a route down into the head of the first major unnamed drainage west of the Unkar Overlook. Use care, and you shouldn't have much problem picking your way back down to the Colorado River.

Assuming the Colorado River isn't rumbling along at 30,000 cfs or more, you can follow the left-hand (south) side of the river through the tammies, along upward-sloping steps of Hakatai Shale all the way to Escalante Creek. (If high water has covered this section along the river, you'll have to take the high route by contouring the talus from Unkar Overlook to Escalante Creek. I have not hiked the high route, so a description of it is not included here. It's marked infrequently by cairns, but if you've got the canyoneering experience to be hiking the Escalante Route, you shouldn't encounter any major problems finding the safest path.)

The bed of Escalante Creek drops off near the Colorado River. Cairns mark the way through a series of three pouroffs standing between you and the beach below. If for some reason you can't find the cairns, eyeball the safest route—and don't get rimrocked down-climbing something you can't climb back up. Each of these three obstacles can be negotiated by locating and following the weakest lines, which have a tendency to diagonal off to the west.

You can follow the beach at Escalante Creek all the way to Papago Creek, assuming it's not buried by high water. Call Grand Canyon National Park River Sub-District at (800) 959-9164, or visit www.nps.gov/grca/river, for up-to-date river flow information. If you study the route closely, there is a line that climbs out of the mouth of Papago Creek and traverses the sandstone ledges above. It has a tendency to diagonal up and west to the top of the rockslide facing downstream, which is your descent route back down to river level. From the bottom of this rockslide, it's another 30-minute hike along the beach to Hance Rapids and the foot of the New Hance Trail and the east end of the Tonto Trail.

ADDITIONAL CONSIDERATIONS: If you're planning to do the Escalante Route, you may find it safer and easier to descend the Tanner Trail on the first leg, traverse the Escalante Route, then exit via either the New Hance Trail or the Grandview Trail (and two seasonal springs in the east arm). If you encounter difficulties negotiating either of the two cliff sections, consider trying the high route or catching a ride around them with river runners.

PRIMARY ACCESS TRAILS & ROUTES:	Tanner Trail, New Hance Trail, and Tonto/Grandview Trail.
ELEVATION:	2,720 feet to 2,600 feet, at river level.
TOTAL ELEVATION LOSS & GAIN:	2,000 feet plus or minus (approximately 1,000 vertical feet each way for the route described).
MILEAGE:	Approximately 10 miles one way.
WATER:	Colorado River, Grandview and J. T. springs on the east arm of the Grandview Trail below Redwall Formation.

Cache Points:	None.
Seasons:	Fall through spring. Summer's hot.
Maps:	Desert View and Cape Royal quadrangles (7.5 minute).

Tonto Trail—Red Canyon to Garnet Canyon

The mouth of Red Canyon at Hance Rapids marks the beginning of the Tonto Plateau and the 95-mile-long Tonto Trail. The Tonto Plateau is the broadest terrace coursing east- and westward through the Grand Canyon, except for certain sections of the Esplanade Sandstone near the west end where the Tonto Plateau tends to diminish. This desert plateau may look flat when viewed from the lofty heights of the South or North rim, but don't be fooled. The nonmaintained Wilderness Trail that snakes its way across the Tonto Plateau is rugged, circuitous, and undulating, with abrupt ascents and descents. In its broadest sections, usually between major and minor drainages, the Tonto Trail has a tendency to contour the outer rim of the Tonto Plateau, frequently skirting the very edge of the Tapeats Sandstone; if there is flat hiking on the Tonto trail, this is where it'll be. The steepest sections, however, appear when the trail contours each of the tributary canyons, creeks, and drainages cut by headward erosion. Going into these drainages the trail generally makes an abrupt descent, while coming out of them it has a tendency to climb abruptly. If there's a debilitating nature to the Tonto Trail, it's in trekking in and out of each and every tributary creek and canyon that drains into the Colorado River. What looks close is far, primarily because there are few shortcuts across these drainages; about when you think you've found one, it generally cliffs-out in the Tapeats Sandstone. Consequently, each and every minor drainage usually has to be contoured before you reach the head of the major drainages. And what before may have looked so close—when you were standing on the Tonto Plateau looking across the mouth of one of these tributaries—will suddenly strike you as being very far. Then, that may have something to do with the manner in which the Tonto Trail was constructed.

Of it George Wharton James wrote in 1905 in *The Grand Canyon of Arizona:* "The trail made centuries ago by mountain sheep, small bands of which are still to be found in the remoter corners of the Canyon—then followed by the Indians, whose moccasin feet made less impression upon it than did the hoofs of the sheep. And in the two or three decades just passed, a few white men trod it. Perhaps Powell, or some of his men, or Stanton, walked where we now walk, or ride, and surely some of those early mining prospectors of the Canyon—Ashurst, McClure, Marshal, Hance, Boucher, Berry, Brashear—once went this way."

Whatever your own impressions of hiking the Tonto Plateau may be, the Tonto Trail is the major east-west *camino* through the Grand Canyon.

Red Canyon to Hance Creek

This leg of the Tonto Trail is perhaps its steepest and rockiest stretch. Standing at the mouth of Red Canyon, look to your west and you can see the trail climbing out of the west side of Red Canyon. Pick it up at the top of a large sand dune before it climbs a steep section of Hakatai Shale. Between the Hakatai Shale and Mineral Canyon, you'll have to pick your way from one cairn to the next as the trail probes its way through the slumps, landslides, and rockfalls. Once through this craggy section, you'll skirt the Bass Formation near the mouth of Mineral Canyon for a few minutes before tying together once again with the Hakatai Shale, which will take you about halfway up the east side of Mineral Canyon. You'll cross Mineral Canyon here.

(Hiking down this section from Hance Creek to Red Canyon, you may get sidetracked on an old burro trail while crossing this section. They generally go down Mineral Canyon to the Colorado River, not over to Red Canyon.) Once across Mineral Canyon, the trail climbs back through the Hakatai Shale to a place called Shady Overhang, which is located at the head of an unnamed canyon between Mineral Canyon and Hance Creek; it's a good lunch or rest spot.

From Shady Overhang, the trail climbs up through the Tapeats Sandstone and finally tops out on the Tonto Plateau below 4,961-foot Ayer Point. You'll stay on the Tonto Plateau, skirting the Tapeats Sandstone along the east side of Hance Creek until you're just about opposite the saddle, or neck, of 5,246-foot Horse Shoe Mesa. This is where the trail leaves the Tonto Plateau and descends back through the Tapeats Sandstone and links up the eastern spur of the Grandview Trail coming down from Horse Shoe Mesa, J. T. Spring, and Grandview Spring.

ADDITIONAL CONSIDERATIONS: If you're planning on making a loop hike using the New Hance, Tonto, and Grandview trails, and you haven't hiked the New Hance Trail before, you might find it easier and safer to descend the New Hance Trail and exit the Grandview Trail. There is no permanent water on the New Hance Trail for the climb out, but you can get water at J. T. Spring and Grandview Spring about halfway up the Grandview Trail on your way out.

PRIMARY ACCESS TRAILS & ROUTES:	New Hance Trail and eastern spur of Grandview Trail.
ELEVATION:	2,600 feet at Hance Rapids to approximately 3,800 feet at junction of eastern spur of Grandview.

TOTAL ELEVATION LOSS & GAIN:	Approximately 1,200+ feet vertical elevation gain.
MILEAGE:	Approximately 4 ½ miles one way.
WATER:	Colorado River and J. T. and Grandview springs.
CACHE POINTS (if hiked out-and-back from Grandview trailhead):	Hance Creek and Shady Overhang.
SEASONS:	Fall through spring. Summer's hot.
MAP:	Cape Royal Quadrangle (7.5 minute).

Hance Creek to Cottonwood Creek

When the prospectors abandoned their mines during the late 1800s, they turned loose herds of exotic African burros. The burros prospered in the warm inner Canyon, and several decades later their population numbered in the hundreds. But their very presence threatened the native, and more timid, desert bighorn sheep by destroying its habitat. And until National Park Service biologists destroyed more than 2,000 burros, and Cleveland Amory saved hundreds of others, they also played havoc with many of the inner-Canyon trails—most notably the Tonto Trail. That's ironic because *Equus asinus* did as much to develop and maintain large sections of the Tonto Trail as did the prospectors who once led them. However, once burros were turned loose to roam at will, they braided many sections of the Tonto Trail into a confusing array of dead ends, cul-de-sacs, and seemingly aimless wanderings. That later presented the hikers and canyoneers with the dilemma of choosing which of the nonmaintained trails to follow.

Today all but a handful of these clever animals are gone from the park, though there remain several sections of the Tonto Plateau that still bear the marks of their feral wanderings. One of these sections is the stretch of Tonto Trail between Hance Creek and Cottonwood Creek, which contours the base of 5,246-foot Horse Shoe Mesa. While there is never any doubt where you are geographically, there are several short sections on the north side of Horse Shoe Mesa that require more care in following the cairns that mark the best of several trail alternatives.

Cave of the Domes Trail leading up the north side of Horse Shoe Mesa is picked up shortly after contouring around the east arm of Horse Shoe Mesa, and the west arm of the Grandview Trail is picked up as soon as you reach Cottonwood Creek. Like the east arm of the Grandview Trail, both of these trails will take you back up to Horse Shoe Mesa, where you can link up with the main stem of the Grandview Trail.

ADDITIONAL CONSIDERATIONS: This section of the Tonto Trail is most frequently done as a loop hike, using the Grandview Trail as the main trail to enter and exit the Canyon. However, if you're doing a loop around Horse Shoe Mesa, you might find it easier and safer to go down either the west arm of the Grandview Trail or Cave of the Domes Trail and come out the east arm at Hance Creek, so you can replenish your water at J. T. or Grandview springs.

PRIMARY ACCESS TRAILS & ROUTES:	Grandview Trail and New Hance Trail.
ELEVATION:	Approximately 3,800 feet at Hance Creek to 3,800 feet atop Tonto to 3,800 feet at Cottonwood Creek.
TOTAL ELEVATION LOSS & GAIN:	Approximately 200 vertical feet each way.

MILEAGE:	Approximately 3 ½ miles from east arm to west arm trail junctions.
WATER:	J. T. and Grandview springs and Colorado River.
SEASONS:	Fall through spring. Summer's hot.
MAP:	Cape Royal quadrangle (7.5 minute).
CACHE POINTS (if hiked from Grandview Trail):	Horse Shoe Mesa.

Cottonwood Creek to South Kaibab Trail

Assuming an old feral burro trail doesn't lead you off on a half-day tangent, it's 18 miles along the main arm of the Tonto Trail from Cottonwood Creek to the Tonto Trail junction with the South Kaibab Trail. Compared to the 40-odd-mile stretch of the Tonto Trail between the Boucher and South Bass trails, this popular stretch is relatively easy to follow, though care is required on several sections.

From Cottonwood Creek, it's 3.43 miles to the head of Grapevine Creek. This creek is significant from a couple of standpoints: it's the only perennial water source on this stretch of the Tonto Trail; and it's the longest tributary drainage cutting through the Tonto Plateau below the South Rim—longer than Hance Creek to the east and Slate Creek and Serpentine Canyon far to the west. From that standpoint alone, it can be particularly debilitating to walk from one side of Grapevine Creek to the other at the end of a weary day. So don't expect to flash Grapevine Creek in an hour, because it *is* farther than it looks. You should also pay particular care in following the cairns when hiking into and out of the east and west sides of Grapevine Creek because the trail is not as clearly defined in the narrower sections of Tapeats Sandstone as it is on the broader stretches of the Tonto Plateau.

It's 5.82 miles from Grapevine Creek around the base of 5,362-foot Lyell Butte to Burro Creek, and if you haven't been tempted to try a shortcut on the meandering Tonto Trail, the notion just might strike you while you're hiking out the west side of Grapevine Creek. There you'll be faced with the classic question that's faced every canyoneer who's spent any time hiking the Tonto Plateau: "Is it shorter and faster to go up and over the talus, or easier to go all the way around along the rim of the Tapeats Sandstone?" It's a question many have answered the hard way. In this particular instance, the carrot being dangled in front of you is the 4,200-foot Muav Limestone saddle between the east arm of 5,362-foot Lyell Butte and a lower butte, designated on your map as 4392. Unless you're prepared for adventure, go around. Boulder Creek is one of three seasonal water sources you may be able to make use of on this stretch of the Tonto Trail if you plan your hike for mid-spring. (Check with the BIC on conditions of this seasonal water source and others.)

From Boulder Creek to Lonetree Canyon it's 2.88 miles, and there aren't any real mysteries in following this section of trail going into Lonetree Canyon, the second seasonal water source.

It's 3.09 miles from Lonetree Canyon to the east arm of Cremation Creek, the last seasonal water source. The only puzzle on this stretch is after you climb out through the Tapeats Sandstone on the west side of Lonetree Canyon and regain the Tonto Plateau; there you'll regain several feral variations of the true Tonto Trail. Let cairns, footprints, and common sense be your guide.

From the east arm of Cremation Creek to the west arm it's a well-marked .82 mile. Don't let the sudden appearance of

Hakatai Shale in the middle and west arms throw you off. From the east arm, the trail climbs out of the Tapeats Sandstone, over a pinched-out section of Tonto Plateau, then descends back into the Hakatai Shale in the middle arm; from the middle arm, it climbs over another pinch of Tonto Plateau before descending back into the Hakatai Shale in the west arm. If you encounter any problems with this section, it may have to do with the refracted heat that can be oppressive in this tributary canyon. Cremation Creek was once a vast urn for ancestral Puebloans who reportedly cremated their dead on the South Rim and hurled the ashes into the abyss.

Once you've started out the west arm of Cremation Creek, it's only 1.63 miles to the junction of the Tonto Trail; the way should be obvious.

ADDITIONAL CONSIDERATIONS: It's imperative you plan your trek along the South Kaibab, Tonto, Grandview loop to coincide with reliable seasonal water sources. You also need to consider whether to do this loop east to west or vice versa. If you've checked with the BIC and their records indicate the only water source you can rely on along this stretch is the perennial one in Grapevine Canyon, you would do well to consider hiking down the South Kaibab across the Tonto Plateau, then out the Grandview Trail; that way, you could make better use of Grapevine Creek as your primary water source—and perhaps layover day—before climbing out the west arm of the Grandview Trail.

PRIMARY ACCESS TRAILS & ROUTES:	Grandview Trail and South Kaibab Trail.
ELEVATION:	Approximately 3,800 feet at Cottonwood Creek to 4,000 feet at South Kaibab Trail.

TOTAL ELEVATION LOSS & GAIN:	Approximately 1,000 feet one way.
MILEAGE:	18 miles one way.
WATER:	Grapevine Creek.
CACHE POINTS:	None.
SEASONS:	Fall through spring. Summer can be deadly.
MAPS:	Grandview Point, Cape Royal, and Phantom Ranch quadrangles (7.5 minute).

South Kaibab Trail to Bright Angel Trail

The 4.1-mile stretch of the Tonto Trail between the South Kaibab and Bright Angel trails is not maintained, but it is the most well worn and easily identifiable stretch of the Tonto Trail along its entire 95-mile course. Pipe Spring and Burro Springs, both perennial water sources, are located midway between the South Kaibab and Bright Angel trails.

ADDITIONAL CONSIDERATIONS: If you're in good shape but only have time for a day hike, the 13-mile-long South Kaibab, Tonto, Bright Angel trail loop is a good outing. Waterwise, it's best to descend the South Kaibab Trail and exit the Bright Angel Trail.

PRIMARY ACCESS TRAILS & ROUTES:	South Kaibab Trail and Bright Angel Trail.
ELEVATION:	Approximately 4,000 feet at South Kaibab Trail to 3,800 feet at Indian Gardens.
TOTAL ELEVATION LOSS & GAIN:	Approximately 200 vertical feet one way.
MILEAGE:	4.1 miles one way.

WATER:	Pipe Spring, Burro Springs, and Indian Gardens.
CACHE POINTS:	None.
SEASONS:	Fall through spring. Summer's hot.
MAPS:	Phantom Ranch and Grand Canyon quadrangles (7.5 minute).

Bright Angel Trail to Hermit Creek

The 12-mile-long stretch of Tonto Trail between the Bright Angel and Hermit trails is as easy to follow as the 4.1-mile section of Tonto Trail between the Bright Angel and South Kaibab trails. Mileages for this section (from Indian Gardens) are as follows: 2.52 miles to Horn Creek campsite (seasonal water); 7.29 miles to Salt Creek campsite (seasonal water); 9.38 miles to Cedar Springs campsite; 10.70 to Monument Creek campsite (perennial water); and 12.32 miles to the Granite Rapids campsite or 12.05 miles to the Hermit–Tonto trail junction.

ADDITIONAL CONSIDERATIONS: This is the most popular multi-day loop hike in Grand Canyon National Park; if you plan your hike when seasonal water sources on this loop are reliable (normally the spring), you're going to have to book reservations far in advance. However, if your schedule coincides with the drier hiking seasons and records at the BIC indicate that Monument Creek is the only reliable water source, consider hiking down the Bright Angel Trail and out the Hermit Trail to make better use of Monument Creek as your primary water source—a good spot for a layover day, too—before climbing out the Hermit Trail.

| PRIMARY ACCESS TRAILS & ROUTES: | Bright Angel Trail and Hermit Trail. |
| ELEVATION: | Approximately 3,800 feet at Indian |

Gardens to 3,200 feet at Hermit
Trail junction.

TOTAL ELEVATION LOSS & GAIN:	Approximately 1,000 feet one way.
MILEAGE:	12 miles one way.
WATER:	Indian Gardens, Monument Creek, Colorado River.
CACHE POINTS:	None.
SEASONS:	Fall through spring. Summer's hot.
MAP:	Grand Canyon Quadrangle (7.5 minute).

Hermit Creek to Boucher Trail

This section of the Tonto Trail is becoming increasingly popular with hikers because it's a relatively short 6.3 miles, and because a challenging loop hike can be done by using a single trailhead. In the case of the Hermit, Tonto, Boucher trail loop, that's Hermits Rest, which is easily accessible. However, because this section of the Tonto Plateau is one of the narrowest below the South Rim, the trail can be difficult to follow because it contours steep talus slopes. Consequently, more care is required in scouting the way for cairns and footprints than on more heavily used sections of the Tonto Trail.

From the Hermit Trail junction to Travertine Canyon, it's a shade under 4 miles; the 2.75-mile section from Hermit Creek to Monument Creek has a tendency to play tag with the Tapeats Sandstone most of the way, except where the trail hooks back over the Tonto Plateau before descending into the mouth of Travertine Canyon.

It's 2.34 miles from Travertine Canyon to the Boucher Trail junction, and the first piece of this section has a tendency to hug the Tapeats Sandstone until you reach the north side of

4,860-foot Whites Butte, where it regains the Tonto Plateau for a mile or so before descending into Boucher Creek, a perennial water source.

ADDITIONAL CONSIDERATIONS: This loop is most frequently done by descending the Boucher Trail and exiting the Hermit Trail—primarily because most people find it easier to climb out the more popular Hermit Trail than the less frequently used Boucher Trail. Knowledgeable canyoneers do it both ways, and strong day hikers have trekked it in 8 to 9 hours.

PRIMARY ACCESS TRAILS & ROUTES:	Hermit Trail and Boucher Trail.
ELEVATION:	Approximately 3,200 feet at Hermit Trail junction to 3,200 feet at Boucher Trail junction.
TOTAL ELEVATION LOSS & GAIN:	Approximately 300 vertical feet one way.
MILEAGE:	6.3 miles.
WATER:	Hermit Creek, Boucher Creek, and Colorado River.
CACHE POINTS:	None.
SEASONS:	Fall through spring. Summer can be unforgiving.
MAP:	Grand Canyon Quadrangle (7.5 minute).

Boucher Trail to South Bass Trail

If there is a no-man's-land character to any section of the Tonto Trail, it's the 30-mile stretch between Boucher Creek and the South Bass Trail. The reason is simple: If you get into trouble anywhere on this stretch and can't walk out under your own power, you have to either call or signal for help, or—

failing that, due to poor reception or visibility or stormy conditions—send your partner for help, out either the Boucher Trail to Hermits Rest or the South Bass Trail to the remote Pasture Wash roads. Another emergency alternative that can be considered during the river-running season is to hike to the Colorado River for help, using either Boucher Creek, Ruby Canyon, Serpentine Canyon, or the South Bass Trail.

Emergency considerations notwithstanding, this leg of the Tonto Trail offers its own unique rewards to experienced canyoneers in the form of solitude and the opportunity to experience the Canyon's natural rhythms for more than a few hours at a time. A multiday trek along this route should be well planned and not taken lightly.

From the Tonto and Boucher Trail junction, it's less than half a mile to the Boucher Creek camp. The Boucher Rapids trail junction is .36 mile down Boucher Creek at its confluence with Topaz Canyon. To reach Boucher Rapids, turn right at this junction and boulder-hop a little more than a mile to the Colorado River. To continue west along the Tonto Trail, however, you have to hike up the west side of Topaz Canyon for about a quarter of a mile until it starts climbing back up through the Vishnu Schist and Tapeats Sandstone and regains the Tonto Plateau southeast of 4,721-foot Marsh Butte.

It's approximately 5 miles from Boucher Creek to Slate Creek, the first perennial water source on this route. This section of the Tonto Trail isn't indelible, but you shouldn't have any problems following it all the way to the South Bass Trail as long as you exercise good judgment in trail and route finding. This section of the Tonto Trail stays atop the Tonto Plateau, except where it shortcuts the heads of tributary drainages like Slate Creek, Sapphire Canyon, the two unnamed drainages between Shaler Plateau and Le Conte Plateau, and Ruby and Serpentine canyons. These shortcuts have a tendency to make abrupt descents and ascents through the Tapeats Sandstone before linking up with the next section of Tonto Plateau. All of the shortcuts should be marked with cairns and/or footprints.

From Slate Creek it's 4 ½ miles to the head of Agate Canyon; the only thing to remember is that the trail in Agate Canyon follows the contact point between the Tapeats Sandstone and Tonto Plateau before climbing back atop the Tonto Plateau and descending into Sapphire Canyon. From Agate Canyon to Sapphire Canyon it's 2.05 miles; the trail shortcuts the head of Sapphire Canyon, then climbs back atop the Tonto Plateau and stays there all the way to the head of Turquoise Canyon 2.72 miles farther. Turquoise Canyon is the second perennial water source on this route and a good objective for your first day's hike west of Boucher Creek. From Turquoise Canyon to Jasper Canyon it's 2.4 miles, and from Jasper Canyon to Jade Canyon it's another .73 mile; these are the two unnamed drainages between Shaler Plateau and Le Conte Plateau that were named by river runners who refer to the 6-mile stretch of river between Agate Canyon and Serpentine Canyon as "the gems"; the trail shortcuts both Jasper and Jade canyons.

From Jade Canyon to Ruby Canyon it's 2.69 miles; the trail shortcuts the head of Ruby Canyon, which is also the first seasonal water source west of Boucher Creek. It's 1.54 miles between Ruby Canyon and Quartz Canyon, and 1.93 miles between Quartz Canyon and Emerald Canyon; these are the two unnamed drainages on the map between Ruby Canyon and Serpentine Canyon. The trail does not shortcut either of these canyons, but generally rims the top of the Tapeats Sandstone.

It's 1.37 miles from Emerald Canyon to Serpentine Canyon, the next seasonal water source; the trail only cuts off a small section of Serpentine Canyon before beginning the 3.81-mile haul to Bass Canyon.

ADDITIONAL CONSIDERATIONS: If you're not trekking all the way from one end of the Grand Canyon to the other and just want to do this remote loop using the Boucher and South Bass trails, consider going in on the South Bass Trail and out the Boucher or Hermit trail.

PRIMARY ACCESS TRAILS & ROUTES:	Boucher Trail and South Bass Trail.
ELEVATION:	Approximately 3,200 feet at Boucher Trail junction to 3,200 feet at South Bass Trail junction.
TOTAL ELEVATION LOSS & GAIN:	Approximately 2,000 vertical feet one way.
WATER:	Boucher Creek, Slate Canyon, Turquoise Canyon, and Colorado River.
CACHE POINTS:	None.
SEASONS:	Fall and spring. Summer can be deadly, and winter snows usually prevent access to South Bass trailhead.
MAPS:	Grand Canyon, Shiva Temple, and Havasupai Point quadrangles (7.5 minute).

The Apache Trail

Look at the Havasupai Point Quadrangle (15 minute) and you'll notice a trail immediately west of the upper end of the South Bass Trail that heads over to 6,322-foot Apache Point. According to Frank J. Taylor and Miner Raymond Tillotson (the latter a former superintendent of Grand Canyon National Park) who coauthored the 1930s classic *Grand Canyon Country,* "in the earlier days, came the Apaches on their expeditions to raid the stores of corn and other foodstuffs harvested by the Havasupai Indians." Their reported raids no doubt had something to do with naming the Apache Trail. This was the same trail that, Harvey Butchart wrote in *Grand Canyon Treks*, "Captain Burro started to build ... which would go from the Bass Trail to his home in Supai." At one time the trail traversed the Esplanade Sandstone situated approximately 1,500 vertical feet below the South Rim; thus it provided both the Havasupai and William Wallace Bass with an easier means of traversing the hanging terrace from east to west.

However, what once existed on the ground, and what still exists on most topographical maps, no longer exists *in situ* today. The Apache Trail is, for the most part, a route that requires as much care and route-finding ability as the Escalante Route. To complicate matters, access to Apache Point at the western end of the Apache Trail has to be approved in advance by the Havasupai tribe, whose Traditional Use Area includes the access roads that lead to both Topocoba Hilltop and Apache Point (for Havasupai contact information, permits, and fees, see page 192). Consequently, if you're an experienced enough canyoneer to be trekking the Apache Trail but for some reason cannot obtain permission to cross Havasupai land, the only other way to follow this route is to hike it out and back from the South Bass Trail. Unless you plan your trek during pleasant spring weather, when seasonal and emergency water sources are often most reliable, there isn't a practical way to carry enough water to complete this arduous multiday route.

From the South Bass Trail, the route clings to the steep talus of the Hermit Shale all the way around both 6,600-foot Chemehuevi and 6,400-foot Toltec points; if you never knew what a Sidehill Gianther was before you tackled this route, you will after you complete it. The main reason is that your left foot is usually 2 feet higher than your right, which makes for interesting locomotion—and cramps to be worked out later. The only water source on this first stretch is a seasonal one located in the first drainage west of Chemehuevi Point, but you'll have to use as much care finding it as you will following the Apache Trail.

Just about the time you reach the northernmost arm of the three separate points that comprise 6,408-foot Montezuma Point, the trail drops back down to the Esplanade Formation for about half a mile, then climbs back up to the Hermit Shale in the first drainage south of that northernmost arm. It stays on the Hermit Shale until you reach 6,000-foot Point Huitzil, where it descends back down to the Esplanade Formation in the first major drainage south of this point. The South-Bass-to-Point-Huitzil leg is physically the most difficult stretch of the Apache Trail. But the route-finding challenge isn't over until you reach Apache Point.

West of Point Huitzil, the Apache Trail stays on the Esplanade Formation around 6,200-foot Point Centeotl and 6,365-foot Point Quetzal; since the Esplanade Formation is virtually devoid of continuous stretches of soil, the only way to know if you're on the historic course of the trail is to look for the occasional rock cairns; they provide the only real clues that this actually was a trail at one time. Failing that, stay on the Esplanade Formation until you reach the second major drainage south of Apache Point; the route goes up the north side of this drainage and regains the Hermit Shale where it remains until you reach the head of the first major drainage south of Apache Point. It uses this steep drainage to climb through the Coconino Sandstone, and contours the Toroweap Formation around to the west until you find the breaks in the Kaibab Limestone, which will offer access to the top of 6,322-foot Apache Point.

ADDITIONAL CONSIDERATIONS: This remote route requires careful planning, good physical conditioning, and a thorough background in canyoneering and route-finding techniques.

Assuming you've obtained permission to cross and hike in the Havasupai Traditional Use Area, take the Apache Trail west from the South Bass Trail to Apache Point, then a compass bearing west through the pinyon-juniper to 5,409-foot Topocoba Hilltop, then down the Topocoba Trail to Supai. This is an excellent way to conclude a multiweek trans-Canyon trek from the Little Colorado Gorge.

One of the most appealing aspects of this route is that it traverses one of the highest terraces in the Grand Canyon, so you don't get that swallowed-up-whole feeling you frequently get hiking remote sections of the Tonto Plateau.

PRIMARY ACCESS TRAILS & ROUTES:	South Bass Trail and Apache Point. (To reach Apache Point you need to shoot a compass bearing from BM 6165, which is located approximately 2 miles north on the road from Mexican Jack Tank.)
ELEVATION:	Approximately 5,400 feet at South Bass Trail to 6,322 feet at Apache Point.
TOTAL ELEVATION LOSS & GAIN:	Approximately 2,500 vertical feet one way.
MILEAGE:	Approximately 18 miles one way.
WATER:	None.
CACHE POINTS:	None.
SEASONS:	Spring and fall. Summer can be deadly; winter access can be impossible.

MAPS: Havasupai Point and Explorers
                        Monument quadrangles (7.5 minute).

NEAREST SUPPLY   Grand Canyon Village, Flagstaff,
POINTS: Williams, Cameron.

Havasupai Lands

One of the most celebrated hikes in the Grand Canyon is the
delightful 8-mile trek to the modern Havasupai village called
Supai; it's situated in a virtual canyon paradise, which has been
described with almost as many colorful adjectives as the Grand
Canyon itself. At one time a dozen trails led down to the aqua-
marine waters of Havasu Canyon, but today there are only
two trails hikers are allowed to use: the popular Hualapai
Trail, the principal means of access for hikers and mule riders
from Hualapai Hilltop to Supai; and the seldom-used
Topocoba Trail—which at one time was followed by William
Wallace Bass carrying mail and supplies from Grand Canyon
Village to Supai.

The reason for the shortage of trails is simple enough: Many
of the old trails and routes to Supai cross the Havasupai's
ancestral lands, and there are many areas within these lands
officially known as the Havasupai's Traditional Use Area that
the Havasupai revere as sacred. Justifiably, the Havasupai don't
want non-Indian visitors in these sacred areas, which they
refuse to identify to outsiders for fear the areas will not be
treated with reverence and will, perhaps, be vandalized or pil-
laged in the process. If their historic encounters with, and broken promises from, the white man are any indication, their
fears are justified. As a result, hiker use is limited to the
Hualapai Trail and the Topocoba Trail. Permission must be
obtained from the Havasupai tribe to hike either of these trails.

Permission to use the Topocoba Trail must also be obtained from the BIC at Grand Canyon National Park.

Hualapai Trail

To reach the Hualapai trailhead at 5,200-foot Hualapai Hilltop, drive 34 miles west of Seligman or 7 miles east of Peach Springs on U.S. 66 to the Supai turnoff. A 62-mile-long paved road heads across the Blue Mountains, Aubrey Cliffs, and Coconino Plateau to Hualapai Hilltop. There are no services on this road.

The 8-mile-long Hualapai Trail is well worn and easy to follow. From Hualapai Hilltop it switchbacks through the Coconino Sandstone and drops approximately 1,100 vertical feet to the floor of Hualapai Canyon in just over a mile of hiking. It stays in the bed of this canyon all the way to its confluence with Havasu Canyon 5 ½ miles farther, in the process descending narrow clefts of Esplanade and Supai Sandstone. There is no perennial water along this stretch, and the first you'll encounter is that trickling out of Havasu Springs near the confluence.

From this point on, the character of the trail changes from that of a dry, sometimes sparsely shaded desert canyon to a lush riparian habitat sprouting from the middle of the Cataract Canyon–Havasu Canyon drainage that begins in Williams, Arizona, 80 miles due south, and empties into the Colorado River. Cataract Canyon and its tributary canyons drain an estimated 3,000 square miles of the Coconino Plateau; in the process, this runoff continues to provide the lifeblood of existence for the Havasupai people, as well as seasonal flash flood danger to the Havasupai, hikers, and river runners if they happen to be playing near the mouth of Havasu Canyon during monsoon flash flood season.

It's 1 ½ miles from Havasu Canyon to the village of Supai, which is located in a verdant U-shaped canyon surrounded by impressive cliffs of Supai Sandstone. Directly east from the village are two towering spires of rock, which the traditional Havasupai know and revere as *wigleeva;* one is said to be male, the other female, and together they watch over the Havasupai people and their crops.

Once in Supai, all hikers must check in with the Havasupai Tourist Enterprise to secure their permits.

ACCOMMODATIONS IN SUPAI: There are two lodges in Supai, the Supai Lodge and Schoolhouse Canyon Lodge; rates vary. A village cafe also operated by the Havasupai offers a menu of Indian fry bread, burritos, and other hot meals. Mail can be sent out of Supai via helicopter and packtrain. Horses can be rented to ride into and out of Supai from Hualapai Hilltop.

CAMPGROUNDS: The Navajo Campground is located 1 ½ miles below (north of) Supai, near 80-foot-high Navajo Falls (9 ½ miles from Hualapai Hilltop). The Havasu Campground is a half-mile beyond. A freshwater spring is located on the west side of Havasu Creek, midway between 100-foot-high Havasu Falls and 190-foot-high Mooney Falls, and is well marked.

Of the three waterfalls, Mooney Falls is the most spectacular. It's located just below Havasu Campground and is reached by descending a steep stairway etched into the travertine and protected by a chain-link guardrail.

Day Hikes

Overnight hiking is not allowed below Mooney Falls. However, the hike to 40-foot-high Beaver Falls (another 3 miles downstream from Mooney Falls) and the hike to the Colorado River confluence (7 miles downstream from Mooney Falls) both make excellent daylong outings if you have the time

Havasu Creek. *Photo © George H. H. Huey*

and energy. Both round-trip hikes are straightforward enough, though attention must be paid each of the numerous times the trail crosses Havasu Creek. Route-finding ability is also necessary when the trail winds around the travertine cliffs on the east side of Havasu Creek above Beaver Falls. If you keep your eyes open for footprints on these craggy sections, and for the cairns that mark all of the creek crossings, you shouldn't have any problems staying oriented.

WARNING: Don't drink the water out of Havasu Creek. It has a high fecal coli count, and it has been known to infect scratches and cuts.

If you decide to hike to the Colorado River, be careful scrambling around the slick Muav Limestone near the Colorado River's edge; hikers have disappeared in the cold, swift-moving current.

ADDITIONAL CONSIDERATIONS: Spring is definitely the most crowded time to be hiking to, or camping below, Supai. So unless you enjoy crowds, plan your visit for another time. The Havasupai flying squirrels are creatures to be reckoned with. No, they don't actually fly, but they make 4- and 5-foot leaps into packs that unwary hikers have carefully suspended from tree limbs with cordage, textbook-fashion. So if you're camping in one of the crowded campgrounds during peak hiking season, and someone in your party isn't watching your packs, these amazing little buggers will probably compromise your security system.

PRIMARY ACCESS TRAILS & ROUTES:	Hualapai Trail, Topocoba Trail, and Colorado River.
ELEVATION:	5,200 feet at Hualapai Hilltop to 3,200 feet at Supai to 1,800 feet at Colorado River.

TOTAL ELEVATION LOSS & GAIN:	4,000 vertical feet (2,000 each way) Hualapai Hilltop to Supai. Approximately 2,800 vertical feet (1,400 feet each way) Supai to Colorado River.
MILEAGE:	8 miles to Supai, 11 miles to Havasu Campground, 14 miles to Beaver Falls, 18 miles to Colorado River.
WATER:	Havasu Springs, Supai, campgrounds, and Colorado River. (*Don't* plan on using river water, as access is extremely dangerous.)
CACHE POINTS:	Secluded areas of Hualapai Canyon.
SEASONS:	All year. Summer is *hot* hiking, but the swimming's great.
MAPS:	Supai, Havasu Falls, and S. B. Point quadrangles (7.5 minute).
NEAREST SUPPLY POINTS:	Seligman, Peach Springs, Supai.

CONTACT: For accommodations, campground reservations, hiking permits, fees, and mule transportation, call the Havasupai tribe at (928) 448-2120 or visit www.havasupaitribe.com. The entrance fee is $20 per person, plus a campground fee of $10 per person per night. Book your reservations 6 months in advance.

8 | North Rim

One of the most overlooked—and rewarding—hiking opportunities in Grand Canyon National Park is the collection of trails and nonmaintained jeep roads that probe the sub-alpine forests of the North Rim. When summertime temperatures turn the inner Canyon into an oven—and hikers who've survived it into ashen-faced apparitions—there is no better place to hike than the cool forests of the North Rim. The ancestral Puebloans made seasonal migrations to the lofty heights of the North Rim long before inner-Canyon rocks became too hot to touch. So if your vacation time is limited to summer months, you'd probably find it far more enjoyable to limit your Grand Canyon hiking to the supernal reaches of the North Rim. Unlike the heavily visited South Rim, which in contrast offers only a handful of hiking opportunities atop the Coconino Plateau, the North Rim's Kaibab Plateau offers a wide variety of rim trails that can keep the most avid backpacker busy for a month; they include everything from the half-mile-long day hikes out to Cape Royal and Bright Angel Point to multiday treks that lead from 8,424-foot Saddle Mountain on the east to Muav Saddle on the west and beyond.

RIM TRAILS—EAST

Bright Angel Point Trail

From the North Rim Visitor Center, a half-mile round-trip hike on the paved Bright Angel Point Trail leads to spectacular views from 8,255-foot Bright Angel Point.

Quaking Aspen, North Rim. *Photo © George H. H. Huey*

Uncle Jim Trail

The trailhead for the Uncle Jim Trail is located on the North Rim entrance road 2 miles north of Grand Canyon Lodge and begins on the east end of the North Kaibab Trail parking lot. The first mile of this well-marked 5-mile loop is also the first mile of the Ken Patrick Trail; it skirts the rim of Roaring Springs Canyon, offering splendid views en route to the junction of these two trails. A sign at this junction reads "Old Kaibab Trail 2.5, Uncle Jim Point 1.2." Turn right (south), and about a quarter mile beyond you'll come to another junction where you have the option of taking the left fork (which makes a beeline through the woods to 8,402-foot Uncle Jim Point) or the right fork (which continues skirting the rim of Roaring Springs Canyon). Either way, the short, challenging hike out to Uncle Jim Point leads you to a fine picnic-style scenic vista.

Ken Patrick Trail

The 12-mile point-to-point hike along the Ken Patrick Trail from the North Kaibab Trail parking lot to 8,819-foot Point Imperial is more akin to orienteering and route finding than a well-marked afternoon hike. From the junction of the Ken Patrick and Uncle Jim trails, the trail contours the west slope of the Roaring Springs drainage. Though the trail remains easy enough to follow for the next couple of miles, it's rocky and makes sudden descents and ascents where it follows the bed of the Roaring Springs drainage.

Three and a half miles out from the parking lot trailhead, you'll reach the Old Bright Angel trailhead. From here the trail becomes more difficult to follow to the Cape Royal Road—though if you're attentive you'll follow the correct course through the New Mexico locust. Care must be taken where the trail is intersected by old fire roads; where the real fun begins, though, is where the Ken Patrick is covered with "blow-down," and there your hiking consists of crawling under or climbing over fallen timber.

Once you've reached the Cape Royal Road, cross it, then descend the trail back into the trees. From this paved, serpentine crossing, the trail skirts the rim of the Canyon all the way to Point Imperial, and it once again offers exposed views en route.

Even though this trail doesn't go to the bottom of the Canyon, it offers the same adventurous elements of many inner-Canyon routes.

Cape Royal Trail

From the Cape Royal trailhead (located 23 miles via paved road from the Visitor Center), a half-mile round-trip hike on the paved Cape Royal Trail leads to 7,685-foot Cape Royal overlooking 7,699-foot Wotans Throne.

Saddle Mountain to Point Imperial Trail

This is actually an old fire road, and it's located in the same cul-de-sac as the Nankoweap trailhead at the end of USFS Road 610. The turnoff for Road 610 is located a mile south of the Kaibab Lodge on the North Rim entrance road 4 miles north of the NPS Entrance Station. It's about 15 miles on USFS 610 to road's end at the eastern edge of the old Grand Canyon National Park boundaries. From this cul-de-sac, head south until you pick up the old fire road that generally contours the rim for 2 miles to 8,819-foot Point Imperial.

This short trail can be used a number of ways: as an addition to the Ken Patrick Trail; as an out-and-back hike from Point Imperial; or as the beginning of the Saddle Mountain to Muav Saddle hike (page 201). Off-season, it provides an excellent means of winter access to the North Rim when the National Park Service closes the North Rim Entrance Station and road; USFS Road 610 from De Motte Park lies outside park boundaries and remains open until it's buried by the first snow.

RIM TRAILS—WEST

Transept Trail

This well-marked 1.5-mile-long trail is one of the real rewards for staying in what might be a crowded campground. It leaves the North Rim Campground just west of the general store and contours the edge of the Transept to Grand Canyon Lodge. Next to Phantom Creek, the Transept is the largest tributary drainage of Bright Angel Canyon, and a hike along its rim offers views as spectacular as any secluded vista in Grand Canyon National Park.

Widforss Trail

If you enjoyed an out-and-back hike along the Transept Trail and want to get an even more secluded view of this magnificent drainage, the 10-mile out-and-back hike along the enchanting Widforss Trail is the ticket. It's well marked, has gentle gradients, and makes one of the best day hikes on the North Rim. To reach the Widforss Trailhead, drive a mile north of the North Rim Campground and turn left on the dirt road adjacent to the North Kaibab parking lot; it's a mile to the trailhead, located on the north side of this road.

From the parking area, the trail should be obvious all the way to 7,822-foot Widforss Point; it climbs gently, skirts the north and northeastern arms of the Transept, then heads south through the woods, terminating several miles later at the head of Haunted Canyon; it's as inspiring a lunch stop as any on the

North Rim, with excellent views of 7,184-foot Manu Temple and 7,212-foot Buddha Temple.

Powell Plateau

One of the most appealing aspects of the North Rim is that it drains—and thus erodes—into the Grand Canyon, unlike the South Rim, which has a tendency to drain away from the Canyon. In addition to the uplifting and faulting of the area north of the Grand Canyon, this erosion has created significant plateaus in Arizona. From west to east they are Shivwits, Uinkaret, Kanab, and the Kaibab Plateau, which comprises most of the North Rim. Extending south from the Kaibab Plateau are three subsidiary plateaus: Fishtail, Powell, and Walhalla. Of the three, Powell Plateau is perhaps the most appealing to explore on foot. While Fishtail Plateau is smaller and more remote than Powell, it's topographically lower in elevation, more arid, and for the most part is covered with pinyon-juniper. Walhalla, on the other hand, is a bit larger, but the paved access out to Cape Royal inhibits, to some extent, what would be the natural charm of the area had it otherwise remained more remote. Powell Plateau has the best of both Fishtail and Walhalla plateaus; it's remote, but it's situated at over 7,661 feet in elevation. Until a recent forest fire, its entire northern third was covered with one of the most impressive untouched stands of ponderosa pine on the heavily logged North Rim; this forest of ponderosa, intermixed with oak, starts merging with pinyon-juniper about midway south across the plateau until you reach its southern end, where pinyon-juniper becomes the dominant vegetation.

One of the most unique aspects of this isolated plateau, however, is not its vegetative mix, but its significance as a temporary habitation site for the ancestral Puebloans between

A.D. 1050 and A.D. 1150. According to the data collected by Richard W. Effland, Jr., A. Trinkle Jones, and Robert C. Euler and published in *The Archaeology of the Powell Plateau,* 85 sites were recorded on Powell Plateau, with an average density of 33 sites and 71 rooms per square mile. These scientists suggest "that there were 650 to 700 rooms used by prehistoric people living on the plateau." Do not disturb any of these sites if you happen across one.

Powell Saddle Trail
To reach 7,565-foot Swamp Point and the trailhead for both the Powell Saddle and the North Bass trails, take USFS Road 422 west from Arizona 67; the turnoff is located a mile south of the Kaibab Lodge. Take USFS Road 422 to USFS Road 270 and turn left (south). Follow USFS Road 270 to USFS Road 223, turn right (west), and take 223 to USFS Road 268B. Road 268B will eventually take you out to Swamp Point and the trailheads. (Please note: There are several North Kaibab National Forest maps in circulation with conflicting information on this stretch of road. Get the latest edition with the correct road numbers, which can be ordered at www.fs.fed.us/r3/kai/.)

From Swamp Point, the trail drops 800 vertical feet in the mile of switchbacks it takes to reach 6,711-foot Muav Saddle. This is the geological confluence of the Crazy Jug and Muav faults, which provides a natural passageway for the North Rim trans-Canyon route (page 217). The trail up to Powell Plateau is marked by a large cairn in Muav Saddle: turning left (east) will get you started down the North Bass Trail, while turning right (west) and heading along the crest of Muav Saddle will get you started on the Powell Saddle Trail. Immediately below the west side of Muav Saddle is a rickety old cabin built by the CCC, which is sometimes used by cross-country skiers during late winter and early spring. The CCC also built the trail up to

Powell Plateau, which switchbacks 1 ½ miles through the Toroweap Formation and New Mexico locust until it tops out in the ponderosa forests 900 vertical feet above. Once atop the plateau, the trail is marked by blaze marks on those trees not destroyed by recent fires. The blaze marks aren't at all frequent, however, and you'll have to look for each of these marks before proceeding if you're intent on staying on the historic course of this trail as it skirts the west rim of White Creek until it begins disappearing somewhere in the head of Dutton Canyon.

ADDITIONAL CONSIDERATIONS: The hike out to Powell Plateau makes a fine day hike from Swamp Point. But since you've taken the effort to drive all the way out to Swamp Point, you might as well spend a day and a night atop this incredible plateau and experience an altogether different kind of Grand Canyon hiking.

PRIMARY ACCESS TRAILS & ROUTES:	Powell Saddle Trail, North Bass Trail (from the river), Saddle Canyon route (from Thunder River).
ELEVATION:	7,565 feet at Swamp Point to 6,711 feet at Muav Saddle to 7,661 feet atop Powell Plateau.
TOTAL ELEVATION LOSS & GAIN:	Approximately 3,600 feet (1,800 vertical feet each way).
MILEAGE:	Approximately 5 miles one way to Dutton Canyon.
WATER:	Below east side of Muav Saddle near base of Coconino at head of White Creek. Secondary trail leads to it.
CACHE POINTS:	Muav Saddle.

SEASONS:	Spring through fall. Winter access is difficult from either South or North Rim due to snow.
MAPS:	Powell Plateau and King Arthur Castle quadrangles (7.5 minute).
NEAREST SUPPLY POINTS (for all North Rim trails & routes):	Fredonia, Page, Vermilion Cliffs, Jacob Lake, North Rim

Saddle Mountain to Muav Saddle

Just as it's possible to traverse the inner Canyon eastward and westward below the North and South rims, it's also possible to traverse the Grand Canyon atop the North Rim. Of many possible variations, one practical and enjoyable route is the 39-mile Saddle Mountain to Muav Saddle route; it makes use of rim trails and old fire roads to traverse one of the prettiest forests in the Southwest. It offers some of the more incredible views to be seen in any life zone—be it desert, canyon, or mountain environment.

The Saddle Mountain to Muav Saddle route traverses a fair-sized piece of the 350-square-mile Kaibab Plateau. Capped by a layer of Kaibab Limestone, the 250-million-year-old fossilized seabed acts as a veritable sponge for the 27 inches of precipitation that fall on the North Rim on average each year. In the process, this moisture—which falls mainly in the form of snow—fills a subterranean aquifer that recharges cascades below the North Rim like Vaseys Paradise, Cheyava Falls, Roaring Springs, Tapeats Creek, and Thunder River. While this route will take you through a subalpine forest and fern-decked meadows (or "parks," as they're called in these parts), you're still going to have to concern yourself with water because the Kaibab Limestone is so porous that surface water is scarce.

From east to west, the route is as follows:

a. Saddle Mountain to Point Imperial: 3 miles; at-large camping; no water.

b. Point Imperial to North Kaibab trailhead parking lot via Ken Patrick Trail: 12 miles; selected camping (check with North Rim BIC); seasonal water at Neal Springs and North Rim Campground.

c. North Kaibab trailhead parking lot to Widforss trailhead parking lot: 1 mile; camping at North Rim Campground; water at North Rim Campground.

d. Widforss trailhead parking lot to Crystal Ridge / Milk Creek area via Marble Flats and Point Sublime Trail: approximately 9 miles; camping at large, with fine choices between Milk Creek and Crystal Creek; seasonal water en route (check map and North Rim BIC); use Bright Angel and De Motte Park quadrangles (both 15 minute) and follow your nose if winter snows have knocked down road and trail signs.

e. Crystal Ridge / Milk Creek area to Muav Saddle via Kanabownits Spring, Crescent Ridge, Big Springs Canyon, BM 8356, and Swamp Ridge (USFS Road 268B): approximately 14 miles; camping at large, with fine choices at Crescent Ridge; seasonal water en route (check map and North Rim BIC); use De Motte Park and Powell Plateau quadrangles (both 15 minute) and North Kaibab National Forest Map.

ADDITIONAL CONSIDERATIONS: This is only one possible route of many that traverse the Kaibab Plateau; there are as many alternate routes as there are old fire and logging roads to be explored on foot, horseback, or even in a vehicle. For further information, maps, and road conditions for the North Kaibab, visit www.fs.fed.us/r3/kai/.

RIM-TO-RIVER MAINTAINED CORRIDOR TRAILS

The only rim-to-river trail below the North Rim currently maintained by National Park Service trail crews is the 14-mile-long North Kaibab Trail. Without a doubt it's the most heavily used trail below the North Rim. Mule-riding concessions also use this trail and have the right-of-way here. If you encounter a mule train, take the high side of the trail before it reaches you.

North Kaibab Trail

The first known modern man to pioneer a route down Bright Angel Creek from the North Rim was François Emile Matthes, a cartographer who surveyed the area in 1902 for the U.S. Geological Survey. The route Matthes and his men used descended the short, northern arm of Bright Angel Canyon and crossed Bright Angel Creek 94 times before reaching the Colorado River. An original section of this trail, called the Old Kaibab Trail, can be reached by taking the Ken Patrick Trail 3 ½ miles from the North Kaibab Trail parking lot; this now-abandoned stretch of trail links up with the modern North Kaibab Trail at the confluence of Roaring Springs and Bright Angel Canyon.

In 1903 the Grand Canyon Transportation Company was formed by E. D. Woolley, who had an epiphany about bringing tourists across the Canyon to visit the remote North Rim; his line of ascent was the route Matthes had descended the year before. Serious trail construction didn't begin until 1924, however, and when the entire cross-Canyon trail was completed in 1928, "the total cost," according to Tillotson and Taylor's *Grand Canyon Country,* "rim to rim, was approximately $147,500, exclusive of the Kaibab Suspension Bridge, which added $39,500."

To reach the head of the North Kaibab Trail, drive 2 miles north of Grand Canyon Lodge; the parking lot is on the right (east) side of the road. The course along the North Kaibab, like the South Kaibab, its counterpart below the South Rim, is easy to follow all the way to the Colorado River; the only difficulties you may encounter, apart from its length and steepness, are rockslides that periodically cover upper sections of the trail during spring thaw or after summer monsoons.

The steepest section of the North Kaibab Trail is the 4.7-mile stretch from the trailhead down Roaring Springs Canyon to its confluence with Bright Angel Canyon, a stretch that drops some 3,600 vertical feet. En route to the confluence you'll pass Roaring Springs Campground on the right. The buildings and house you'll pass on the left are occupied and maintained by Park Service personnel who operate the Roaring Springs pumphouse, which supplies Grand Canyon Village with water via a cross-Canyon pipeline.

From this confluence it's another 2 miles down Bright Angel Creek to Cottonwood Campground; there's a seasonally staffed ranger station there. A mile beyond you'll come to the Ribbon Falls Trail junction and footbridge; the nonmaintained trail leading to Ribbon Falls is marked by cairns, as is the ford of Bright Angel Creek farther to the south. (During heavy spring runoff it's extremely dangerous to attempt fording Bright Angel Creek; stick to the footbridge.)

It's another 6 miles down Bright Angel Creek to the Phantom Ranch / Bright Angel Campground area; less than a mile north of Phantom Ranch, you'll pass the junction of the Clear Creek Trail (see page 222).

ADDITIONAL CONSIDERATIONS: The hike down the North Kaibab Trail to Roaring Springs and back is an excellent day hike, as is the hike up from Bright Angel Campground to Ribbon Falls

Ribbon Falls. *Photo © George H. H. Huey*

and back. The North Kaibab Trail is frequently used by hikers in combination with the South Kaibab or Bright Angel Trail to make a cross-Canyon hike. If you're hiking north-to-south, you'll find it easier and safer to hike out the Bright Angel Trail. If you're hiking south-to-north, on the other hand, you may find it easier to descend the South Kaibab.

PRIMARY ACCESS TRAILS TRAILS & ROUTES:	North Kaibab trailhead, Old Kaibab Trail, Bright Angel Trail, and South Kaibab Trail.
ELEVATION:	8,200 feet at trailhead to 2,450 feet at Colorado River.
TOTAL ELEVATION LOSS & GAIN:	11,480 feet (5,740 vertical feet each way).
MILEAGE:	14 miles one way.
WATER:	Roaring Springs, Bright Angel Creek, Transept Spring, Ribbon Springs (heavy lime), Phantom Creek, Bright Angel Campground.
CACHE POINTS:	Secluded areas of Roaring Springs and Ribbon Falls Trail junction.
SHUTTLES:	Rim-to-rim; call (928) 638-2820 for schedules and fees.
SEASONS:	June through September from the North Rim; all year from the South Rim—though expect deep snows and harsh conditions above Roaring Springs during winter months.
MAPS:	Bright Angel Point and Phantom Ranch quadrangles (7.5 minute).

RIM-TO-RIVER NONMAINTAINED
WILDERNESS TRAILS

There are only three nonmaintained rim-to-river trails on the North Rim that see any regular use: the popular Thunder River Trail (Bill Hall variation); the increasingly popular Nankoweap Trail; and the seldom-used North Bass (formerly known as the Shinumo and White trails). Unlike the majority of nonmaintained rim-to-river trails on the South Rim, however, which have relatively easy access and tend to be clustered in one general area, these North Rim trails require long drives over secondary roads to reach their remote trailheads. For the most part, the North Rim trails are both longer and have a greater elevation loss and gain than those on the South Rim; they also visit relatively seldom explored areas of Grand Canyon National Park, where the consequences of poor planning, insufficient canyoneering experience, or an error in judgment can have disastrous consequences. Whatever preparation you did before hiking the South Rim miner trails, do half again as much before you tackle the Nankoweap, North Bass, or Thunder River trails.

Nankoweap Trail

Of the four rim-to-river trails that plummet off the North Rim, the Nankoweap Trail should receive the colorful history award. It was constructed by Major John Wesley Powell, geologist Charles Doolittle Walcott, and others during the winter of 1882 so Walcott could study "the Grand Canyon Series of rock layers." It was down the Nankoweap, which Walcott called "a perfectly frightful trail," that Utah horse thieves reportedly linked their Butte Fault route across the eastern Grand Canyon with the Tanner Trail on the south side of the Colorado River.

But perhaps the most outlandish tale concerning the Nankoweap Trail involves government lion hunter Colonel C. J. "Uncle Jim" Owens, who was responsible for shooting 532 mountain lions on the North Rim at the turn of the 19th century. As a result of such drastic wildlife conservation measures, the Kaibab deer population exploded from around 4,000 to an estimated 100,000 in 1924, according to J. Donald Hughes's *The Story of Man at the Grand Canyon*. One hundred twenty-five cowboys and Navajo trackers were hired to herd 3,000 to 8,000 deer down the Nankoweap Trail, across the Butte Fault, and up the Tanner Trail to the South Rim. Even with the best Navajo trackers beating the brush and firing pistols into the air, the wild and half-starved mule deer would have none of it. This fact was headlined on page one of the Thursday morning, December 18, 1924, issue of the *Arizona Republican*:

KAIBAB DEER DRIVE IS CALLED OFF
Snowstorm Ends Plans of M'Cormick
Motion Picture Men Return to Flagstaff in
Blinding Snowstorm; Deer Scatter Widely

Even Tinseltown had gotten in on the act, which did nothing to alleviate the disaster of thousands of starving deer.

To reach the Nankoweap trailhead, take USFS Road 610, located a mile south of the Kaibab Lodge on the North Rim entrance road, and follow it east approximately 15 miles to the road's end.

From the end of USFS Road 610, cairns mark the trail's descent east off the rim to a saddle in the Toroweap Formation some 500 vertical feet below; from this saddle, you'll climb back up to a small hill to the east identified on your Nankoweap Quadrangle as 8839, contour the north side of it, then descend into an east/northeastern drainage. This drainage will provide you with a passage through the Coconino Sandstone immediately below. At the base of the Coconino, follow a ridge of Hermit Shale east for about a half mile before you drop down to the saddle in the Esplanade Sandstone at the base—immediately west—of 8,424-foot Saddle Mountain.

For canyoneers wishing to explore the eastern Grand Canyon after winter snows have buried USFS Road 610, and for cross-country skiers who want to tour the North Rim without having to make the 40-mile trek in from Jacob Lake, winter access to the Saddle Mountain area is relatively easy. Take U.S. 89A approximately 21 miles west from Marble Canyon and turn left (south) onto USFS Road 445, which is also called the Buffalo Ranch Road. Follow USFS Road 445 approximately 25 miles to USFS Road 445G; turn right (west) onto 445G, and follow it another 4 or 5 miles to the road's end. Be attentive for surveyors' flags and widely spaced cairns and you shouldn't have too much trouble following the southern arm of Saddle Canyon the 3 miles or so it takes to climb up to the Saddle Mountain saddle.

The Nankoweap Trail drops off the south side of the Saddle Mountain saddle through the Esplanade Sandstone and contours the Supai Sandstone for approximately 3 miles before it begins its corkscrew descent through the Redwall on the west side of 5,888-foot Tilted Mesa; the stretch along the Supai Sandstone is dangerously exposed in two sections and takes inventive forks in one or two other stretches, so extra care and caution should be exercised along this stretch. Below the Redwall, pick your way down through the landslide, a pinch of limestone, and the Galeros Formation to the bed of Nankoweap Creek. Perennial water flows from the Muav Limestone into Nankoweap Creek, which normally surfaces along the 3-mile stretch of creekbed you'll follow from the foot of the Nankoweap Trail to the Nankoweap Delta adjacent to the Colorado River.

ADDITIONAL CONSIDERATIONS: This difficult trail, which should not be attempted by inexperienced canyoneers, provides access to the Butte Fault Trail and is the first leg of the North Rim trans-Canyon route (see page 217).

PRIMARY ACCESS TRAILS & ROUTES:	USFS Road 610 from the North Rim, USFS Road 445G from Houserock Valley, Colorado River, and Butte Fault Trail (route).
ELEVATION:	8,848 feet at Nankoweap trailhead to 2,787 feet at Colorado River.
TOTAL ELEVATION LOSS & GAIN:	Approximately 12,200 feet (6,100 vertical feet each way).
MILEAGE:	14 miles one way.
WATER:	Nankoweap Creek and Colorado River.
CACHE POINTS:	Saddle Mountain saddle, top of Redwall, and Nankoweap Creek.
SEASONS:	Early fall and late spring. Summers have proven deadly, and winter access can be difficult and treacherous.
MAPS:	Point Imperial and Nankoweap Mesa quadrangles (7.5 minute) and North Kaibab National Forest Map.

North Bass Trail (a.k.a. Shinumo Trail and White Trail)

According to "Grand Canyon Nature Notes" dated September 8, 1933, a prospector by the name of White was the first to use the route up Shinumo and White creeks, which linked the Colorado River with the North Rim. Around 1887, William Wallace Bass developed White's route into a trail so that tourists who stayed at Bass Camp would also have a means of visiting the beautiful, yet remote, North Rim. Nineteenth-century travel writer George Wharton James describes a pack trip he took with Bass along the Canyon's first cross-Canyon trail system in *The Grand Canyon of Arizona*: "Another two or three weeks' delightful experience can be gained by arranging to go down Bass's Trail [the South Bass Trail], cross on his cable ferry, go up the Shinumo Trail to Powell Plateau, watch herds of protected and preserved deer and antelope, look lovingly upon the succulent and delicious pine-hens that live upon pinion nuts and roost in the branches of the pine trees of the Kaibab forest, and pleasantly saunter along out to Point Sublime."

A hike down the North Bass isn't much different today than it was in Bass's time more than a century ago; it's remote, difficult, and wildly beautiful. Unlike most other rim-to-river trails, which periodically expose themselves to the expansive breadth of the Grand Canyon, the North Bass Trail has a distinctly confined character. From Muav Saddle all the way to the Colorado River it follows the course of White Creek and Shinumo Creek—never once exposing itself to the Canyon itself. In short, a trek down the North Bass is more akin to hiking into a distinct wilderness area within the Grand Canyon—a seldom-trod, undiscovered wildland that heeds its own primeval laws and offers its own sublime rewards.

To reach the North Bass trailhead at Swamp Point, see Powell Saddle Trail (page 199) for access information and a description of the trail to Muav Saddle. From Muav Saddle head east along the base of the Coconino Sandstone for about a half mile; the springs that feed White Creek are located along a secondary trail to the east of the steep descent you'll take almost straight down through very loose Hermit Shale. Once through the Hermit, you'll make several switchbacks in the Esplanade Formation before the Muav Fault provides a natural passage through the Esplanade to the Supai below. You'll follow the bed of White Creek as it carves its way through the Supai, bushwhacking half the time, boulder-hopping the other half, with your eyes focused on the route ahead for the next cairn or clue that'll take you to the top of the Redwall on the west side of White Creek. Stay on the west side of White Creek and pick your way through the pinyon-juniper as this wilderness route traverses a series of three saddles before beginning its descent through the Redwall. The Redwall descent should be marked by a totem-sized cairn, so don't attempt a descent of this formation without first locating it.

Below the Redwall switchbacks, the route continues following the west side of White Creek as it descends through the Muav Limestone. Once you reach BM 4001 on your King Arthur Castle Quadrangle, the route crosses the east side of White Creek and stays there the next mile or so it descends through the Bright Angel Shale to BM 3480. Here the trail crosses back over to the west side, where it makes its circuitous descent through the Tapeats Sandstone and upper Vishnu Schist—eventually coming out below the confluence of White and Shinumo creeks. The route crisscrosses Shinumo Creek several times, passing Bass's old camp on the left before gaining a well-marked trail used by river runners; it climbs out of the creek over BM 2917 before switchbacking down to the Colorado River below Bass Rapids.

ADDITIONAL CONSIDERATIONS: If you're hiking the North Bass out and back from Swamp Point, take time to familiarize yourself with the climb back out by stopping every so often to look at the country you're leaving; it's definitely more difficult hiking up the North Bass than it is hiking down it. In an emergency, the best place to catch a ride across the Colorado River with river runners is at the beach camp at the foot of the North Bass below Bass Rapids.

WARNING: This is the most difficult rim-to-river trail or route described in this guide.

PRIMARY ACCESS TRAILS & ROUTES:	Muav Saddle (see page 199), Saddle Canyon, and South Bass via Colorado River.
ELEVATION:	7,565 feet at Swamp Point to 2,200 feet at the Colorado River.
TOTAL ELEVATION LOSS & GAIN:	10,730 feet (5,365 vertical feet each way).
MILEAGE:	14 miles one way.
WATER:	White Creek below Coconino on east side of Muav Saddle, Shinumo Creek, and Colorado River.
CACHE POINTS:	Muav Saddle, top of Redwall, and where trail first crosses Shinumo Creek.
SEASONS:	Late spring and early fall; summer can be unforgiving; winter access from South and North rims difficult; early spring runoff can make fording Shinumo Creek dangerous and/or impossible in several sections.
MAPS:	King Arthur Castle and Havasupai Point quadrangles (7.5 minute).

Thunder River Trail and Bill Hall Trail

Gold may have been discovered "in the sands at the mouth of Tapeats Creek," as the 1869 Powell Expedition reported, but no one has rediscovered it to this day. What prospectors did discover after constructing this trail in 1876, however, and what hikers and river runners continue to discover, is another treasure in the form of three of the most beautiful, cataract-fed creeks anywhere: Deer Creek, Tapeats Creek, and Thunder River. Thunder River, which was said to be former U.S. senator Barry Goldwater's favorite place in Arizona, also has the unique distinction of being the shortest river in the world— tumbling, cascading, and roaring out of the Muav Limestone to Tapeats Creek a half mile and 1,200 vertical feet below.

To reach the Thunder River trailhead at Indian Hollow requires more driving time than either the Nankoweap or North Bass trails, but if the number of hikers using the Thunder River Trail is any indication, the rewards are far greater. Turn west off Arizona 67 a mile south of the Kaibab Lodge onto USFS Road 422, and take this road approximately 18 miles to the turnoff for USFS Road 425. Turn left (south) on USFS 425 and drive approximately 10 miles to the junction of USFS Road 232. The Thunder River trailhead at Indian Hollow is at the end of USFS Road 232. (To reach the Bill Hall trailhead at Monument Point, however, stay on USFS Road 425, turn right on USFS 292, and make another right onto USFS Road 292A and follow it to the end.)

From the Indian Hollow trailhead, at 6,300 feet, the Thunder River Trail contours west along the rim for about a half mile to Little Saddle, where it makes its abrupt descent through the Toroweap Formation, Coconino Sandstone, and Hermit Shale to that broad, enchilada-red terrace called the Esplanade. It then contours its way eastward along the Esplanade for approximately 4 miles before linking up with the Bill Hall Trail coming down off 7,166-foot Monument Point. (Whether you're descending the Thunder River Trail or the Bill Hall Trail, this junction is a good place to cache water for the hike out.)

The Bill Hall Trail from Monument Point to this junction leaves the west end of the Monument Point parking lot and stays atop the rim by heading southwest over a little knoll called Millet 7206 for about a half mile to the southern tip of 7,166-foot Monument Point; there it begins switchbacking through the Toroweap Formation and Coconino Sandstone to the Hermit Shale saddle between 6,602-foot Bridgers Knoll and Monument Point. From the Bridger's Knoll saddle it heads almost straight down through the Hermit Shale to link up with the Thunder River Trail another three-quarters of a mile below.

From the Thunder River/Bill Hall junction the trail is braided in sections, but it continues its serpentine course along the Esplanade below the west slope of Bridgers Knoll.

From a geographical standpoint, you shouldn't go astray whichever slight trail variation you might take along this stretch of Esplanade; however, the area is covered with fragile cryptobiotic soil, and if you're not careful to follow the cairns marking the exact line of the Thunder River Trail, this fragile soil will bear the marks of your footprints for years.

Cairns mark the descent off the Esplanade, west then south across the Supai, and through the Redwall to Surprise Valley. Near the head of Bonita Creek in Surprise Valley you'll come to another trail junction: the trail to the right (west) heads to Upper Deer Creek Falls, Deer Creek Narrows, and Deer Creek Falls where it cascades into the Colorado River (see Tapeats Creek, page 242). The trail to the left (east) is the Thunder River Trail, which is clearly marked as it switchbacks down to the headwaters of Thunder River. No camping is permitted in this area; however, it's a refreshing rest stop before continuing down to the campground below the confluence of Tapeats Creek and Thunder River. It's another 2 miles or so from this campground along Tapeats Creek to the Colorado River. But this well-marked trail, which is frequently used by river runners, crosses Tapeats Creek a number of times, and care must be exercised in fording it during spring runoff.

ADDITIONAL CONSIDERATIONS: The Thunder River/Bill Hall Trail is the last leg of the North Rim trans-Canyon route (see page 217). Fishermen frequently use the Bill Hall Trail to fish the confluence of Tapeats Creek and the Colorado River, and canyoneers sometimes use it as the first, or last, leg of a Kanab Creek Canyon loop trek.

PRIMARY ACCESS TRAILS & ROUTES:	Indian Hollow, Monument Point, and Colorado River via Tapeats and Deer creeks.
ELEVATION:	6,300 feet at Indian Hollow 7,166 feet at Monument Point 2,000 feet at Colorado River
TOTAL ELEVATION LOSS & GAIN:	10,300 feet (5,150 vertical feet each way).
MILEAGE:	17 miles via Thunder River Trail to the Colorado River. 12 miles via Bill Hall Trail to the Colorado River.
WATER:	Thunder River, Tapeats Creek, Colorado River, and Deer Creek.
CACHE POINTS:	Surprise Valley and the Bill Hall/Thunder River trail junction on Esplanade.
SEASONS:	Spring and fall. Thunder River Trail closed by USFS from June 15 to August 30 due to extreme heat. Winter access difficult.
MAPS:	Tapeats Amphitheater, Fishtail Mesa, and Powell Plateau quadrangles (7.5 minute) and North Kaibab National Forest Map (for all North Rim trails and routes).

TRANS-CANYON ROUTES AND WILDERNESS TRAILS

If you have extensive canyoneering experience, feel comfortable trekking and scrambling for days on end over precipitous and uncompromising terrain with tenuous footing, can look at the lay of the land and pick the most natural route across it, *and* have both your wilderness and survival skills down cold in the event you get into trouble, then the virtually trailless trans-Canyon route below the North Rim may be the canyoneering challenge you've been looking for. In most sections it's no less difficult than the North Bass Trail; in fact, put about twelve to fifteen North Bass treks back-to-back and that would be closer to the mark. However, whatever you've done on the relatively accessible South Rim is basically a romp in a park compared to the hazards and rewards of trekking this remote, seldom-explored route. An accident in this inner-Canyon frontier would be like stepping off the face of the earth. Most likely, the grid searches by helicopters, professional trackers, and bloodhounds would fail to find you; if they did, the ravens would probably have gotten to you first. However, if you do undertake this trek—and exercise good judgment—you'll have the exceedingly rare opportunity to glimpse, if only for a few fleeting moments, the Grand Canyon the way it once was seen by the ancient masters of canyoneering, the ancestral Puebloans.

The following section will describe the major trans-Canyon route from the Nankoweap Trail on the east end of the North Rim to the Thunder River Trail on the west end. Each of the individual sections of this route will be described east-to-west and will link one individual section with the next.

Nankoweap Trailhead to the Butte Fault Trail

The Butte Fault Trail is picked up approximately 100 yards above the foot of the Nankoweap Trail when it first joins Nankoweap Creek (see Nankoweap Trail, page 207). Approxi-

mately 11 miles; camping at large, with many choices around
Nankoweap Creek; water in Nankoweap Creek; use Point
Imperial and Nankoweap Mesa quadrangles (7.5 minute).
Escape routes via Saddle Mountain to Point Imperial fire road
and Nankoweap Creek to Colorado River.

Nankoweap Creek to Colorado River via Butte Fault Trail,
East Fork of Carbon Creek, and Lava Canyon
The Butte Fault Trail isn't a trail any more than the North Bass
Trail is; however, it is a very distinct route that follows the geological fault line called the Butte Fault. This was the route horse
thieves rode hell-for-leather with their stolen stock across the
eastern Grand Canyon; if they actually made that ride, they
were outstanding horsemen. From Nankoweap Creek, you
have two choices of routes that closely parallel one another to
reach Kwagunt Creek: either follow the actual hogback of the
Butte Fault on its east or west side up and over the 4,810-foot
saddle between Nankoweap Mesa and Nankoweap Butte down
to Kwagunt Creek; or follow the north/south drainage system
that contours the west side of 6,316-foot Nankoweap Mesa.

Once you get to Kwagunt Creek, you should have a feel for
the Butte Fault and be able to see the lay of the land ahead.
Continue following this fault line generally south below the
Redwall Formation on the west slopes of 5,584-foot Malgosa
Crest, 6,377-foot Kwagunt Butte, 5,403-foot Awatubi Crest,
and 6,394-foot Chuar Butte to the east fork of Carbon Creek
on the northwest side of Temple Butte. The inherent characteristic of this sometimes-debilitating section is that of a slow-
motion roller-coaster ride as you struggle out of Kwagunt
Creek, flank the west side of Malgosa Crest, then plunge down
into Malgosa Canyon, and so on from Malgosa Canyon to
Awatubi Creek, from Awatubi Creek to Sixtymile Canyon, and
from Sixtymile Canyon to the east fork of Carbon Creek.

From the head of the east fork of Carbon Creek at BM 4987, drop into this creekbed and follow it as it contours the west slope of 5,308-foot Temple Butte to its confluence with the west fork of Carbon Creek. Once at this confluence, you can take the west fork all the way to the Colorado River; or you can follow it downstream for about a half mile, where you can eyeball a route over the saddle between the west side of 3,945-foot Chuar Lava Hill and BM 3741 into Lava Canyon, and thence to the Colorado River.

PRIMARY ACCESS TRAILS & ROUTES:	Nankoweap trailhead, Saddle Mountain, and Colorado River.
ELEVATION:	3,400 feet at Nankoweap Creek to 2,700 feet at Colorado River.
TOTAL ELEVATION LOSS & GAIN:	*Loss:* 6,500 vertical feet. *Gain:* 6,100 vertical feet.
MILEAGE:	Approximately 15 to 20 miles.
WATER:	Nankoweap Creek and Colorado River.
SEASONAL WATER:	Kwagunt Creek, Sixtymile Creek, East Fork Carbon Creek, and Lava Canyon.
SEASONS:	Fall through spring, though from a water standpoint spring would be best.
MAPS:	Point Imperial, Nankoweap Mesa, and Cape Solitude quadrangles (7.5 minute).
ESCAPE ROUTES:	Via Nankoweap Trail to North Rim or Colorado River; Kwagunt Creek, East Fork of Carbon Creek, and Lava Canyon to Colorado River.

Lava Canyon to Tanner Canyon via Beamer Trail
If the river level is too high to follow the route along the river's edge, consider crossing the Colorado River and following Beamer Trail to Tanner Canyon (see Beamer Trail, page 163). Approximately 4 miles; camping at large; water in Colorado River; use Cape Solitude and Desert View quadrangles (7.5 minute). *Escape routes* via Tanner Trail (see page 146) or river runners.

Tanner Canyon to Unkar Creek
Hitch a ride above Tanner Canyon Rapids, or cross the river on the west side of Tanner Canyon Delta above Basalt Canyon Creek. Follow the right bank (north side) from Basalt Canyon Creek through heavy stands of tammies along Dox Sandstone to Unkar Creek. Approximately 5 miles; no camping on Unkar Delta; water in Colorado River; use Desert View and Cape Royal quadrangles (7.5 minute). *Escape routes* via Tanner Trail or river runners.

Unkar Creek to East End of North Tonto Plateau
This section gains the 4,400-foot saddle between the 4,802-foot Tabernacle and 6,406-foot Rama Shrine. Immediately west of Unkar Creek is a prominent ridgeline of Dox Sandstone. Climb up this ridgeline (north) to a break in the Tapeats Sandstone and take a narrow strip of Tonto Plateau to the saddle on the north side of the Tabernacle. Approximately 4 miles and 2,000 feet of elevation gain; camping at large; water in Colorado River, sometimes seasonal water in Unkar Creek; use Cape Royal Quadrangle (7.5 minute). *Escape routes* via Tanner Trail or river runners.

The Tabernacle to Clear Creek via North Tonto Plateau
The Tabernacle saddle is the most practical starting point for using the north Tonto Plateau as the main thoroughfare for proceeding westward through the inner Canyon below the North Rim. Because the North Rim drains into the Canyon,

the North Tonto is for the most part narrower, steeper, and rockier than the South Tonto. To make matters more interesting, the tributary drainages on the north Tonto are generally longer and steeper. And due to the fact that the North Tonto is devoid of any trail until you reach the Clear Creek Trail, you'll have to decide if your best route is to follow the outer edge of the Tonto Plateau along the Tapeats rim, or whether you should stay high and hug the base of the Muav in order to shortcut what may seem like long and circuitous miles.

From the Tabernacle saddle, follow the Tonto around the south side of 4,990-foot Sheba Temple to the head of Asbestos Canyon; there's a break in the Tapeats you'll have to eyeball in order to reach seasonal water on the floor of Asbestos Canyon or the Colorado River. To continue westward, take the Tonto from the head of Asbestos Canyon until you reach the base of the saddle on the north side of 5,105-foot Newberry Butte; there's a break through the Muav in this saddle, which will cut a few miles off your Tonto route to the head of Vishnu Creek. If you do this route in the spring, you can generally find seasonal water in the head of Vishnu Creek, which also makes a good camping spot.

It's a long but otherwise straightforward haul from the head of Vishnu Creek around the base of the 5,525-foot Hall Butte, 5,200-foot Hawkins Butte, and 5,572-foot Howlands Butte to the Clear Creek descent, with no shortcuts worth writing home about. The standard descent into Clear Creek is down the drainage running northeast from the 5,400-foot Angels Gate/Wotans Throne saddle; however, if you're a fair climber, there's a steeper descent through the Tapeats into Clear Creek north of The Howlands Butte. Eyeball the route to make sure it's the right chimney before committing yourself. From the bed of Clear Creek at the foot of this descent line, head downstream (west) for a few hundred yards before turning north up the main arm of Clear Creek where you'll pick up the Clear Creek Trail. There is perennial water in Clear Creek. Allow 1 ½ to 2 days minimum; camping at large to Clear Creek; designated sites at Clear Creek; water in Clear Creek and Colorado River at mouth of Unkar Creek and Asbestos Canyon; terrible-tasting seasonal water in floor of Asbestos Canyon at the head of Vishnu Creek; use Cape Royal and Phantom Ranch quadrangles (7.5 minute). *Escape routes* to Colorado River via Unkar Creek and Asbestos Canyon, and to Phantom Ranch via Clear Creek Trail.

Clear Creek to Phantom Ranch via the Clear Creek Trail
This is unquestionably the best section of trail on this entire route, and it's straightforward and easy to follow all the way to the Phantom Ranch beer hall. Approximately 9 miles; selected camping; water in Clear Creek and Phantom Ranch; emergency water sometimes found in Sumner Wash in Tapeats; use Phantom Ranch Quadrangle (7.5 minute).

ADDITIONAL CONSIDERATIONS: The Clear Creek Trail is most frequently used by hikers coming down the South Kaibab and Bright Angel trails, normally a two-day trek from the South Rim. But once you've set up camp at Clear Creek, you can explore Cheyava Falls to the north, the Colorado River to the south, or just hang out and watch cotton tufts blow off the Fremont cottonwood trees.

Phantom Ranch to Crystal Rapids
via Utah Flats and the North Tonto
From the north end of Bright Angel Campground (opposite the aluminum bridge spanning Bright Angel Creek), follow a track up through the Vishnu Schist to a notch through the Bass Formation, which is the passageway to the Hakatai Formation. The tendency is to want to climb high at this point, but stay in the Hakatai around the base of 5,401-foot Cheops Pyramid

until you reach the northwest arm of Ninetyone Mile Creek; climb up this arm to the Tonto.

From Ninetyone Mile Creek, stay on the Tonto around the base of 7,006-foot Isis Temple to the northeast arm of Trinity Creek; this arm will take you to Trinity Creek, where seasonal water can sometimes be found, but it's pretty foul-tasting stuff. You can also use the upper-west arm of Trinity Creek to regain the Tonto, but it's not much good as a shortcut if you don't need water.

Continue on the Tonto around the tentacles of 6,012-foot Tower of Set, the head of Ninetyfour Mile Creek, until you reach the westernmost arm coming down off 6,129-foot Tower of Ra. This arm points to the general direction of the descent to Crystal Creek, but you'll have to eyeball the route down the correct drainage before committing yourself. This descent is longer, looser, and more difficult than the descent to Clear Creek. Allow 1 ½ to 2 days minimum; camping at large; water at Phantom Ranch and Crystal Creek; seasonal water sometimes available in Trinity Creek; use Phantom Ranch, Grand Canyon, and Shiva Temple quadrangles (7.5 minute). *Escape routes* to Phantom Ranch and Crystal Creek at river via this route.

Crystal Creek to Tuna Creek via the North Side of the Colorado River

This little stretch through the Vishnu Schist and quartz is as short, difficult, and time-consuming as any mile-and-a-half on this route, and from Crystal Creek to Tuna Creek it's just a matter of picking and scrambling your way along the path of least resistance. Approximately 1 ½ to 2 miles; not the most ideal place to camp in the Canyon, but suitable spots can be found near Crystal Creek and the mouth of Tuna Creek; water in Crystal Creek and Colorado River; use Shiva Temple and Havasupai Point quadrangles (7.5 minute). *Escape routes* either back the way you came or with river runners who pull over to scout Crystal Rapids on river right several hundred yards above Crystal Creek.

Tuna Creek to the North Bass Trail via North Tonto
From the mouth of Tuna Creek, the first major fault to the west will take you back up through the Vishnu Schist and Tapeats to the Tonto Plateau. Once on the Tonto Plateau, stay on it around 5,832-foot Scorpion Ridge and all the way through and around Monadnock Amphitheater until you reach the western arm of 6,379-foot Evans Butte near BM 3962. There are several faults leading into the Hotauta drainage, but you'll have to eyeball your line of descent to the foot of the North Bass Trail before you commit yourself; this descent is comparable to the Crystal Creek descent in steepness, length, and difficulty, so use extra care following one of several steep lines south of the south arm of Hotauta Canyon. Allow 1 to 1 ½ days minimum; camping at large; water at Colorado River; emergency water sometimes available in second major drainage north of the west pincher of Scorpion Ridge, and below Tapeats in both arms of Monadnock Amphitheater; use Havasupai Point Quadrangle (7.5 minute). *Escape routes* either back the way you came or at Colorado River above and below Bass Rapids.

Bass Rapids to Muav Saddle via North Bass Trail
See the North Bass Trail description (page 210); 14 miles and 5,365-vertical-foot elevation gain; camping at large; water in Colorado River, Shinumo Creek, and White Creek below east side of Muav Saddle; use Havasupai Point and King Arthur Castle quadrangles (7.5 minute). *Escape routes* out Swamp Point Road or at Colorado River.

Muav Saddle to Thunder River Trail
via Saddle Canyon and Tapeats Creek
Head west off 6,711-foot Muav Saddle straight down the drainage through the brush below the old CCC cabin, and follow

it all the way to the Thunder River confluence. There is no trail along this stretch, but it's one of the prettiest stretches on the entire North Rim route. There aren't any real route-finding difficulties either, but several of the upper formations may require doubling back and scouting a descent line when cliffed-out; these pourovers can generally be gotten around on their right (or north) side—specifically in the Esplanade and Supai formations. Surprisingly, the Redwall Limestone presents no difficulties other than an 8-foot jump into a small plunge pool, which can be down-climbed, and it's unquestionably the finest section of Saddle Canyon until you reach Tapeats Narrows. The narrows have to be crossed, as there's no practical way to skirt them above on the right all the way to Thunder River. Make sure your trip isn't planned during peak runoff. If it is, and you've succeeded in somehow fording—bodysurfing—the narrows of Tapeats Creek, there's really no way to safely ford Tapeats Creek below the Thunder River confluence; you'll have to ford Tapeats Creek above this confluence, or find a stout-enough stalk from a century plant and pole-vault it, in order to reach the trunk of a cottonwood tree that spans the mouth of Thunder River and links you back up with the Thunder River Trail. Allow 1 to 1 ½ days; camping at large above Tapeats Narrows, in Tapeats Campground below; water in Muav Saddle springs, Tapeats Creek, and Thunder River; use King Arthur Castle, Powell Plateau, and Tapeats Amphitheater quadrangles (7.5 minute). *Escape routes* via Muav Saddle to Swamp Point, Tapeats Creek to Colorado River; and Thunder River to Monument Point.

Thunder River Trail Exit

See the Thunder River Trail description (page 213); 9 miles to Monument Point via Bill Hall Trail; camping at large above Redwall; water in Thunder River; use Tapeats Amphitheater Quadrangle.

9 | The Colorado River

Many rewarding day hikes lead from the banks of the Colorado River into the stone corridors and amazing tributary canyons that drain into the Colorado between River Mile 0 at Lees Ferry and River Mile 225 at Diamond Creek—and beyond. This chapter is a guide for private and commercial river runners. As an aid for private river runners rafting the Colorado River during the off season, river-to-rim escape routes are noted in event standard emergency procedures prove unsuccessful. All hikes and escape routes are listed by River Mile and, where possible, topographical name in descending order from Lees Ferry to Lake Mead.

For your river journey, consider carrying several companion guides in your ammo box. The popular guides *Grand Canyon River Guide,* by Buzz Belknap and Loie Belknap-Evans (Westwater Books; call (800) 628-1326), and *The Colorado River in Grand Canyon: A Comprehensive Guide to Its Natural and Human History,* by Larry Stevens (Red Lake Books, P.O. Box 1315, Flagstaff, AZ 86002), are illustrated with a Colorado River map detailing, among other points of interest, River Mile numbers, the names and scale of white water rapids, and locations of most of the hikes highlighted in this section. *A River Runner's Guide to the History of the Grand Canyon,* by Kim Crumbo (Johnson Publishing, 1880 South 57th Court, Boulder, CO 80301), details the river's colorful history mile by mile and includes a series of river maps. *Adventuring in Arizona,* by John Annerino (University of Arizona Press; call (800) 426-3797 or visit www.uapress

.arizona.edu), includes an engaging history of river running in the Grand Canyon, and river-mile-by-mile anecdotes and route descriptions.

Contact Grand Canyon National Park at www.nps.gov/grca/river for commercial outfitters, and www.nps.gov/grca/crmp for private river permits.

Lees Ferry Quadrangle (15 Minute)

Mile 0, Lees Ferry, River Right (facing downstream)
Lees Ferry is located on the Colorado River near the mouth of Paria Canyon—the first of four major tributary canyons that drain into the Colorado River in Arizona. While few river runners take the opportunity to explore this canyon before putting on the river, there are several destinations that make pleasant afternoon or early morning strolls. From the wooden bridge crossing the Paria River, you can head north and walk along a dirt road that will take you past "Lonely Dell" and the Lees Ferry cemetery to the southern boundary of the Paria Canyon–Vermilion Cliffs National Monument. From here, a trail hugs the left (west) side of the Paria River, which you can take past several other historic sites around the base of a bluff where the old grade parts with the Paria Canyon route. (For a detailed description of the 42-mile-long hike through Paria Canyon, see *Adventuring in Arizona*.) No spring water available for short day hikes.

Mile 3, Cathedral Wash, River Right
Now off-limits to camping, the mouth of this wash was once used by river runners who put on the river too late in the afternoon to make more than a few miles. It's an enjoyable and straightforward 1 ½-mile hike up this wash to the Lees Ferry road; this route is sometimes used by boatmen to mail one last

letter at the Marble Canyon post office several miles farther.
You can hike to the rim from here in an emergency. No water
en route.

Mile 7.5, Badger Canyon, River Right

You can take a mile hike up the boulder-strewn bed of Badger
Canyon until it dead-ends, for all practical purposes, in an
overhanging section of Kaibab Limestone. No water en route.

Mile 7.5, Jackass Creek, River Left

This canyon is sometimes used by Navajo Indians to fish the
Colorado River, and less successfully by pirate river runners
once netted in NPS stakeouts.

Escape route: Approximately 3 miles to Highway 89A. No
water.

Tanner Wash Quadrangle (15 Minute)

Mile 12, Salt Water Wash, River Left

It's a 4-mile hike up Salt Water Wash to Highway 89A. Cairns
mark the way up the steep, boulder-clogged lower half of this
route until the wash opens up and the walking becomes more
enjoyable.

Escape route: This is the last practical route to reach
Highway 89A and the phone at Marble Canyon Lodge. No
water.

Mile 17, Rider Canyon, River Right

If you lunch or camp at House Rock Rapids, you can take a
charming half-mile hike through the Supai narrows to a chockstone (a boulder wedged in a chimney or narrow canyon) that
can be climbed on the left.

Escape route: Above the chockstone, a 2-mile hike up the
wash leads to a cairned route through the rimrock to House
Rock Valley. It's a 3-mile cross-country walk to Highway 89A.

Emmett Wash Quadrangle (15 Minute)

Mile 20.5, North Canyon, River Right

You can take a mile-long hike up the bed of North Canyon through the sand and talus, then along the Supai Sandstone ledges. No water. Great place for a "rock talk."

Mile 22, Left Bank, River Left

Widely spaced cairns mark the steep, sometimes exposed route through the Supai Sandstone to a good viewpoint approximately 1 mile out from camp. No water.

   Escape route: A route has been linked from the Supai through the Coconino Sandstone to reach the rim and Highway 89A. However, this exposed and waterless route should be avoided by inexperienced canyoneers.

Mile 29, Shinumo Wash, River Left

More commonly known as Silver Grotto. A short side trip can be taken up this beautiful drainage, but a boat may be needed to ferry people from the pull-in immediately below the mouth of Shinumo to the start of this route. Several boulder moves on polished Muav Limestone may require spotting one another, and several cool plunge pools must be swum in order to reach Silver Grotto.

Mile 31.5, South Canyon, River Right

From camp you can take a short walk through South Canyon's Redwall narrows, follow the well-beaten route downstream to Stantons Cave, or wander upstream to contemplate ancestral Puebloan ruins.

Nankoweap Quadrangle (15 Minute)

Mile 34, Nautiloid Canyon, River Left

Named after the fossilized nautiloids found in this canyon. The short side trip up Nautiloid Canyon also involves several boulder moves on polished limestone to reach its terminus at the base of an overhanging section of Redwall Limestone. Depending on the river level, a boat may also be required to ferry people to the start of this enchanting route.

Mile 41, Buckfarm Canyon, River Right

A mile-long hike can be taken up Buckfarm Canyon, which involves some boulder-hopping and ledge walking.

Mile 44.4, Eminence Break, River Left

From the camp at the foot of President Harding Rapids, a steep, rugged prehistoric route crosses the Eminence Break Fault and leads through the Redwall, Supai, Coconino, and Kaibab formations to the 5,500-foot-high rim 2,700 vertical feet above the Colorado River.

Escape route: Not the best.

Mile 47, Saddle Canyon, River Right

This canyon makes a pleasant 2-mile round-trip hike from the river. After the initial climb up from the river, the trail levels off, then threads the holly and redbuds before dead-ending in an appealing little waterfall.

Mile 50, River Right

A deer trail leads from the lower camp at Mile 50 to the mouth of Little Nankoweap Creek, 2 miles downstream. However, you'll probably cover 3 miles en route to Little Nankoweap because the existing trail snakes through dense stands of tammies where the popular breaststroke is required to make any headway. When you're not swimming through the tammies, you'll have the opportunity to either boulder-hop or posthole through the mud.

Mile 53, Nankoweap Canyon, River Right

The steep three-quarter-mile-long hike up to the ancestral Puebloan granaries is the most frequently done hike in the area. However, there are several other options in the area worth doing. From the lower camp at the south end of Nankoweap Delta, frustrated distance runners can follow a well-marked 1 ½-mile lap that climbs over the neck of the delta, drops into Nankoweap Canyon, and follows its right side to river level before contouring the eastern base of this delta back to your starting point. From this lower camp, hikers and runners can also follow a faint trail system downstream for approximately 1 ½ miles.

If these hikes fail to get your land legs back, the Nankoweap/Kwagunt loop hike may do the trick. To start this 10-mile-long trek, you pick up a nonmaintained trail on the left (south) side of Nankoweap Creek. For the most part, it stays on the left side of Nankoweap Creek as it weaves and climbs its way over small boulders and through the cottonwood trees for a little over 2 miles to the confluence of the first major drainage coming down off the northwest side of Nankoweap Mesa. This is the beginning of the Butte Fault (see page 218). Scramble up this distinct ridgeline until it forms a near-perfect razorback; it's "six of one, half a dozen of the other" whether you follow its east or west side, though the west side involves less scrambling. Follow this route as it contours around the southwest side of unnamed Peak 5058 to the 4,810-foot Nankoweap Butte/Nankoweap Mesa saddle. From this saddle a deer trail meanders to the summit of 6,316-foot Nankoweap Mesa, or you have the option of descending into the drainage on the east or west, or continuing down this ridgeline; the drainage on the west sometimes has seasonal water. Continue down to the confluence of Kwagunt Creek, turn left (east), and start boulder-hopping your way back down to the river. Water can frequently be found in Kwagunt Creek, which is a somewhat narrower drainage in its lower end than Nankoweap Creek. Although it is possible to hike the 4 miles back upstream at river level at the mouth of Nankoweap Creek, most river runners day hiking this loop prefer to be picked up at the camp immediately below Kwagunt Rapids at River Mile 56 rather than contend with the exotic riparian jungle between the two creeks.

ADDITIONAL CONSIDERATIONS: The trails in the Nankoweap Delta area are heavily braided. National Park Service volunteers have realigned them to prevent erosion, so please take care to stay on the marked trails.

Mile 56, Kwagunt Creek, River Right
A 2-mile hike up Kwagunt Creek leads to the Butte Fault's storied Horse Thief Trail across Kwagunt Valley.

Vishnu Temple Quadrangle (15 Minute)

Mile 61.5, Little Colorado River Gorge, River Left
There are two popular day hikes up the mouth of the Little Colorado River: the obvious short jaunt to Beamer's cabin on the south bank, in the Tapeats Sandstone; and the 4 ½-mile hike to the Hopi Indians' sacred Sipapuni. In deference to Hopi religious beliefs, the author agrees the area should not be visited—or photographed—by non-Hopi. If you must pass by Sipapuni en route to Salt Trail Canyon 6 ½ miles up from the Colorado River confluence, or coming down the Little Colorado River Gorge from Cameron, please exercise discretion in this area. The Hopi know and revere it as the opening through which mankind originally emerged. (See Little Colorado River Gorge, page 249.)

WARNING: Don't drink the water.

Mile 61.5 to 65.5, Little Colorado River
Gorge to Palisades Creek, River Left
You can day hike the Beamer Trail from the mouth of the Little Colorado River west to Palisades Creek, where you can pick

Colorado River boatman Renny Summer rows his dory into camp at Nankoweap Creek. *Photo © John Annerino*

up a boat shuttle (for a description of the Beamer Trail, see page 163). No water en route.

Mile 64.5, Carbon Creek, River Right

You can take a 1- or 1 ½-mile hike up Carbon Creek to the prominent saddle on the west side of 3,945-foot Chuar Lava Hill; you can return by the same marked (but trailless) route, or loop hike down to the bed of Lava Canyon and continue to the river and a boat shuttle at River Mile 65.5. No water en route.

Mile 65.5 to 68.5, Palisades Creek to Tanner Canyon, River Left

A river trail and route goes from the mouth of Palisades Creek to the mouth of Tanner Canyon; this can be done as an out-and-back day hike from either of these canyons or as a point-to-point hike from Palisades Creek to Tanner Canyon using a boat shuttle.

Mile 68.5, Tanner Canyon, River Left

The 10 ½-mile-long Tanner Trail is sometimes used by private river runners as an interchange to drop off folks who don't have enough time to make a two-week river trip, or to pick up new people who couldn't make it to Lees Ferry before their party shoved off. Shadeless and no water en route.

Escape route: People at the Desert View Watch Tower on the South Rim are easily able to see a mirror flash from the mouth of Tanner Canyon; however, if inclement weather precludes emergency mirror signals or hampers electronic communication, there's an NPS ranger station at Desert View east of the Tanner trailhead, as well as a public phone (for a description of the Tanner Trail, see page 146).

Mile 68.5 to Mile 71, Tanner Canyon to Cardenas Creek, River Left

There's a well-marked river trail that goes from the mouth of

Tanner Canyon to the mouth of Cardenas Creek; it can be hiked either as an out-and-back hike from either of these two areas or as a point-to-point hike from Tanner Canyon to Cardenas Creek using a boat shuttle (see Tanner Canyon to Red Canyon, page 166).

Mile 69.5 to Mile 72.5, Basalt Canyon to Unkar Creek, River Right

During average river flows, it's possible to walk from the mouth of Basalt Canyon through the tammies along the Dox Sandstone to the mouth of Unkar Creek (see Tanner Canyon to Unkar Creek, page 220).

Mile 71, Cardenas Creek, River Left

A steep but popular and heavily used trail goes from the mouth of Cardenas Creek a mile or so up to the Hilltop Ruins Unkar Rapids overlook (see Tanner Canyon to Red Canyon, page 166). No water en route.

Mile 71 to Mile 76.5, Cardenas Creek to Red Canyon, River Left

A difficult cross-country route goes from the mouth of Cardenas Creek to the Unkar Rapids overlook to the foot of the Tonto Trail at Hance Rapids (see Tanner Canyon to Red Canyon, page 166).

Mile 72.5, Unkar Creek, River Right

Several trail variations cross the archaeologically significant Unkar Delta, so take care to use the designated trails in this area. Scientists are still studying this prehistoric ancestral Puebloan settlement, the largest in the inner Canyon. Careless foot travel will destroy valuable archaeological data.

Unkar Creek can be used to reach the east end of the north Tonto Plateau (see Unkar Creek, page 220) and was used by climber and boatman George Bain to make an epic ascent of

7,533-foot Vishnu Temple from the river—and back—in one long day on October 23, 1980.

Mile 75.5. Seventyfive Mile Creek, River Left
An easy quarter-mile hike leads through narrows of Shinumo Quartzite.

Mile 76.5, Red Canyon and Hance Rapids, River Left
Two possible escape routes leave the Hance Rapids area on river left: the New Hance Trail, which climbs up to the South Rim via Red Canyon, and the Tonto and Grandview trails. If you've not been up the New Hance Trail, use the Tonto and Grandview combination; it's easier to follow, and there's perennial water en route. (See the Tonto and Grandview trails description, pages 169 and 152.)

Mile 81.5, Grapevine Creek Camp, River Left
From the camp above Grapevine Rapids you can scramble along the Vishnu Schist on the left bank, gain the mouth of Grapevine Creek, and explore this rugged tributary. This route, which is exposed and loose in several key sections, is not recommended for inexperienced canyoneers or weak rock climbers. Also use Bright Angel Quadrangle (15 minute).

Bright Angel Quadrangle (15 Minute)

Mile 84, Clear Creek
From the small camp above Clear Creek on river right, the route into Clear Creek skirts up and around the dark amphibolite before dropping back down into the bed of this heavily visited creek. The first waterfall is located a half mile or so upstream. This waterfall can be passed on the left (west) side in order to continue up Clear Creek for as far as time will permit. Over the years, several boatmen have hiked up Clear Creek to the east end of the Clear Creek Trail, then over to Phantom

Ranch, where they were picked up by a boat shuttle the same day.

Loop Hike: You can loop hike from the river to Phantom Ranch by boulder-hopping 3 miles up Clear Creek to the east end of the Clear Creek Trail, then following the Clear Creek Trail 9 miles to Phantom Ranch and catching a boat shuttle at River Mile 87.5, Bright Angel Creek. (See Clear Creek to Phantom Ranch, page 222).

Mile 87.5, Bright Angel Creek, River Right

From Roys Beach you can cross the Kaibab Suspension Bridge and hike the River Trail to Pipe Creek and return via the Bright Angel Bridge variant; you can hike upstream a small piece via the Gauging Station Trail, sometimes used by river runners ferrying departing passengers across the river from Last Chance; you can hike the Bright Angel Trail; or you can take the North Kaibab Trail north to the mouth of Phantom Creek, Ribbon Falls, or Roaring Springs. (For the North Kaibab Trail, see page 203.)

EMERGENCY HELP: There's an NPS ranger station near the mouth of Bright Angel Creek. There's also a pay phone, food, and refreshments at Phantom Ranch.

Mile 95 to Mile 96.5, Hermit Creek
to Boucher Creek, River Left

You can hike up Hermit Creek to the Tonto Trail (see page 169) and take the Tonto Trail over to Boucher Creek, which will take you back down to the river and a boat shuttle. This hike is seldom done by river runners simply because Hermit Rapids is one of the best rides on the river before facing the Jaws of Death 3 miles downstream.

Escape routes: Hermit and Boucher trails (see pages 154 and 157).

Mile 98, Crystal Creek

There are two short hikes near the mouth of Crystal Creek, and both have a certain blow-the-heart-out-of-your-chest character to them. The shorter of the two hikes has seldom been missed by river runners since a flash flood formed this frightening rapid in 1966, and it involves a straightforward boulder-hop to the head of Crystal Rapid, where airbags are most frequently used on a Colorado River hike. The second hike is a bit longer, requires rudimentary route-finding ability, and is usually done at a brisk pace by river runners to pick up their head boatman before he ends up swimming Tuna Creek Rapid as well.

Havasupai Point Quadrangle (15 Minute)

Mile 107.5, Bass Canyon, River Left
From the camp immediately above Bass Rapid on river left, you have to scramble downstream along the schist in order to gain the foot of the South Bass Trail because the mouth of Bass Canyon cliffs-out above the river. You can hike up the South Bass Trail to the Tonto Trail junction, and double back due north along the Tonto Trail below 5,209-foot Wallace Butte to a second junction northeast of 4,879-foot Tyndall Dome. This point makes a fine overlook, up canyon or down, before taking the short right (east) fork of the trail back down to the South Bass Trail and camp.

Escape route: The South Bass Trail is an easy-enough escape route, but unless you hike up it during the summer, when the Pasture Wash Ranger Station may be staffed, its value is questionable; it's some 30-odd miles west of Grand Canyon Village via a seldom-used dirt road (for the South Bass Trail description, see page 160).

Mile 108.2, Shinumo Creek Camp, River Right
From the Upper Shinumo Creek Camp, the North Bass Trail climbs up over a prominent ridgeline designated BM 2917 before dropping back down to the bed of Shinumo Creek; it

follows the right side of Shinumo Creek until William Wallace Bass's old camp is reached shortly after.

Do not disturb the old tools and relics in this camp!

Escape route: Assuming you can find your way up the North Bass Trail and reach the trailhead at Swamp Point, it's at least another 20-odd miles via old fire roads to the Kaibab Lodge, so you should weigh all factors carefully before trying to use the North Bass Trail as an escape route (for a description of the North Bass Trail, see pages 210).

Mile 114, River Right

From the camp at Mile 114 you can scramble up a small drainage to the base of the Tapeats and traverse it eastward until you find a break leading up to the Tonto Plateau. Taking a faint burro trail north along this bench for a mile or so will offer good views of 6,281-foot Mount Huethawli on the South Rim and 6,721-foot Wheeler Point on the North Rim. It looks like it would be feasible to follow this section of the Tonto Plateau eastward to Burro Canyon and Shinumo Creek. No water en route.

Mile 116.5, Royal Arch Creek and Elves Chasm, River Left

Elves Chasm: The two short jaunts into Lower and Middle Elves are both obvious enough, since the area is so heavily visited; however, the route up to Middle Elves involves several exposed traverses on polished Elves Chasm gneiss.

WARNING: Don't drink the water!

Royal Arch Creek: The route to Upper Elves Chasm and Keyhole Arch leaves the proximity of the second tributary drainage downstream from Garnet Canyon on river left. (A small low-water camp at the foot of this rugged route was flushed downstream in a 1983 flood control exercise by the Bureau of Reclamation.) The route follows a faint trail up to a break in an obvious travertine deposit; this exposed section is protected somewhat by a rope anchored to a boulder that may or may not be anchored itself. Once atop this section, it's a relatively straightforward trek for a mile or so along this bench to a 7-foot-high stone monument. Turn left (south) and head along the east rim of Royal Arch Creek, where an exposed move or two in the Muav Limestone will take you to the upper floor of this drainage; if you continue downstream, you'll hike under a precarious-looking rock stack and natural arch at the head of a waterfall that feeds Middle Elves Chasm immediately below. From the rock stack, look up to the east and you'll see Keyhole Arch in the Redwall rim above. No water en route.

Mile 120, Blacktail Canyon, River Right
The most frequently done hike in this area is the short hike up the floor of this charming little canyon. However, you can find a route, somewhat exposed, through the Tapeats Sandstone near the mouth of Blacktail Canyon on its east side; this line will provide access to the Tonto Plateau, which you can follow at least as far eastward as the camp at Mile 119. However, the descent off the Tonto Plateau through the Tapeats Sandstone requires careful scouting before you'll be able to eyeball the least intimidating line back down to river level at Mile 119. (This upper route should not be attempted by weak climbers or inexperienced canyoneers.) From Mile 119, you can loop back along the river to the mouth of Blacktail Canyon. No water on Tonto.

Powell Plateau Quadrangle (15 Minute)

Mile 132, Stone Creek, River Right
From the camp immediately below the mouth of Stone Creek, at Dubendorff Rapids, you can make at least two rewarding hikes in the area. Two miles of hiking up the course of Stone Creek will take you to one of the prettiest waterfalls in the Canyon, or you can find the break in the Bass Formation and

Hikers in Blacktail Canyon. Photo © George H. H. Huey

take a faint trail several miles west along the Hakatai Shale, around Hundred and Thirty-three Mile Creek to the rim overlooking the mouth of Tapeats Creek. From the Tapeats Creek overlook, a more frequently used trail follows the east side of Tapeats Creek and will eventually take you to the creek itself.

Mile 133.5, Tapeats Creek, River Right

This is one of the must-stops for river runners, and it is frequently the location for a layover day for others, because Tapeats Creek provides access to three hikes in the area: the popular, well-marked 4-mile trail to the headwaters of Thunder River, which leaves the west side of Tapeats Creek and climbs immediately through the Diabase and Bass formations before linking up with the well-trod trail to Thunder River (cairns mark several creek crossings); the more arduous trek up from the confluence of Thunder River and Tapeats Creek to Tapeats Cave; and the loop hike from Thunder River, across Surprise Valley, to Deer Creek Falls and a boat shuttle at River Mile 136, Deer Creek. You can also hike the Tonto Plateau from Tapeats Creek south into Hundred and Thirty-three Mile Creek 2 ½ miles to Stone Creek.

Escape routes: The Bill Hall Trail is another one of those straightforward but arduous and remote escape routes. The trek from Monument to the Kaibab Lodge can be an interminably long one if Big Saddle Camp is unoccupied (see the Thunder River and Bill Hall trail descriptions, page 213).

Kanab Point Quadrangle (15 Minute)

Mile 136, Deer Creek, River Right

There are four enticing trips to do in this area. The mile-long romp up through Deer Creek Narrows is the most frequently done hike; the trail up to the Narrows is more obvious than the pictographs of white hands that adorn its Tapeats Sandstone walls. If you want a cold, wet, and exciting canyoneer's peek at the head of Deer Creek Falls, use your nylon bowline or a perlon climber's rope to belay one another for a short descent into the narrows. The trail up from the Narrows, over Surprise Valley to Thunder River, is more strenuous but becoming increasingly popular. One of the most rewarding and least frequently done day hikes in the area, however, is the short, steep trek from Surprise Valley up to the 4,545-foot summit of Cogswell Butte. From the Cogswell Butte saddle on the west end of Surprise Valley, take the most prominent north-south ridgeline from the saddle and follow it cross-country toward the summit of Cogswell Butte. En route you'll have to make an 8-foot-long boulder move in the Redwall before zigzagging your way through the Supai, but the hike presents no real technical difficulties if you use good route-finding judgment. From the summit of Cogswell Butte, you'll have an incredible view of 7,410-foot Steamboat Mountain to the east, and neighboring Swamp Point, Muav Saddle, and 7,661-foot Powell Plateau; to the south, you can take in virtually all of Great Thumb Mesa—from Apache Point to the mouth of Havasu Creek; to the west, 6,125-foot Fishtail Mesa can be readily picked out; and to the north, Indian Hollow and 6,602-foot Bridgers Knoll can be seen. Allow 25 minutes each way from Surprise Valley.

Escape route: Any escape route from the river via the Bill Hall Trail (page 213) should be carefully considered.

WARNING: Watch out for poison ivy on the Deer Creek Trail near river level; it's the only place in the Grand Canyon, other than Vaseys Paradise, at River Mile 32, where the stuff grows.

Mile 143.5, Kanab Creek
It's approximately 4 miles up Kanab Creek to the falls of Whispering Falls Canyon. This is an enjoyable hike through a fairly wide canyon, draped here and there by several traver-

tine falls on its west side; you have to cross Kanab Creek a number of times, but you'll also get to skirt across some neat Muav ledges.

From the mouth of Whispering Falls Canyon you can trek up Kanab Creek some 50-odd miles to Kanab, Utah, much the way Major John Wesley Powell and his men did in 1872 when he concluded his second voyage down the Río Colorado at the mouth of Kanab Creek. For a detailed description of that route, see *Adventuring in Arizona*.

Mile 145.5, Olo Canyon, River Left

You have to perform two neat tricks to get into the mouth of this gem—both of which can be unnerving if someone in your party hasn't been down the river before. The first involves climbing up a dangling rope ladder; the second involves a somewhat slippery and exposed climb up a modern set of "Moki steps" that have been etched into a 20-foot-high travertine falls. Both of these climbs are easy enough technically, but unless everyone in your party is a strong climber, bring a rope to belay one another up and down these two abrupt drops.

WARNING: Several river runners have taken serious falls here.

Escape route: If somebody *does* get injured in a fall, the quickest escape route is the run to Supai, which usually entails running Upset Rapid with the injured person (which can be a problem for first-time boaters running the Colorado River between 1,000 to 16,000 cfs), making the pull in at Havasu (which can also be a problem for first-time boaters), then running 7 ½ miles to the Havasupai Ranger Station and the phone above Mooney Falls (also a problem, since you probably wouldn't start up Havasu until dark). Although Olo Canyon is probably one of the more enticing tributary canyons in the Grand Canyon, make sure your exits are safely covered.

Mile 148, Matakatamiba, River Left

Also known as Matkat, this is another tributary canyon that has been eroded and polished through the Muav Limestone. And while it's more heavily visited than Olo Canyon, it's also a good alternative for inexperienced canyoneers simply because it's an easy and enjoyable hike that covers similar terrain as that of Olo. (*Please note:* In deference to the Havasupai Indians' religious beliefs, the author agrees the area a mile above the mouth of Matakatamiba should not be visited by non-Havasupai; they know and revere this sacred area, and many others, around Great Thumb Mesa.)

Tuckup Canyon Quadrangle (15 Minute)

Mile 156.5, Havasu Canyon, River Left

The 4-mile hike to Beaver Falls is the most frequently done hike by river runners in Havasu Canyon; the way is obvious, though you will have to look for cairns that mark the five creek crossings you'll make en route to Beaver Falls. If you're a fair swimmer and treat your boatman right, maybe he or she will take you into the Green Room. Mooney Falls is certainly the most spectacular falls in Havasu Canyon, and in order to reach it you have to climb up and traverse the travertine deposits on the east side of Beaver Falls, then ford Havasu Creek another three times before reaching the base of Mooney 1 ½ miles farther. You can also use the Kanab Point Quadrangle (15 minute).

Escape routes: It's 7 ½ miles to the Havasupai Ranger Station and the private phone above Mooney Falls; Supai is another 1 ½ miles beyond this ranger station.

EMERGENCY RADIO FREQUENCIES:
  Lees Ferry to Havasu—122.9
  Havasu to Pierce Ferry—123.05

WARNING: Flash floods are a deadly hazard during summer monsoons. Don't drink the water in Havasu Creek, and if you have any open cuts, don't swim in it.

Mile 164.5, *Tuckup Canyon, River Right*
If you miss the Havasu pull-in, you get to hang out at Tuckup Canyon, in which case you'll have plenty of time to discover the area for yourself.

BEYOND HAVASU
After the big hiking day in Havasu, folks start thinking about running River Mile 179.5 rapid. Although there are many hiking opportunities below Havasu Canyon, they don't seem to be hiked as heavily as the areas above Havasu Canyon; then again, maybe River Mile 179.5 rapid has a lot to do with the sudden lack of hiker enthusiasm. Here are some areas worth exploring:

Mile 166.5, *National Canyon, River Left*
A short hike can be taken up its bed to an enchanting boulder problem.

Mile 168, *Fern Glen, River Right*
Another short but charming hike. Donald Davis reports in his notes *A Traverse of the Colorado River from Lee's Ferry to Lake Mead*, "There is a way out as prospectors were here in 1932."

Mile 171, *Stairway Canyon and Fault, River Right*
In those same notes the former ranger Davis also poses the possibility that Gateway and Mohawk canyons may have been used together as a cross-Canyon route. This may even have been a cross-Canyon route the Paiute Indians used when, as J. Donald Hughes writes in *The Story of Man at the Grand Canyon*, they "sometimes ventured into the Grand Canyon in search of rock salt and mescal, and sometimes crossed it to contact the Havasupais to the south." Or it could have been the route Mormon pioneer and explorer Jacob Hamblin used

when, as author Hughes further notes, he "induced the Kaibab Paiute Chief, Chuar, to locate springs and trails for Powell, including one down to the Colorado River in the Grand Canyon near Toroweap."

Mile 179.5, Lava Falls and Trail, River Right

With the possible exception of prospector James White, who may have successfully run the biggest drop on the Colorado River on a crude log raft two years before Major John Wesley Powell's first successful descent, few river runners have missed this short, usually hot, hike through the black lava to a heart-thumping overlook.

Escape route: 1 ½ miles up the Toroweap Trail and 6 miles by dirt road to the seasonally staffed Tuweep Ranger Station (see Toroweap Trail, page 277); no water en route. Another emergency option is line-of-sight radio contact or mirror flashes with chopper pilots using the helipad on river left at Mile 183 or with fixed-wing aircraft flying over the area.

Mile 188, Whitmore Wash, River Right

Several commercial river outfitters use this steep, 2-mile-long trail to "interchange" outgoing passengers with incoming passengers, which is worth noting from an emergency standpoint, if not a hiking one. However, a deal may have been struck with the Hualapai Indians to use a helipad on reservation land on the south side of the river (river left), in which case line-of-sight radio contact or mirror flashes may be your best bet.

Mile 211.5, Fall Canyon, River Right

You can hike a mile up Fall Canyon, strewn with boulders of Bright Angel Shale, to a pourover at trail's end.

Mile 225.5, Diamond Creek, River Left

Takeout. Peach Springs is located 22 miles up the Diamond Creek Road.

Escape route: Even during the off-season you should be able to hitch a ride through the Hualapai heartland in the event help is not readily available at Diamond Creek.

WARNING: Flash floods are a deadly hazard during summer monsoons.

Mile 229, Travertine Falls and Canyon, River Left
A short hike leads to Travertine Falls. A half-hour climb past Travertine Falls leads to the Tonto Plateau; you can follow the Tonto west for several spectacular miles. Old burro trails frequently skirt the very edge of the Tapeats Sandstone.

Mile 235, Bridge Canyon, River Left
This was yet another dam-threatened area in the Grand Canyon. It's 15 minutes up to the Tonto Plateau, which you can take at least as far west as Separation Canyon several miles distant.

Mile 246, Spencer Canyon, River Left
To gain the Tonto Plateau, ascend the first major drainage upstream from the mouth of Spencer Canyon on the east side; it'll take approximately 20 minutes to reach this section of Tonto, which, if you proceed eastward, has more difficult footing than either the Travertine or Bridge Canyon sections of the Tonto Plateau. It also has one of the densest stands of teddy bear cholla you're likely to encounter on the Tonto Plateau anywhere in Grand Canyon National Park and vicinity.

Emergency considerations below Spencer Canyon: Recreational traffic and NPS patrols usually ply the still waters upstream to Spencer Canyon and beyond. You shouldn't have much problem hitching a ride back to Pearce Ferry, or to the phone at Meadview Ranger Station.

10 | Little Colorado River Gorge

First kayaked by Brad Dimock and Tim Cooper in March 1978, the Little Colorado River Gorge is a dark serpentine chasm on the scale of Marble Canyon. Its headwaters begin atop 11,403-foot Mount Baldy—*dzil ligai* ("white mountain"), sacred to the Apache. That's nearly 300 miles above the confluence of the Little Colorado with *the* Colorado in the eastern Grand Canyon. The upper end of the Little Colorado River offers some outstanding backpacking opportunities in the spruce, aspen, and ponderosa forests of the White Mountains.

The last 57 miles of the Little Colorado River gorge are the most appealing from a canyoneering standpoint, a remote adventure equal to the 57-mile trek down Kanab Creek in charm and difficulty. From Cameron to the Colorado River confluence, the Little Colorado River Gorge barrels its way down what kayaker Tim Cooper described in *Mountain Gazette* as a "gradient more than three times as steep as the river into which it flows." In the process the Little Colorado cuts its way through Permian formations "of resistant sandstones, limestones, and shales that form the upper walls of the Grand Canyon."

To begin this multiday trek, drive to Cameron, Arizona, 74 miles north of Flagstaff on U.S. 89. The riverbed can be reached by taking the dirt road just south of the Cameron Bridge on its east side. From the Cameron Bridge the way is obvious all the way to the Colorado River confluence 57 miles downstream; there's never really any danger of getting lost.

There are two more important considerations, however: water sources and the season. There is no perennial water between the Cameron Bridge and the first spring above Blue Springs 35 miles downstream. The water from Blue Springs is high enough in carbonates to render it almost unpalatable unless doctored with a powdered drink mix—unless you're in a dire emergency. That fact, perhaps more than any other, will determine the best season for undertaking this trek. Unless it's a dry year, with little runoff coming off the White Mountains and Colorado Plateau, spring is out of the question; the gorge will either have enough water in it for expert kayakers to boat it (around 750 cfs is considered ideal for this difficult run, assuming you have a permit to boat the Colorado River below the confluence), or it will be so muddy that your trek will become a nightmare of postholing through ankle-deep muck from one waterhole to the next. From mid-May to the first week of June—again, depending on the runoff—there is a narrow window during which the gorge can be trekked: when the mud has been sunbaked to near-ideal footing and when there may be enough water holes to preclude the necessity of carrying more than a gallon or gallon and a half of water at a time. However, you must be physiologically adapted to heat stress, because the temperature in the gorge exceeds 105°F, and upstream winds blasting across your exit route along the Beamer Trail can make several sections unnerving for non-hang-gliders. The remainder of the summer is out of the question. Flash-flood dangers have proven deadly for *veteran* canyoneers during monsoon season. Unless you hit that late spring/early summer window, you should consider planning your trek down this gorge for late October through January, when the temperatures are far cooler and your chances of reaching the first water source (with the water you can carry on your back) may be best.

The Route

Stay in the riverbed and follow the path of least resistance. The gorge gets exciting when it starts cutting through the Coconino Sandstone, about 8 ½ miles downstream; this is the narrowest stretch of the gorge, and you can see how rapidly it drops—an average of 28 feet per mile. There are some test holes in this section, drilled by Bureau of Reclamation engineers as a possible dam site; they also built the footbridge you'll see spanning the Narrows 70 feet above. Like the Narrows in Paria Canyon, this is a dangerous section to be hiking during any kind of runoff; it's sheer-walled and a mere 30-odd feet wide.

A half mile or so downstream from the Narrows, the gorge widens again and sluices through broken sections of Coconino. Between approximately Miles 9 and 11, you'll be able to see the first scenic overlook high above on the southern rim. If you get into trouble along this stretch, use your signal mirror to flash for help.

When I trekked this route from Cameron to the head of the Tanner Trail in late May one year, I began seeing water pretty regularly from this point on down.

About 11 miles out there's a gauging station on the left; from here to the cable crossing another half mile or so downstream there's a section of trail that stays about 50 feet above the bed on its west side and connects the gauging station with the cable crossing and an old green shack. If you've got plenty of water, there are some nice places to camp in this area, but if you're running low, you'd probably better crank out a few more miles down to Dead Indian Canyon.

From Cameron to Dead Indian Canyon the footing is generally excellent—assuming you hit the right conditions—and is comprised of hard-packed silt or dried mud. But it sometimes gets gnarly when the Little C. begins making abrupt descents, in which case you'll either be threading or jumping over boulders. About 2 miles downstream from Dead Indian Canyon the gorge begins cutting through the Supai Sandstone, and at Mile 23 it makes a dogleg turn through Hellhole Bend. About 7 or 8 miles below Hellhole Bend the gorge passes through the Redwall Formation.

There are good camping areas about a half mile upstream from Waterhole Canyon; it makes a good objective for day 2 if you're trucking for water but don't quite have enough spit left to make it to Blue Springs. You should encounter your first springs just below Waterhole Canyon, about 35 miles downstream from Cameron. Between Waterhole Canyon and Blue Springs, another 5 miles or so downstream, you'll go through a narrow Redwall section that has no less than a half dozen springs gurgling out of the wall on its east side. If your feet haven't been wet to this point, they soon will be—all the way to the Colorado River.

Approximately 42 miles downstream from Cameron you'll reach Blue Springs; it bubbles out of the west wall into several travertine pools. While these travertine pools aren't as high as the spectacular falls of Havasu Canyon, the color of the water is far prettier. This makes an excellent rest and swimming spot. Tough miles lie ahead. From Blue Springs the roughest hiking you'll encounter on this trek—next to Hell's Half Mile below Waterhole Canyon—will be the 7 or 8 miles down to the mouth of Salt Trail Canyon. An air mattress might come in handy for the numerous deep fords you'll have to make before reaching the first travertine dams, which provide natural footbridges from one side to the other; it's these travertine dams that provide the greatest obstacle to foot travel (and kayak descents), but if you scout the way, you'll usually find passage along the left bank.

Below the last of these dams, your best course will probably be to stay on the river left all the way to Salt Trail Canyon. There are several dense stands of tammies and arrowweed on the river right that are difficult to get through, especially at the end of a long third day of hiking. Salt Trail Canyon and several other camping areas are immediately below.

From Salt Trail Canyon, plan on another day of trekking down to the Beamer Trail and on to the foot of the Tanner Trail (see page 146), the exit route for this section of the Little Colorado River Gorge. Camping is not allowed within the boundaries of Grand Canyon National Park at the confluence of the Little Colorado and the Colorado River.

ADDITIONAL CONSIDERATIONS: The 16-mile roundtrip hike from the Cameron Bridge to the Narrows makes a challenging day hike, and the 23-mile round-trip hike to Cable Crossing is a good overnighter.

PRIMARY ACCESS TRAILS & ROUTES: Cameron Bridge and Tanner Trail. Contact Navajo Nation Parks at www.navajonationparks .org and the Grand Canyon National Park at www.nps.gov/ grca/backcountry for current access information, permits, and fees. See J. H. Butchart's "The Lower Gorge of the Little Colorado," in *Arizona Highways,* September 1965, pp. 34–42, for trail descriptions and access information for the following abandoned rim-to-river trails: Horse Trail, Moody Trail, Paiute Trail, and Indian Maid Trail.

ELEVATION:	Approximately 4,100 feet at Cameron Bridge to 2,700 feet at the Colorado River.
TOTAL ELEVATION LOSS:	1,400 vertical feet.
MILEAGE:	57 miles from Cameron to confluence. Bureau of Reclamation counts miles upstream from confluence, with Colorado River being Mile 0 and Cameron Mile 57.
WATER:	Blue Springs area.
SEASONS:	Mid- to late May, and late October through January. Summer can be deadly, and spring walking can be atrocious, depending on runoff.
MAPS:	Cameron, Coconino Point, Blue Springs, and Vishnu Temple quadrangles (all 15 minute).
ESCAPE ROUTES:	Cameron, Colorado River confluence, Beamer and Tanner trails to South Rim.
EMERGENCY SIGNALS:	Best spot for mirror flashes to be observed is line of sight from bed of Little Colorado River to rim vistas 9–11 miles below Cameron.
NEAREST SUPPLY POINTS:	Cameron, Flagstaff, Page, South Rim.

11 | Pipe Spring National Monument, Grand Canyon–Parashant National Monument, and Western Grand Canyon

Into the earth, and into the sky—running.

—*Anonymous*

Once the ancestral lands of the Southern Paiute Indians, the untamed 11,000-square-mile Arizona Strip still forms one of the loneliest and most desolate tracts of land in the Southwest. Comprised of four major plateaus—the Kaibab, Kanab, Uinkaret, and Shivwits—this vast, sparsely populated region of Great Basin desert reels southward from the Vermilion Cliffs 60 miles to the edge of the western Grand Canyon. Today, it includes Pipe Spring National Monument, Grand Canyon–Parashant National Monument, and western Grand Canyon National Park.

Major John Wesley Powell was the first non-Indian to explore what he called "that difficult region" in 1870, and he had two pressing reasons for doing so: he wanted to investigate the fate of William Dunn, Seneca, and O. G. Howland, three men who'd abandoned his first Colorado River expedition at Separation Canyon in 1869; and he wanted to explore the possibility of establishing resupply caches for his second expedition down the Colorado River in 1871. To do so, Powell hired Mormon missionary, explorer, and polygamist Jacob

Hamblin to act as his liaison with the Kaibab Paiute who would actually lead Powell's overland expedition through the uncharted region.

Venturing southward from the prehistoric way station of *Mutungw* ("Yellow Rock Water"), Powell embarked on one of the most unusual murder investigations and reconnaissances in the annals of Western history: during his nine-day journey he would climb the area's highest mountain, drink from sacred water holes, descend into the depths of the western Grand Canyon, and be told face to face by the very men who killed them that the Dunn-Howland trio had been murdered. Powell completed this rugged adventure months before embarking on his second Colorado River expedition, an expedition that would end with Powell and his men venturing the entire length of Kanab Creek in 1872.

Yet more than a century later, it's still possible to follow in the footsteps of Powell and the astute Kaibab Paiute guides who led him into that exciting, seldom-traveled region; this chapter will show you the way.

Access

For all hikes and treks described in this chapter, use the Mount Trumbull Road. The well-marked turnoff is located 6 miles west of Fredonia. It is 5 miles east of Pipe Spring National Monument on Highway 389. (For a detailed description of the historic tour along what was once known as the Sunshine Road, see *Adventuring in Arizona*.)

Travel Advisory

The condition of all-weather Mount Trumbull Road, and the remote and rugged four-wheel tracks that branch from it, dictate the accessibility of the hikes and treks described in this chapter. The dry months of spring and fall are best. Deep snow is common in the higher elevations near Mount

Trumbull and Mount Logan mid-winter, while summer mon-soons can inundate long stretches of Mount Trumbull Road with tire-ripping detritus from flash floods and axle-burying ponds of standing water. There are no facilities, so come pre-pared with adequate provisions of food, gas, water, tools, and a shovel. Also bring a copy of the AAA map "Guide to Indian Country."

PIPE SPRING NATIONAL MONUMENT

When Powell first rode to the ancient Kaibab Paiute water hole of Mutungw on September 13, 1870, he wrote, "We fol-lowed this Indian trail toward the east all day, and at night camped at a great spring, known to the Indians as 'Yellow Rock Water.'" To Mormon militiamen who built a fort there in 1868, it was known as Pipe Spring. William "Gunlock Bill" Hamblin reportedly shot the bottom out of Dudley Leavitt's pipe from 50 paces there in 1852, hence the name. Yet, from the dawn of civilization, this ancient spring has been one of the most dependable water sources for travelers journeying across the vast ancestral lands of the Southern Paiute: for the Kaibab Paiute, who journeyed from one water hole to the next, hunting, gathering, and growing small plots of maize, beans, and squash; for Mormon missionary families strug-gling along the Honeymoon Trail from St. George, Utah, southward to the Little Colorado River valley; for hordes of forty-niners who headed down Kanab Creek to the Colorado River hell-bent on finding the mother lode at river's edge; and for Powell's own overland expedition, as well as his 1871–72 topographical survey that would ultimately give birth to the "new west."

More than a century after the one-armed Powell last rode out of Yellow Rock Water, Pipe Spring still makes the best jumping off spot for modern adventurers headed south in the footsteps of Powell and the Kaibab Paiutes who led him to what one expedition member called "the Edge of the World" and back. A tour of this Mormon redoubt will enlighten those interested in seeing how the early Euro-American settlers adapted to what to them was a hard country by applying farming and ranching practices that would, in one disastrous decade following 1863, displace and decimate the Kaibab Paiute people. Until that tragic turning point, when nearly a thousand Kaibab Paiutes perished from disease and starvation (a nearly 90-percent population "reduction"), the Kaibab Paiute practiced what ethnographers call "total fauna-flora and horticulture utilization patterns." For those interested in learning how these Native People effectively utilized the region's indigenous plants and animals to live in harmony with the same land Anglo settlers fought for, overgrazed, and stripped of the very foodstuffs the Kaibab Paiutes depended on, the self-interpreting Muuputs Canyon and Tukuputs Canyon trails are a must. Petroglyph panels near the end of the Muuputs Canyon Trail reflect the degree to which the Kaibab Paiute still revere their ancestral lands; while Powell's Monument high atop the Tukuputs Canyon route will provide you with the same view once seen by Powell's survey when they built such monuments along the rim of the Vermilion Cliffs to map the region in 1871–72.

Directions

From the entrance to Pipe Spring National Monument, drive or walk two-tenths of a mile north to a large sign on the left (west) that reads "Kaibab Paiute Educational Hiking Trails: Admittance by brochure only. Available at campground and snackbar." From this sign, follow the dirt road west to the fork of the Muuputs Canyon and Tukuputs Canyon trails.

Muuputs ("Owl") Canyon Trail (day hike)

From the trail fork, follow the flash flood–scoured streambed a quarter mile to a second fork marked "North" and "West." The north fork leads to several petroglyph panels of ancient figures dancing across stone and a sign that reads "Sacred Area. Stop Here." The west fork leads to a third panel of petroglyphs at the head of Muuputs Canyon. Located near the foot of a dry cascade, this must be an unusually beautiful sight when the stream is flowing. Return to the trail forks.

Tukuputs ("Cougar") Canyon Route (day hike)

If following the Muuputs Canyon Trail is like journeying into the earth, tracking the Tukuputs Canyon route is like climbing into the sky. From the forks, turn left (southwest) and follow the wash until cairns lead you to the crest of the ridgeline. Follow this trailless, though well-marked, route to the Powell Monument at marker No. 12, a pile of stones above the 5,700-foot elevation contour; here Powell's men discovered that Pipe Spring lay in the territory of Arizona, and not in Utah, as was originally thought. Pipe Spring became the site of Arizona's first telegraph station, the Deseret Telegraph Company. Of his 1872 ascent to this point, topographer Stephen Vandiver Jones wrote, "Friday, February 2nd. From Geodetic point A to south end base line 6 P. Climbed mountains back of Pipe Spring to Monument A. Took some bearings." This bare-bones description of the breathtaking climb would later contribute to the region's first topographical map, Reconnaissance Map, *ARIZONA KAIBAB SHEET* (March 1886).

Even if summer thunderstorms are hammering the Arizona Strip, you can still make out the region's highest plateau, the 8,000-foot Kaibab Plateau, which the Paiute called *Kaivaavich* ("mountain lying down"). Immediately below your vantage, at the foot of Tukuputs Ridge, the Paiute's verdant oasis of Mutungw is the only patch of green that can be seen in the sea of parched sagebrush desert Anglos have since named The Strip. And farther south, you can eyeball the route Powell and his Paiute guides took from Pipe Spring 50 miles to Mount Trumbull and beyond.

Down the ridge at marker No. 10 you can see the wagon wheel ruts of the Honeymoon Trail rolling into and out of Pipe Spring to the east and slashing across the landscape as far west as you can see. Return the way you came.

PRIMARY ACCESS:	Pipe Spring National Monument.
ELEVATION GAIN & LOSS:	Muuputs Canyon: Approximately 200 vertical feet each way; Tukuputs Canyon: Approximately 900 vertical feet each way.
MILEAGE:	Muuputs Canyon: 1 mile round-trip from Pipe Spring; Tukuputs Canyon: 3 miles round-trip from Pipe Spring.
WATER SOURCE:	Pipe Spring; none en route.
ESCAPE ROUTE:	Back the way you came.
SEASONS:	All year.
BOOKLET:	*Kaibab Paiute Educational Hiking Trails.*
MAPS:	Kaibab, Pipe Spring, Pipe Valley, and Moccasin, AZ, quadrangles (7.5 minute, 1988 Provisional Editions) and Reconnaissance Map, *ARIZONA KAIBAB SHEET* (March 1886).

NEAREST SUPPLY POINTS FOR ALL TRAILS AND ROUTES DESCRIBED IN THIS CHAPTER:	Pipe Spring National Monument and Fredonia, Arizona, and St. George, Utah.
MANAGING AGENCY:	Kaibab Paiute Tribe and Pipe Spring National Monument. Contact Pipe Spring National Monument at www.nps.gov/pisp for current access information, permits, and fees.
BACKCOUNTRY INFORMATION:	Booklet serves as permit to hike these trails.
BIOTIC COMMUNITY:	Pinyon-juniper woodland.

GRAND CANYON–PARASHANT NATIONAL MONUMENT

Established by President Bill Clinton on January 11, 2000, the 1.1-million-acre Grand Canyon–Parashant National Monument sits in the heart of the Arizona Strip. Wild, remote, and rugged, it is a modern no-man's-land that lures adventurers, backpackers, and spirited individuals who've grown weary of the crowds, traffic congestion, and smog that characterize many of the region's other parks and monuments.

U-nu-pin Pi-ka-vu ("Witches Pool") (day hike)

One of the first things Powell wrote about when he headed south from Pipe Spring on the morning of September 14, 1870, was the paucity of water sources in the region: "Not more than a half-dozen are known in a district of country large enough to make many good-sized counties in Illinois. There are no running streams, and these springs and water-pockets—that is, holes in rocks that hold water from shower to shower—were our only dependence." A noted explorer, Powell relied on the knowledge of Chu-ar and Shuts, two Kaibab Paiutes, to lead his party along the ancient footpaths from one aboriginal water hole to the next. At twilight on day two, Powell finally reached Witches Pool, 40-odd miles south of Pipe Spring; it was one of the Kaibab Paiute's most storied water holes. Of his September 15 visit, Powell wrote, "During the rainy season the water rolls down the mountain-sides, plunging over precipices, and excavating a deep basin in solid rock below. This basin, hid from the sun, holds water the year round.... The Indians call it U-nu-pin Pika-vu, that is, Elfin Water-Pocket."

Directions

To reach U-nu-pin, ride your horse south across Antelope Valley, by way of Wild Band Pockets and the Uinkaret Plateau, for two days, as Powell did. Or drive 44 ½ miles south on the Mount Trumbull Road; from this pullout (located 4.2 miles south of the junction with the Colorado City Road), a four-wheel-drive track heads west from the Mount Trumbull Road. Park here.

Trail Log

Head west along the double-rutted track, which crosses an open meadow marked by two abandoned dwellings, 1 ½ miles to a second gate; 50 yards or so west of this gate, a second 4WD track branches off and heads north toward the base of a 5,921-foot hill. Follow this track across the shimmering-hot black lava for a half mile. The track winds among the pinyon-juniper, beavertail cacti, and staghorn cholla to a wash that contours the base of the hill Powell climbed and described as "a huge pile of volcanic scorria, loose and light as cinders from a forge, which gave way under my feet as I climbed with great labor." Turn west at the base of this slag heap and follow the wash upstream another quarter mile to U-nu-pin. A ragged stand of live oak, clustered beneath a 50-foot-high basalt cliff, marks the spot, but Elfin Water-Pocket is located another 30 yards upstream. Fortunately, this aboriginal rain catchment has not been "improved upon," as early settlers and stockmen have done to most other water holes on the Arizona Strip, and today Witches Pool retains the same allure it had when cartographer Clarence Dutton retraced Powell's route to the western Grand Canyon in 1871. Dutton wrote: "In every desert the watering places are memorable, and this one is no exception. It is a weird spot. Around it are the desolate Phlegraean fields, where jagged masses of black lava still protrude through rusty, decaying cinders. . . . The pool itself might well be deemed the abode of witches." That's exactly what Chu-ar told Frederick S. Dellenbaugh, one of Powell's expedition members, when he visited the spot: "They said the locality was a favourite haunt of witches." But you'll never really know unless you, too, visit it.

PRIMARY ACCESS:	Via Mount Trumbull Road.
ELEVATION GAIN & LOSS:	300+ vertical feet each way.
MILEAGE:	Approximately 4 ½ miles round-trip.
WATER SOURCES:	U-nu-pin (before drinking, purify and strain out the "wigglers" Powell nonchalantly drank).
ESCAPE ROUTE:	Back the way you came.
MAPS:	Mt. Trumbull NE Quadrangle (7.5 minute) and Reconnaissance Map, ARIZONA MT. TRUMBULL SHEET (March 1892).

MANAGING AGENCY:	Bureau of Land Management. Contact Grand Canyon–Parashant National Monument at www.nps.gov/para/index.htm for current access information, permits, and fees.
BACKCOUNTRY INFORMATION:	Permit not required; camping and campfires not allowed within ½ mile of water hole.
BIOTIC COMMUNITY:	Pinyon-juniper woodland.

Mount Trumbull Wilderness, Uinkaret Mountains (peak ascent)

When Powell climbed the small hill of volcanic rubble looming over Witches Pool on the morning of September 16, he was looking for the most practical way to approach and climb 8,029-foot Mount Trumbull. He wrote he hoped he "could get a good view of the great mountain from this point, but it was like climbing a chair to look at a castle. I wished to discover some way by which it [Mount Trumbull] could be ascended, as it was my intention to go to the summit before I started for the settlements." Climbing and naming Mount Trumbull (after U.S. senator Lyman Trumbull), however, was one of the last things Powell accomplished before he returned to Pipe Spring. You may want to emulate the sequence of his treks by heading to the ancient Paiute encampment of Big Springs before descending into the Grand Canyon and then climbing Mount Trumbull; or, you may want to conserve your gasoline by following the sequence described in this chapter.

Next to the 7,700-foot Kaibab Plateau, 8,029-foot Mount Trumbull is the highest summit on the Arizona Strip. When Lt. Joseph Christmas Ives first viewed this isolated range in 1858 from a point far to the south, he named it the North Side Mountains because it was situated north of the Colorado River; the Kaibab Paiute, however, called the range the *Uinkaret Kaib* ("Pine Mountains"), the name the range now bears. Long the domain of the Paiute, and earlier the ancestral Puebloans, the peak was no doubt climbed by these Native Americans hundreds of years before Powell made the first recorded ascent.

What's not known for certain, however, is which route Powell used to reach the summit from Witches Pool. After his successful descent into the western Grand Canyon, followed by an all-night powwow with the Shivwits Paiutes, Powell rode back to Witches Pool with Captain F. M. Bishop. From there, Powell's route most likely took them west 2 ½ miles because Powell described riding across a volcanic field of cinder cones. If that's true, then Powell and Bishop probably climbed the north slope of Mount Trumbull. Powell wrote, "Then we rode through a cedar forest up a long ascent until we came to cliffs of columnar basalt. Here we tied our horses, and prepared for a climb among the columns. Through crevices we worked still toiling up, till at last we were on the mountain."

This summit cap of basalt cliffs can be clearly seen from Witches Pool, and you can strike out for the summit from it. However, the standard approach to the mountain is from the vicinity of Nixon Spring on the south side of the mountain.

Directions
On Mount Trumbull Road, 46.7 miles south of Highway 389, the road forks. Turn right and follow the Mount Trumbull Road 7 miles to the official trailhead located near Nixon Spring. Park here.

Trail Log
Much of the later history of Mount Trumbull and the Uinkaret Mountains dates to 1874, when Mormon lumbermen logged 1

million board feet of timber on the mountain and hauled it by oxen teams 80 miles over the Temple Trail to St. George, Utah, in order to build St. George's first temple. You can still drive Temple Trail northwest from Nixon Spring today.

To reach the summit of Mount Trumbull, however, follow the steep rocky trail from the trailhead. The trail switchbacks up the southwest escarpment of the mountain through cinder slides covered with manzanita, pinyon, and juniper. About the time you reach the 7,600-foot elevation contour, the trail becomes a gentle path that contours the southeast/east slope of the mountain through a wonderful forest of ponderosa pine. But just about the time you start thinking the path is actually going to lead you to the elusive summit, it disappears in a stream of yellow plastic ribbons that veer south off the shoulder of the mountain. And like Powell, you're left to your own good sense to find the summit; Powell wrote, "A thousand acres of pinelands spread out before us, gently rising to the other edge. There are two peaks on the mountain. We walked to the foot of the one that seemed the highest, then made a long hard climb to the summit." Today, this forest crowns the 7,900-acre Mount Logan Wilderness portion of the monument, and if you have any problems locating the summit in its midst, just head west along the summit ridge to higher-and-higher ground until you're on the true summit—it's marked by a benchmark and a pile of stones hiding two summit registers, so there's no fudging the high point. A note inside one of the registers touched upon the dilemma most hikers encounter in trying to find Mount Trumbull's exact high point: on 6-27-91, Larry Nelson of St. George, Utah, wrote, "I don't know how I found the summit, but here I am."

And there *you* are, surrounded on three sides by a curtain of ponderosa pine and live oak and a burned-out stand of withered black snags. The only real view you have from the summit of Mount Trumbull is to the north-northeast. If thunderstorms don't obscure your vision, the Vermilion Cliffs are the most prominent landmark on the northern horizon. According to Dellenbaugh, Powell named them "Vermilion on account of their rich red color." You'll also be able to make out most of Powell's route from Pipe Spring at the foot of the Vermilion Cliffs to the base of Mount Trumbull: it parallels, to the west, the deep fissure in the earth called Kanab Creek.

But if you've climbed Mount Trumbull for the unobstructed 360-degree panorama Powell had, you'll have to rely on his description. Powell wrote, "And there, oh! what a view was before us. A vision of glory. Peaks of lava all around below us; the vermillion cliffs to the north, with their splendor of color; the Pine Valley Mountains to the north-west, clothed in mellow perspective haze; unnamed mountains to the southwest towering over cañons bottomless to my peering gaze; and away beyond, the San Francisco Mountains lifting their black heads into the heavens."

Powell lost some of his credibility as a reporter when researchers discovered he sandwiched his 1869 and 1871–72 Colorado River expeditions into a single account written to sound like one adventure, not to mention his blatant omission of the names of several expedition members who didn't see eye-to-eye with him. If you don't want to take Powell at his word on the summit view, the views en route back down the trail once it breaks out of the ponderosa and drops over the 7,600-foot elevation contour are exceptional.

SOUTHWEST: You can make out the forested ridge that connects 7,866-foot Mount Logan with 7,702-foot Mount Emma, named after Powell's wife.

SOUTH: You can make out the volcanic fields encircling the dormant volcanoes of Mount Trumbull, Mount Logan, and, clustered among them, what Roderick Pattie described in the now-classic *The Inverted Mountains,* "nearly 170 distant cones, many perfect in form." Back beyond the western Grand Canyon's south rim, which forms the brink of the 6,000-foot-high Coconino Plateau, you can pick out what appears to be 7,168-foot Picacho Butte near Seligman and, if the refracted afternoon light isn't warping the view, 7,626-foot Granite Mountain near Prescott, more than 150 miles distant.

SOUTHEAST: You have a commanding view of Toroweap Valley, from Tuweep Ranger Station south to Toroweap Point; of the Kanab, which, in its 60-mile stretch from Fredonia to its confluence with the Colorado River, grows from a creek to a chasm; and across the Canyon, 130 miles southeast, the 12,633-foot San Francisco Mountains.

EAST: You can see lone 7,324-foot Red Butte, sacred to the Havasupai and once epicenter of the Grand Canyon uranium mining controversy. Far up-Canyon you can also see as far east as 7,646-foot Shiva Temple, unmistakably marked by 6,613-foot Osiris Temple.

But not everyone comes to Mount Trumbull for the vista; in the summit register, a woman wrote, "I came to Mount Trumble [*sic*] to fight the spring and mountain fires. There [*sic*] out now, why am I still here! It's beautiful up here. I love it and hope to visit it again someday. Until Then, Jenifer Randall, 7-16-89."

PRIMARY ACCESS:	Via Mount Trumbull Road and Wilderness trailhead; secondary access via Witches Pool.
ELEVATION GAIN & LOSS:	1,600 vertical feet each way.
MILEAGE:	Approximately 2 ½ miles one way.

WATER SOURCES: None en route.

CACHE POINT: 7,600-foot elevation contour.

ESCAPE ROUTE: Back the way you came.

MAPS: Mt. Trumbull NW and Mt. Trumbull NE quadrangles (7.5 minute) and Reconnaissance Map, ARIZONA MT. TRUMBULL SHEET (March 1892).

MANAGING AGENCY: Bureau of Land Management. Contact Grand Canyon–Parashant National Monument at www.nps.gov/para/index.htm for current access information, permits, and fees.

BACKCOUNTRY INFORMATION: Permit not required; be extremely careful with fires.

BIOTIC COMMUNITIES: Pinyon-juniper woodland and montane conifer forest.

Mount Logan Wilderness, Sawmill Mountains (peak ascent)

That Powell neglected to describe his ascent of 7,866-foot Mount Logan in his *The Exploration of the Colorado River and Its Canyons* makes you wonder if that climb was of less importance to him than his climb of Mount Trumbull. Be that as it may, Powell apparently didn't climb Mount Logan during his September 14–22 overland expedition, because accounts by both Dellenbaugh and Almon Harris Thompson have him climbing Mount Logan on November 11, during a second trip south from Pipe Spring. Dellenbaugh wrote, "The Major, Prof. [Thompson] and [Stephen Vandiver] Jones climbed Mount Logan for more data and took a general sur-

vey of the country, while I went out on foot, climbed, measured, and located eight large cinder-cones." So if you're trying
to follow the exact sequence of Powell's movements during
his first overland expedition (Pipe Spring, Witches Pool, Big
Springs, Inner Canyon, and Mount Trumbull), you can save
Mount Logan for the end; or if you're concerned about con-
serving gas, follow the sequence of hikes highlighted thus far.
Either way, a visit to the summit of this 14,600-acre wilderness makes for a pleasurable outing and will provide you with
an outstanding view of the route Powell took to reach the
Colorado River.

Directions
From the Mount Trumbull trailhead, drive 4 miles south on
Mount Logan Road to the unmarked fork for Mount Logan/
Big Springs, turn right (west), and 2 miles beyond you'll reach
the summit car park for Mount Logan. In fact, if there's one
disturbing aspect to the Mount Logan Wilderness portion of
the monument, it's that the trail up Mount Logan is actually a
road that leads to within a half mile of the summit: a bane for
purists, a delight for car campers.

Trail Log
Whether you drive or walk to the wilderness boundary near
the 7,600-foot elevation contour at road's end, it's a breathtaking place to picnic or camp. The forested volcano of Mount
Trumbull lies immediately to the north. You can follow the
route of the Temple Trail west from the mountain's base across
Potato Valley, past Death Valley Lake, until it disappears in the
distant Main Street Valley.

From road's end, head west up an old fire road, which narrows to a charming forest path after a hundred yards or so.
This trail skirts the exposed northern rim of Mount Logan and
courses through bristling stands of ponderosa, still home to the

bushy-tailed Kaibab squirrel. Fearing that a natural calamity would threaten the dwindling native squirrel population, biologist Dave Brown reportedly transplanted sixteen Kaibab squirrels to Mount Logan between 1971 and 1974. However, I didn't see any during my visit two decades later.

Between March 27 and November 11, Frederick S. Dellenbaugh climbed Mount Logan no less than three different times. While he never described his exact route, he made one enlightening entry in his *A Canyon Voyage: The Narrative of the Second Powell Expedition*: "In spite of the exceedingly rugged surface ... [the lava field] was marked by deeply worn trails running to and from a small spring situated in the middle of it. Beside this spring one of the men ... found a human skeleton, covered with fragments of lava, with the decayed remains of a wicker water-jug between the ribs, marking some unrecorded tragedy."

Thick stands of pinyon, juniper, and ponderosa now obscure much of the horizon from south/southeast to north, so you have to dance around the summit cap or walk farther south along the western rim of Mount Logan to identify any topographical features of note in the horizon other than 7,702-foot Mount Emma 7 miles south. What you should be able to see from atop what Dellenbaugh called "Signal Station Number 7" is 6,990-foot Mount Dellenbaugh 25 miles southwest. Dellenbaugh couldn't have been happier that Major Powell also saw that mountain, because "when they came down [from Mount Logan] the Major said he had seen a fine, isolated mountain to the west which he had called after me, and I naturally felt much pleased with the honour of having my name stamped on the map."

Dellenbaugh stamped his footprints on several other prominent features that can be seen from the summit of Mount Logan: 50 miles northwest you can see the dark gray mass of the 8,075-foot Virgin Mountains. Sometime after April 27, Dellenbaugh and Professor Thompson left St. George and "made a long, hard ride and climb" to reach the base of Mount Bangs, which they climbed the next day. Dellenbaugh and Prof. Thompson got caught in a blinding April snowstorm while climbing Utah's 9,000-foot Pine Valley Mountains 70 miles north-by-northwest of here; Dellenbaugh wrote, "Above, below, and around us was a great blank whiteness. Dismounting and cautiously advancing on foot we discovered that we were at the brink of a very high cliff."

What really grabs your attention from this vista is the bald western escarpment of Mount Logan plunging 2,000 vertical feet into Hells Hole immediately to the west. The Painted Desert–like cliffs of this yawning inferno form the headwaters of Whitmore Canyon, which drains into the Colorado River 20 miles downstream. It was along the floor of this rugged drainage that Powell and his men were undoubtedly guided to the river after leaving the Paiute encampment of Big Springs on the south side of Mount Logan. Powell wrote, "The valley is high up in the mountain, and we descended from it by a rocky, precipitous trail down, down, down ... leading our ponies, and stumbling over the rocks." But you'll have to head off the mountain to Big Springs yourself to pick up the next leg of Powell's route to the river.

PRIMARY ACCESS:	Via Mount Logan Road, from Mount Trumbull Road.
ELEVATION GAIN & LOSS:	200 vertical feet each way.
MILEAGE:	1 mile round-trip.
WATER SOURCES:	None en route; seasonal water pump at Nixon Spring.
ESCAPE ROUTE:	Back the way you came.

MAPS: Mt. Logan and Mt. Trumbull
                               NW quadrangles (7.5 minute)
                               and Reconnaissance Map,
                               ARIZONA MT. TRUMBULL
                               SHEET (March 1892).

MANAGING AGENCY: Bureau of Land Management.
                               Contact Grand Canyon–Para-
                               shant National Monument at
                               www.nps.gov/para/index.htm
                               for current access information,
                               permits, and fees.

BACKCOUNTRY
INFORMATION: Permit not required.

BIOTIC COMMUNITIES: Pinyon-juniper woodland and
                               montane conifer forest.

Big Springs, Sawmill Mountains (day hike)

Perhaps more than any other location, Big Springs was the most important stop Powell made during his exploratory journey of the Arizona Strip. It was here at this ancient Kaibab Paiute encampment that Powell and his men were led down Whitmore Canyon to the bottom of the Grand Canyon where they had hoped to establish a resupply point for their second Colorado River expedition the following year. Here also, after almost perishing of thirst during a nearly disastrous trek to the river and back, Powell finally met the Shivwits Paiutes who told him the fate of the Dunn-Howland party. On the morning of September 17, Powell wrote, "Early the next morning the Indians came to our camp. They had concluded to send out a young man after the Shi-wits. The runner fixed his moccasins, put some food in a sack, and some water in a little wicker-work jug lined with pitch, strapped them on his back, and started off at good round pace."

Today, Big Springs is a burned-out swath of sage bearing little resemblance to the "lovely little park for their home, a meadow in front, and a grove of tall pines behind" that Powell wrote of. Situated beneath the southwestern escarpment of the 7,866-foot Sawmill Mountains, the onetime Kaibab Paiute encampment faces the chasm formed by the Colorado River and the flying terraces of stone that fan out from it. To the Paiute, life in their ancestral lands was everything: "We love our country; we know not other lands.... The pines sing, and we are glad. Our children play in the warm sand; we hear them sing, and we are glad. The seeds ripen, and we have to eat, and we are glad. We do not want their [white man's] good lands; we want our rock and the great mountains where our fathers lived."

Unfortunately, the only sign that marks this ancient Paiute village is a pipe-fed cattle trough constructed by the descendants of the same settlers who pushed the Kaibab Paiutes from their cherished ground. Yet if you can maintain a grasp of the big picture, it's still possible to follow the inner-Canyon routes of Paiute runners who, according to one ethnographer, reportedly could run antelope to death. But where ancient footpaths once traversed these rugged canyons, forested highlands, and distant plateaus, jeep roads have been laid. And with the choking, leg-ripping stands of sage limiting cross-country travel, you'll have little choice but to follow these modern trails if you want to run in the footsteps of these great runners or struggle in those of Powell to the Colorado River, what the Paiute called *Paga*, "Big Water."

Directions
From the Mount Logan / Big Springs road junction (4 miles south of the Mount Logan Road), turn left (southeast) and fol-

low this forest track as it contours around Petty Knoll through the pass formed by it and Slide Mountain. If Powell's description tells no lies, his route also crossed this pass, but he made a detour to climb 7,586-foot Slide Mountain before descending into Big Springs: "We rode along the trail another half-hour until we came to a pass between two high cinder cones, of which I concluded to climb the one on the left.... I rode my horse as far as possible, and then tugged up afoot to the summit, from which I could see the Grand Canyon." Whether or not you also climb this cinder cone for the view, it's 2.1 miles to Big Springs from the Mount Logan Road.

Trail Log

From Big Springs, run or walk a half-mile southeast back up to the Whitmore Canyon Road junction. Follow the Whitmore Canyon Road approximately three-quarters of a mile to another 4WD track coming in from the left (south). This 4WD track will, in a little over 3 miles, lead you to the forested crest of the 8,029-foot Uinkaret Mountains; these mountains form the natural boundary for Grand Canyon National Park to the east and the Mount Logan Wilderness to the west and north. If it's no longer possible to experience what once captivated the Kaibab Paiute at Big Springs, you can still feel the natural power of the mountains here in the *Uinkaret Kaiv* ("Place of Pines"), far from the destructive hand wrought upon this land by strangers. Here, in this remote forest, with the wind howling through the trees, you can still feel the power of what the Shivwits told Powell late one night: "Last year we killed three white men. Bad men said they were our enemies. They told great lies. We thought them true. We were mad.... We are very sorry. Do not think of them; it is done; let us be friends.... When white men kill our people, we kill them. Then they kill more of us. It is not good. We hear that the white men are a great number. When they stop killing us, there will be no Indians left to bury the dead."

Return the way you came.

PRIMARY ACCESS:	Via Mount Logan Road.
ELEVATION GAIN & LOSS:	Approximately 1,000 vertical feet each way.
MILEAGE:	Approximately 9 miles round-trip.
WATER SOURCES:	Big Springs, in season.
ESCAPE ROUTE:	Back the way you came.
MAPS:	Mt. Logan and Mt. Trumbull NW quadrangles (7.5 minute) and Reconnaissance Map, ARIZONA MT. TRUMBULL SHEET (March 1892).
MANAGING AGENCY:	Bureau of Land Management. Contact Grand Canyon–Parashant National Monument at www.nps.gov/para/index.htm for current access information, permits, and fees.
BACKCOUNTRY INFORMATION:	Permit not required.
BIOTIC COMMUNITIES:	Pinyon-juniper woodland and montane conifer forest.

WESTERN GRAND CANYON NATIONAL PARK

Bordered on the east by the deep, rugged course of Kanab Creek Canyon, on the north by a sea of Great Basin Desert, on the west by the stark plateaus and canyons of Grand Canyon–Parashant National Monument, and on the south by sheer cliffs that plummet 3,000 feet to the Colorado River, the western Grand Canyon remains the wild canyon country that first lured prospectors, surveyors, and developers into the heart of what's popularly known as "the Grand Canyon." It's just the kind of country that tugs at the souls of artists, desert rats, canyoneers, and adventurers. Go see for yourself!

Toroweap Trail (a.k.a. Lava Falls Trail) (trek)

There's little doubt that the Kaibab Paiute did not lead Powell to the Colorado River via the Toroweap Trail because when Powell asked them if there was a way into the Canyon, he wrote that they told him "years ago, a way was discovered by which parties could go down, but that no one had attempted it for a long time; that it was a very difficult and dangerous undertaking to reach the 'Big Water.'" That's a more fitting description of the Toroweap Trail than Powell's account of his trek to the Colorado River from Big Springs, which more accurately describes the length and nature of Whitmore Canyon. Yet few people realize that the Toroweap Trail was first used as a way to the "Big Water" by the Kaibab Paiute and not by the modern river runners who now call it the Lava Falls Trail.

However, as far as can be discerned, Dellenbaugh and Captain Pardyn Dodds made what was probably the first recorded descent of this ancient Paiute route in 1870. Dellenbaugh wrote, "On the 20th [of April] Dodds and I climbed down the cliffs about three thousand feet to the water at a rapid called Lava Falls." That's as succinct and as accurate a description of the Toroweap Trail as there is, along with Roderick Pattie's in *The Inverted Mountains*: "the shortest and doubtless one of the roughest [trails] down to the Colorado River." He was right about that.

Still, if you're up to the challenge—and the trail register indicates many are—there are two good reasons to follow the

Toroweap Trail: As a journey, it follows the historic route of Powell's men to the river and that of the Kaibab Paiute who first pioneered it—and how better to emulate these early canyoneers than to follow in their footsteps; as a destination, it ends at one of the most spectacular rapids in North America, which has tested river runners since James White made his controversial first descent of the Colorado River on a log raft almost two years before Powell completed his first Colorado River Expedition.

Directions

From the Toroweap Ranger Station (53 miles south of Highway 389, via the Mount Trumbull Road), drive south on the Toroweap Point Road 3.5 miles and turn right (west) at an unmarked turnoff. The Toroweap Trail is another 2.4 miles through the dustbowl formed by Toroweap Lake, along the west slope of 5,102-foot Vulcans Throne, to the black crust of the Canyon rim. Vulcans Throne was named by eminent geologist Clarence Dutton in 1871 when he retraced Powell's general route from Pipe Spring toward Toroweap Point. It is reportedly a worthwhile mile round-trip scramble for taking in the views of the western Grand Canyon. In the work Dutton produced from that geological survey, called *The Tertiary History of the Grand Canyon District, with Atlas,* he wrote, "there stands a basaltic cinder cone immediately upon the brink of the inner gorge. Its altitude above the surrounding plane is 580 feet. The summit is readily gained, and it is an admirable stand-point from which the entire panorama may be viewed. We named it Vulcan's Throne."

Trek Log

Whether you follow this rugged route to emulate Powell's men and the Kaibab Paiute, or because you just want to reach the Big Water, the Toroweap Trail is anything but an aesthetically pleasing "hike," as most people define the term. Plummeting an astonishing 2,600 vertical feet in a mile and a half, the Toroweap Trail is an avalanche of a route waiting to throw you to your knees during the descent—and to wring the last drop of moisture out of you during the debilitating crawl out.

There is little more to say about the viper-plagued route snaking its way through glass-black lava other than follow the rock cairns during the decent and, once you turn around, the white crosses shining the way back out of this fearsome hole. The crosses were undoubtedly white-washed in place by a grateful pilgrim as memorials to all those canyoneers who, like Major Powell, nearly perished of thirst climbing over skin-burning black lava. Whatever reasons you have for using this route, you are strongly advised to cache water during the descent, say, a quart for every 500 to 700 vertical feet you descend.

"The way is difficult and at times well calculated to daunt the most active climber.... Very seldom is it possible to descend in safety the walls of the Grand Canyon," wrote Dutton of the route. To help measure your progress along the mournful procession of crosses and stone memorials, the following topographical features are highlighted from rim to river's edge:

Vulture Valley: So called for the proliferation of turkey vultures cruising this canyoneer boneyard, Vulture Valley is actually a steep slope leading from the trailhead down to the brink of the topographical formation called Lava Falls. (Allow a minimum of 15 minutes while ascending this section.)

Lava Falls: Two grungy boulder moves must be negotiated in descending Lava Falls from Vulture Valley to Finger Rock Ridge. (Allow 15 minutes for the ascent.)

The Chute: From Finger Rock Ridge, you have the rottenest section on the Toroweap Trail—a knee-wrenchingly steep chute filled with ankle-knocking, feet-pulverizing rock. Two grungy boulder moves must also be negotiated on this leg to reach the river's edge alive. (Allow 30 minutes during the ascent.)

River's Edge: Now that you're this far, the scramble across the boulder slide through the mesquite, barrel cactus, and creosote to Lava Falls Rapid will seem like a walk in the park. (Allow 10 minutes on return.)

You can lunch in the shade beneath the boatman overlook and wonder how in the world you're going to crawl out of here, or you can stare at the steepest rapid in North America, which many believe was first run by a sunburned and emaciated prospector named James White. In *The Big Drops: Ten Legendary Rapids,* Roderick Nash and Robert Collins wrote, "Think of a weakened, dazed man, looking up from his logs at the line across the river, listening to the boom of Lava, and thinking, in desperate condition, that he might as well hang on and hope for the best. Then the sickening first drop and brown water tearing at his body and smashing it against the wood and, finally, the calm below and wondering how much more he could take before death. He took enough to get out barely alive and tell a tale nobody would, at first, believe. We do." So do I.

Return the way you came, and be grateful you don't have to try running Lava on a raft made of three cottonwood logs lashed together.

PRIMARY ACCESS:	Via Toroweap trailhead.
ELEVATION LOSS & GAIN:	2,600 vertical feet each way.
MILEAGE:	1 ½ miles each way.
WATER SOURCES:	None en route; Colorado River.

CACHE POINTS:	Vulture Valley, Lava Falls, Finger Rock Ridge.
ESCAPE ROUTE:	Back the way you came; or, in a dire emergency, try flagging down a commercial river outfitter in season or one of the dozens of air-tour operators barnstorming this section of the Canyon.
MAPS:	Vulcans Throne Quadrangle (7.5 minute) and Reconnaissance Map, ARIZONA MT. TRUMBULL SHEET (March 1892).
MANAGING AGENCY:	Grand Canyon National Park. Contact Grand Canyon National Park at www.nps.gov/grca for current access information, permits, and fees.
BACKCOUNTRY INFORMATION:	Permit required for overnight camping; fires not allowed.
BIOTIC COMMUNITY:	Mojave desert scrub.

Tuckup Trail, via Saddle Horse Springs (day hike)

Whether Powell ever actually set foot on 4,552-foot Toroweap Point is not certain. But his cartographic point man, Clarence Dutton, did. And when he sat on the edge of that sheer cliff that drops like a stone twenty-eight hundred-and-fifty-two vertical feet into the gaping chasm formed by the Colorado River, he wrote, "It would be difficult to find anywhere else in the world ... such dramatic and inspiring surroundings." He was right about that.

So was Dellenbaugh when he described it as "the Edge of the World." It is. Yet, to reach the very edge requires a journey (but then, it always has). If you're anywhere in Arizona but the Strip, you practically have to drive to Utah to reach it, the most remote and spectacular vista in Arizona. Still, people come; not many, maybe hundreds. The curious. The foreign tourists in rented sedans. Photographers, especially, like the daunting view; only some of them get possessive. Take the modern landscape photographer who, rumor has it, wanted to have a brass nameplate mounted on the edge of Toroweap Point because he felt other photographers were "stealing his picture." He didn't know, or maybe he didn't think any other photographer would find out, that John K. Hillers beat them all to the punch. Hillers was one of Powell's expedition photographers, and on April 1, 1872, he took the first picture from Toroweap Point. So maybe a brass plate with Hillers's name should be embedded in stone here, instead.

Whether or not you ever take a picture from Toroweap Point, or bore the life out of your friends with a three-hour webcam broadcast from here, you must go. If you do nothing else, just sit there. Take your time. Let the Canyon whisper its secrets to you. But go see the Edge.

For those who want to dance along the Edge, you can trace the Saddle Horse Springs and Tuckup trails. Both no doubt had their beginnings with sheepherder and prospector Henry Covington. According to a documentary film script by Elinor Lin Mrachek, Covington "prospected along the rim and the inner gorge around 1917." That's not all Covington did—somewhere over the Edge, the polygamist reportedly "kept one of his wives in an old Indian cave near his mine." But Covington wasn't the only one hanging honeymoon suites over the Edge. According to Mrachek, cattleman Al Craig refurbished two caves near the bottom of the Canyon and called it the "Son-of-a-Bitch Hotel" because it was so difficult and dangerous to reach "few have ever spent the night or would have the courage to ever return." If you're interested in bunking your honey in either of these honeymoon aeries, you can start looking for them by tracing the Saddle Horse Springs or Tuckup trails.

Directions

To reach the Edge of the World, drive south from Highway 389 60 miles on the Mount Trumbull and Toroweap Point roads.

Saddle Horse Springs Trail

A half-mile north of the Toroweap Point campground there's an unmarked pullout on your right (east). Follow the old 2WD track east and then north, as it contours the rimrock of Esplanade Sandstone and the cairns that still mark the route. About a mile from the roadhead you'll see a one-inch steel pipe drop over the rock shelf. Follow the pipe into a small drainage where the pipe abruptly dives over the rimrock. Turn right (south) here and follow the old trail 50 yards or so south to another break in the Supai. Hop down this five-foot step, turn left (north), and follow the pipeline trail along the base of an overhanging Supai cliff 100 yards north to Saddle Horse Spring.

Reminiscent of Dripping Springs off the Boucher Trail, Saddle Horse Spring is far more spectacular because it's perched on the brink of a cliff that drops in a series of steplike walls a thousand feet into Saddle Horse Canyon. At the time of this writing, this hanging oasis of clear, knee-deep water supported wild grapes, cane, and thick tufts of grass.

Return the way you came; or, if you want to continue your exploration of the Tuckup Trail from Saddle Horse Spring, follow the pipeline trail back atop the Esplanade, then strike out west cross-country over the caprock for a half-mile until you reach the Tuckup Trail.

Tuckup Trail

From Toroweap Point east to Buckhorn Spring, the Tuckup Trail contours the Esplanade formation for some 60 miles. Author and canyoneer Michael Kelsey called it "an old live-stock trail," while author and historian Byrd Howell Granger wrote, "It is possible that this canyon is what Lt. Edward Fitzgerald Beale called Tucker's Pass, naming it for the black-smith on his 1857–58 expedition." The trail no doubt origi-nated as an inner-Canyon footpath for the Paiute or even the ancestral Puebloans; stockmen and miners no doubt used these ancient trail systems, which are adorned with remarkable pic-tographs, to link the precious springs and water holes along the hanging terrace of Esplanade.

To reach the Tuckup Trail, either follow the route out of Saddle Horse Spring, or pick up the trail heading out of the campground north of Toroweap Point.

Reminiscent of the Esplanade west of both the Thunder River and South Bass trails, the first several miles of the Tuckup Trail are actually an old road. Heavily wooded with pinyon and juniper and gnarly stands of yucca stabbing the sky, this path is as enjoyable and exciting a run as you're likely to embark upon in the Grand Canyon. The trail unwinds before you, making gentle flying twists and turns as it contours around the rust-red rim of the Esplanade below 5,855-foot Toroweap Point. Even on a musty July evening, the running was so effortless and tranquil that I was drawn farther and far-ther east until I suddenly realized I was becoming increasingly dehydrated and needed to turn around before the return jour-ney became a struggle. Given the time and provisions, this enchanting track can be followed as far east as you want to fly.

PRIMARY ACCESS:	Via Toroweap Point Road.
ELEVATION GAIN & LOSS:	Saddle Horse Spring, 200 vertical feet each way. Tuckup Trail to west fork of Cove Canyon, 400 vertical feet each way.
MILEAGE:	Saddle Horse Spring: 1 mile each way. Tuckup Trail to west fork of Cove Canyon: approximately 4 ½ miles each way.
WATER SOURCES:	Saddle Horse Spring.
ESCAPE ROUTE:	Back the way you came.
MAPS:	Vulcans Throne Quadrangle (7.5 minute), Reconnaissance Map, ARIZONA MT. TRUMBULL SHEET (March 1892), and Topographic Map of the GRAND CANYON NATIONAL MONUMENT, ARIZONA (scale 1,48000, 1944 edition). The latter shows old water pockets and a mine trail that may lead you to the Son-of-a-Bitch Hotel.
MANAGING AGENCY:	Grand Canyon National Park. Contact Grand Canyon National Park at www.nps.gov/grca for current access information, permits, and fees.
BACKCOUNTRY INFORMATION:	Permit required for overnight camping; fire only permitted in campground grills.
BIOTIC COMMUNITY:	Great Basin desert scrub.

Climbers of Temples and Buttes in the Grand Canyon Region

compiled by John Annerino, edited by George Bain

Name	Map	Formation	Elevation	First Known Ascent
Akaba, Mount	HF	Coconino & Toroweap	5,248'	George Bain, solo, 11-4-80
Alarcon Terrace*	PP	Supai	4,922'	Donald G. Davis, 6-7-73
Alsap Butte	PI & WP	Supai	7,494'	Davis, 6-14-72
Angels Gate	CR	Coconino	6,761'	Dave Ganci & Chuck Graff, 3-30-72
Apache Point*	EX	Kaibab	6,296'	*Party & date unknown*
Apollo Temple+	CR	Supai	6,252'	J. Harvey Butchart, 7-17-65
Awatubi Crest	CS	Supai	5,403'	Bruce Grubbs & Jim Haggart, 1-8-78
Ayer Point	CR	Redwall & Temple Butte	4,961'	Davis, 6-26-72
Banta Point	WP	Redwall & Muav	6,530'	Jim Ohlman, 6-11-78

(continues on next page)

CLIMBERS (continued)

Name	Map	Formation	Elevation	First Known Ascent
Barbenceta Butte	PI	Supai	4,697'	Butchart, 8-27-63
Battleship, The+	GC	Hermit	5,850'	*Party & date unknown*
Berry Butte	CR	Supai	5,682'	Ohlman, Bob Packard & Al Doty, 11-15-98
Bourke Point	PI	Redwall	6,545'	Richard Dutt & Ohlman, 3-22-77
Brady Peak	WP	Coconino	8,121'	Larry Trieber, Chris Beal & Haggart, 6-75
Brahma Temple	BAP	Coconino & Toroweap	7,551'	Clarence "Doc" Ellis & Davis, 5-15-68
Bridgers Knoll	TA	Coconino & Toroweap	6,602'	Chuck Johnson & Butchart, 6-3-65
Buddha Temple	BAP	Coconino & Toroweap	7,212'	Mark Brown, Chuck Parker, & Grubbs, 1973
Burro, Mount	S	Toroweap & Kaibab	5,127'	Butchart, 4-11-66
Carbon Butte	CS	Butte Fault	4,459'	Dirk Springorum & Butchart, 6-12-63

Name	Code	Formation	Elevation	First Ascent
Cardenas Butte*	DV	Esplanade	6,281'	Butchart & NAU Hiking Club, 3-25-61
Castor Temple	HP	Coconino & Toroweap	6,221'	Doty & Davis, 4-19-71
Cheops Pyramid	PR	Redwall & Muav	5,401'	Merrell Clubb, 1960
Chiavria Point*	WP	Redwall & Muav	6,214'	Butchart, 6-8-73
Chuar Butte	CS	Hermit, Coconino, Toroweap & Kaibab	6,394'	Grubbs & Haggart, 1-9-71
Chuar Lava Hill	CS	Cardenas	3,945'	Butchart, 6-10-59
Claude Birdseye Point	ST	Coconino & Toroweap	6,982'	Doty , 6-14-78
Clement Powell Butte	BAP	Hermit	6,444'	Jim Kirshvink & Ohlman, 4-23-78
Cochise Butte	WP	Redwall	6,530'	Butchart, 6-7-73
Cogswell Butte+	TA	Supai	4,545'	Butchart, 8-18-67
Colonnade, The	BAP	Coconino & Toroweap	7,602'	Doty, 9-5-70
Colter Butte	WP	Supai	7,254'	Ohlman, 3-23-77
Comanche Point	DV	Toroweap Pinnacle	6,800'	Trieber & Grubbs, 4-75
Confucius Temple	ST	Coconino & Toroweap	7,081'	Butchart, 9-3-73

(continues on next page)

CLIMBERS (continued)

Name	Map	Formation	Elevation	First Known Ascent
Cope Butte+	GC	Redwall	4,528'	Johnson, *date unknown*
Cork, The	SBP	Basalt	4,335'	J.D. Green, 4-21-83
Coronado Butte+	CR	Toroweap & Kaibab	7,162'	"Captain" John Hance & tourist, prior to 1900
Dana Butte+	GC	Redwall	5,031'	Dave Bucello, Ken Walters, Paula Martini, Kirshvink & Ohlman, 5-7-78
Deva Temple	BA	Coconino & Toroweap	7,353'	Butchart, 7-18-59
Diamond Peak	DP	Redwall	3,512'	Charles F. Lummis & his dog, 1884
Diana Temple	P	Toroweap & Kaibab	6,683'	Butchart, 7-30-60
Dome, The	FGC	Coconino, Toroweap & Kaibab	5,489'	Glen Rink & Bain, 12-21-80
Dox Castle	P	Temple Butte	4,780'	B. J. Boyle, Dan Hartley, Terry Hutchins, Brian Rasmussen, Drew Smith, Dave Vanderburgh, Kirshvink & Ohlman, 10-25-80

Dragon, Little	ST	Kaibab	8,121'	Doty, 8-27-77
Dragon, The+	ST	Kaibab	8,049'	Butchart & Springorum, 9-1-64
Dragon Head+	ST	Toroweap & Kaibab	7,765'	Butchart & Springorum, 9-1-64
Dunn Butte	CR	Supai	5,721'	Hartley, Kirshvink, Ohlman & Smith, 11-28-80
Duppa Butte	WP	Redwall	6,692'	Packard & Butchart, 5-31-73
Ehrenberg Point	PI	Redwall	6,800'	Kirshvink, Ohlman & Walters, 5-23-78
Elaine Castle*	KAC	Coconino & Toroweap	7,431'	Davis, 6-27-69
Escalante Butte*	DV	Hermit & Coconino	6,536'	Butchart & Sholing, *date unknown*
Espejo Butte	DV	Coconino & Toroweap	6,200'	Butchart & Ohlman, 9-6-75
Evans Butte	HP	Hermit	6,379'	Butchart, 10-76
Excalibur	KAC	Hermit & Coconino	7,052'	Bain & Rink, 5-28-81
Explorers Monument	EX	Supai	4,572'	Hartley, Kirshvink & Ohlman, 3-18-80
Fan Island	KAC	Redwall	5,092'	Hartley, Kirshvink & Ohlman, 3-21-80

(continues on next page)

CLIMBERS (continued)

Name	Map	Formation	Elevation	First Known Ascent
Fishtail Mesa*	FM	Coconino & Toroweap	6,126'	U.S. Forest Service, *date unknown*
Fiske Butte	EX	Supai	4,748'	Doty, 10-74
Flatiron Butte	SBP	Toroweap	5,325'	Ohlman parry, 4-18-81
Fossil Mountain	HP	Kaibab	6,729'	Clubb & Doty, *date unknown*
Freya Castle	CR	Coconino & Toroweap	7,288'	Allyn Cureton & Butchart, 6-24-62
Galeros Butte	CS	Temple Butte	6,499'	Haggart, 1-78
Geikie Peak	HP	Redwall	5,005'	Bucello, Ohlman & Walters, 12-17-77
Guinevere Castle*	KAC	Coconino & Toroweap	7,281'	Butchart, 8-25-65
Gunther Castle	CS	Supai	7,199'	Butchart, Davis, Doty, & Ellis, 6-4-69
Hall Butte	CR	Supai	5,525'	Ellis parry, 12-27-72
Hancock Butte	PI	Esplanade	7,683'	Doty, 10-2-76
Hattan Butte	BAP	Supai	5,973'	Hartley & Ohlman, 12-19-80

Name	Code	Formation	Elevation	Named by
Hawkins Butte	PR & CR	Supai	5,200'	Kirshvink & Ohlman, 11-25-77
Hayden, Mount	PI	Coconino	8,362'	Rick Petrillo & Bob Sigler, 10-69
Hillers Butte	BAP	Supai	5,895'	Kirshvink & Ohlman, 4-23-78
Holy Grail Temple	KAC	Coconino	6,711'	Grubbs & Trieber, 10-23-76
Horse Shoe Mesa Butte*	CR	Supai	5,246'	Billingsly, Butchart & Mitchell, 12-4-66
Horus Temple	ST	Esplanade & Hermit	6,150'	Scott Kronberg, Grubbs & Haggart, 1-3-77
Howlands Butte, The	PR	Supai	5,572'	Ellis, 1-6-72
Hubbell Butte	WP	Esplanade	6,740'	Butchart & Springorum, 4-25-63
Huethawali, Mount*	EX	Coconino & Toroweap	6,281'	William Wallace Bass & tourist, before 1900
Hutton Butte	WP	Redwall	6,704'	Kirshvink, Ohlman & Smith, 3-19-81
Isis Temple	ST	Coconino	7,006'	Doty, 9-26-70
Juno Temple*	WP	Hermit	6,896'	Butchart, 9-3-61

(continues on next page)

CLIMBERS (continued)

Name	Map	Formation	Elevation	First Known Ascent
Jupiter Temple*	WP	Hermit & Coconino	7,084'	Butchart & Springorum, 4-26-63
Kibbey Butte*	WP	Hermit	7,801'	Butchart & Cureton, 5-31-61
King Arthur Castle*	KAC	Coconino & Toroweap	7,344'	Clubb, 8-17-61
King Crest*	PP	Coconino & Toroweap	6,820'	Doty, 10-1-77
Krishna Shrine	CR	Esplanade	6,131'	Butchart, 9-5-62
Kwagunt Butte	CS	Coconino, Toroweap & Kaibab	6,377'	Dennis Abbink, Grubbs, Haggart & Trieber, 3-24-79
Lava Butte	CS	Tapeats	4,242'	Butchart & Springorum, 6-12-63
Little Pup Pinnacle	DV	Toroweap	7,200+'	Mark Brown, Kronberg & Trieber, 3-74
Lone Mountain	WP	Hermit	4,241'	Jim Sears, 3-75
Lyell Butte	PR	Supai	5,362'	Doty, 1-24-70
Malgosa Crest	CS	Coconino	5,584'	Grubbs & Trieber, 3-17-77
Manu Temple	BAP	Coconino	7,184'	Ellis, 1-10-72
Marcos Terrace*	EX	Supai	5,140'	Davis, 5-23-74

Marion Point+	PI	Redwall	6,400'	*Party & date unknown*
Marsh Butte	GC	Redwall	4,721'	Mitch McCombs & Pete Baertlein, 10-29-77
Masonic Temple*	KAC	Hermit	6,242'	Doty, 9-25-80
Mencius Temple	ST	Coconino & Toroweap	7,001'	Stevens & Walquist, 9-3-73
Mollies Nipple	WP & SE Toroweap		5,551'	Green, 4-17-84
Monument Creek Pinnacle	GC	Trinity Gneiss	3,200'+	Walt Gregs, Spider Herbert & Bill Trevitchick, 11-6-72
Nankoweap Butte*	PI	Sixtymile	5,430'	Butchart, 8-28-63
Nankoweap Mesa*	NM	Coconino, Toroweap & Kaibab	6,316'	Butchart, 8-28-63
Newberry Butte	CR	Temple Butte & Redwall	5,105'	Butchart, 11-10-63
Newton Butte	PR	Esplanade & Hermit	5,742'	Doty, 8-71
Novinger Butte	PI	Supai	6,922'	Butchart & Davis, 6-15-72
Ochoa Point+	DV	Tapeats	4,761'	Ohlman party, 1-12-79
O'Neill Butte	PR	Hermit	6,071'	British Columbia climbers, 1962
Osiris Temple	ST	Hermit & Coconino	6,613'	Davis, 3-13-66
Oza Butte+	BAP	Kaibab	8,068'	*Party & date unknown*

(continues on next page)

CLIMBERS (continued)

Name	Map	Formation	Elevation	First Known Ascent
Paguewash Point*	KP	Kaibab	5,663'	Doty, 8-3-81
Pattie Butte	PR	Supai	5,315'	Jim David & Butchart, 9-19-61
Pollux Temple*	P	Coconino & Toroweap	6,251'	Doty, 3-69
Poston Butte+	WP	Esplanade	6,469'	Butchart & Springorum, 4-25-63
Powell Plateau*	KAC & PP	Kaibab	7,661'	Ancestral Puebloan
Racetrack Knoll	FM	Supai	4,884'	Butchart, 6-3-78
Rama Shrine	CR	Hermit	6,406'	Butchart, 9-22-62
Red Point*	TIN	Hermit	5,162'	Butchart, Kirschvink & Ohman 1-2-79
Saddle Mountain*	PI	Toroweap	8,424'	John W. Powell & Charles Doolittle Wallcott, winter 1882
Sagittarius Ridge	HP	Hermit	6,297'	Doty, 8-1-81
Schellbach Butte	BAP	Supai	6,034'	Kirschvink & Ohman, 2-25-78
Scorpion Ridge	HP	Supai	5,832'	Doty, 8-21-81
Scylla Butte	HP	Muav	3,844'	Kirshvink & Ohman, 3-18-78

Sheba Temple	CR	Temple Butte & Redwall	4,990'	Butchart, 6-3-70
Shiva Temple*	ST	Hermit, Coconino, Toroweap & Kaibab	7,646'	Emery Kolb & Gordon Berger, 9-37
Siddartha	TP	Coconino & Toroweap	4,989'	John Annerino, Bain, & Rink, 10-17-82
Siegfried Pyre	WP	Coconino & Toroweap	7,922'	Babb & Davis, 6-7-70
Sinking Ship*	GP	Toroweap & Kaibab	7,344'	Reider Peterson & Butchart, 9-25-65
Sinyella, Mount	HF	Coconino & Toroweap	5,441'	UCLA climbers, 1958
Solomon Temple	CR	Temple Butte & Redwall	5,121'	Butchart, 6-3-70
Spoonhead, Mount*	TH	Kaibab	5,682'	Gary Weesner, Kirshvink & Ohlman, 2-7-81
Steamboat Mountain	PP	Coconino, Toroweap & Kaibab	7,410'	Marshall Demick & Butchart, 10-17-64
Sullivan Peak	PI	Coconino	8,321'	Lee Dexter & Steve Studebaker, 10-11-75
Summer Butte+	PR	Redwall	5,126'	Johnson, *date unknown*
Swilling Butte	WP	Supai	6,785'	Scott Baxter, Butchart, Packard & Walquist, 10-13-73
Tabernacle, The	CR	Muav	4,802'	Butchart, 9-2-61

(continues on next page)

CLIMBERS (continued)

Name	Map	Formation	Elevation	First Known Ascent
Temple Butte	CS	Esplanade & Supai	5,308'	Grubbs & Haggart, 1-7-78
Thor Temple	WP	Esplanade & Hermit	6,741'	Doty, 5-14-77
Thumb	PS/NE	Redwall	5,305'	Green, 4-1-81
Tower of Babylon	RR	Kaibab	6,469'	Gibson party, 10-17-20
Tower of Ra	ST	Esplanade & Hermit	6,129'	Art Christiansen, Barbara Zinn & Haggart, 6-5-77
Tower of Set	GC	Esplanade & Hermit	6,012'	Grubbs & Haggart, 11-26-77
Tritle Peak	WP	Toroweap & Kaibab	8,388'	Doty, 10-24-70
Tyndall Dome	HP	Redwall & Muav	4,879'	Doty, 5-14-72
Venus Temple	CR	Supai	6,281'	Butchart, 7-17-65
Vesta Temple	P	Coconino & Toroweap	6,299'	Doty, 3-21-70
Vishnu Temple	CR	Coconino & Toroweap	7,533'	Merrell D. Clubb & son Roger, 7-13-45
Vulcans Throne+	VT	Basalt	5,102'	Clarence Dutton, 1871
Wallace Butte	HP	Supai	5,209'	Doty, 5-14-72
Wheeler Point	PP	Kaibab	6,721'	Doty, 7-4-81

Summit	Location	Elevation	First Ascent
Whites Butte+	GC	4,860'	Butchart & Cureton, 1-1-61
Widforss Point	BAP	7,822'	Doty, 5-31-78
Wodo, Mount	S	5,132'	Mark Price, John Ritchey & Butchart, 2-13-71
Wolf Pinnacle	DV	7,200'	Grubbs & Trieber, *date unknown*
Woolsey Butte	PI	7,302'	Butchart, 7-27-62
Wotans Throne*	CR	7,721'	George B. Andrews, Elliott Humphrey, Preston Swapp, Walter Wood & wife, 9-37
Zoroaster Temple	PR	7,123'	Ganci & Rick Tidrick, 9-23-58
Zoroaster Temple, Southwest Face	PR		Annerino, Bain & Ganci, 5-6-78

* Archaeological evidence indicates these summits were first climbed by Native Americans.

+Summit cairns indicate these summits were first climbed by prospectors, early tourists, and others.

On August 8, 1967, Harvey Butchart wrote there were "old cairns already on Poston, Escalante, Sumner, Cope, Cogswell, and perhaps King Arthur," when he made the first recorded ascents of those summits.

Sources: John Annerino, author's collection and "Climbs in the Grand Canyon: A Historical Introduction Combined with a Personal Account of the Climbing Possibilities in the Grand Canyon of the Colorado River, Arizona," *Mountain 77* (January/February 1981): 25–35; George Bain, personal communication, 2004.

(continues on next page)

ABBREVIATIONS for USGS 7.5 Minute Quadrangles, scale 1:24,000

Abbreviation	Name	Edition
BAP	Bright Angel Point	1988
CR	Cape Royal	1988
CS	Cape Solitude	1999
DV	Desert View	1988
DP	Diamond Peak	1967
EX	Explorers Monument	1988, Provisional Edition
FGC	Fern Glen Canyon	1988, Provisional Edition
FM	Fishtail Mesa	1988, Provisional Edition
GC	Grand Canyon	1988
GP	Grandview Point	1989, Provisional Edition
HF	Havasu Falls	1988, Provisional Edition
HP	Havasupai Point	1988, Provisional Edition
KP	Kanab Point	1988, Provisional Edition
KAC	King Arthur Castle	1988, Provisional Edition
NM	Nankoweap Mesa	1988, Provisional Edition

PS/NE	Peach Springs NE	1967
PR	Phantom Ranch	1988
P	Paiute Point	1988, Provisional Edition
PI	Point Imperial	1988, Provisional Edition
PP	Powell Plateau	1988, Provisional Edition
RR	Robbers Roost	1980
SBP	S. B. Point	1988, Provisional Edition
ST	Shiva Temple	1988
S	Supai	1988, Provisional Edition
TA	Tapeats Amphitheater	1988, Provisional Edition
TP	Tatahatso Point	1988, Provisional Edition
TIN	Tincanebitts Point	1971
TH	Topocoba Hilltop	1988, Provisional Edition
VT	Vulcans Throne	1967
WP	Walhalla Plateau	1988
WTP	Whitmore Point	1967
WTP/SE	Whitmore Point SE	1967

About the Contributors

Janet R. Balsom is Chief of Cultural Resources at Grand Canyon National Park. Janet received her bachelor's in anthropology from the State University of New York at Buffalo in 1980 and received her master's in anthropology from Arizona State University in 1984, where she wrote a thesis on Grand Canyon archaeology. Janet has worked as an archaeological consultant for Arizona State University and the State of New York Archaeological Survey, and she has interned at the Arizona State Historic Preservation Office. She currently serves as a committee member on the Arizona State Historic Sites Review Committee.

George Bain, editor of "Climbers of Temples and Buttes in the Grand Canyon Region," is a mechanical engineer, veteran Colorado River boatman, and passionate climber who has spent the last 30 years climbing 96 named temples, peaks, and buttes in the Grand Canyon. Among many firsts, George's one-day solo ascent of 7,533-foot Vishnu Temple from the banks of the Colorado River on October 26, 1980, remains unrepeated. He is currently ticking off a handful of remaining Grand Canyon summits.

George H. H. Huey is an acclaimed photographer whose images celebrate the landscape and natural history of the West. His stunning photography books include *The Southwest,* with Paul Robert Walker (National Geographic Books, 2002), *Grand Views of Canyon Country,* with David B. Williams (Canyonlands Natural History Association, 2000), *Wild Cactus,* with Rose Houk (Artisan, 1999), and many fine publications for the Western National Parks Association. George is currently sailing the seven seas.

Larry E. Stevens is the author of *The Colorado River in Grand Canyon: A Comprehensive Guide to its Natural and Human History.* An environmental consultant based in Flagstaff, Arizona, he has worked as a commercial white water guide on the Colorado River in the Grand Canyon for many years and has worked for the National Park Service and the Museum of Northern Arizona. He received a bachelor's degree from Prescott College and a master's degree from Northern Arizona University.

Michael Young was adopted by the Colorado Plateau decades ago. He has rowed the plateau rivers for years watching the multiple expressions of the rock face and measuring with the yardstick of geologic time. He is currently leading environmental education seminars for the Elderhostel at Yavapai College in Prescott, Arizona.

Selected Bibliography

Grand Canyon Natural History Association titles cited in this bibliography may still be available through the Grand Canyon Association. Visit www.grandcanyon.org for availability, price, and ordering information.

Abbey, Edward. *Hidden Canyon: A River Journey* (photographs by John Blaustein, introduction by Martin Litton). New York: Penguin Books, 1977.

Ahrens, Bill. "Trailblazers, 55-day Canyon Trek Takes Pair through Eons of Time." *Arizona Republic,* November 16, 1980, B-1, B-6.

Andrews, George B. "Scaling Wotan's Throne." *Natural History* 40, no. 5 (December 1937): 723–24, 776.

Annerino, John. *The Photographer's Guide to the Grand Canyon* (photographs by the author). Woodstock and New York: Countryman Press and W. W. Norton, 2005. www.countryman press.com.

———. "The Grand Canyon Explored." *National Geographic Adventure* 6, no. 2 (March 2004): 66–68.

———. *Grand Canyon Wild: A Photographic Journey* (photographs by the author). Woodstock and New York: Countryman Press and W. W. Norton, 2004. www.countrymanpress.com.

———. *Adventuring in Arizona*. Tucson: University of Arizona Press, 2003. First published 1991 by Sierra Club Books. www.uapress .arizona.edu.

———. *Desert Survivor: An Adventurer's Guide to Exploring the Great American Desert*. New York & London: Four Walls Eight Windows, 2001. www.4w8w.com.

———. *Canyons of the Southwest: A Tour of the Great Canyon Country from Colorado to Northern Mexico* (photographs by the author). Tucson: University of Arizona Press, 2000. First published 1993 by Sierra Club Books. www.uapress.arizona.edu.

———. *Running Wild: An Extraordinary Adventure of the Human Spirit* (photographs by Christine Keith, forward by Charles Bowden). New York: Thunder's Mouth Press, 1998.

———. *People of Legend: Native Americans of the Southwest* (photographs by the author). San Francisco: Sierra Club Books, 1996.

———. *Hiking the Grand Canyon: A Sierra Club Trail Map*. San Francisco: Sierra Club Books, 1993.

———. "Whitewater Women" (photographs by the author). *Phoenix Magazine* 27, no. 8 (August 1992): 82–89.

———. *High Risk Photography: The Adventure behind the Image* (photographs by the author). Helena, MT: American and World Geographic Publishing, 1991.

———. "Angels Gate, Traverse of the Gods" (photographs by the author). *Arizona Highways Magazine* 61, no. 6 (June 1985): 32–37.

———. "Climbs in the Grand Canyon: A Historical Introduction Combined with a Personal Account of the Climbing Possibilities in the Grand Canyon of the Colorado River, Arizona. Appended is a table of summits within the Canyon confines." *Mountain* 77 (January/February 1981): 15, 25–35. Sheffield, UK.

Anthony, Harold E. "The Facts about Shiva Temple—The Real Story of One of the Most Popular Scientific Adventures in Recent Years." *Natural History* 40, no. 5 (December 1937): 709–21, 725–76.

Baars, Donald L. *The Colorado Plateau: A Geologic History*. Albuquerque: University of New Mexico Press, 1983.

Babbitt, Bruce. *Grand Canyon: An Anthology*. Flagstaff, AZ: Northland Press, 1978.

Bain, George. Personal communication, 2004.

———. "A One Day Solo Ascent of Vishnu Temple from the Colorado River." Flagstaff, AZ, unpublished manuscript, January 1985.

Barlett, Katharine. "How Don Pedro Tovar Discovered the Hopi and Garcia Lopez de Cardenas Saw the Grand Canyon, with Notes upon Their Probable Route." *Plateau* 12, no. 3 (January 1940): 37–45.

Bass, William Wallace. *Adventures in the Canyons of the Colorado: By two of its earliest explorers, James White and W. W. Hawkins*. Grand Canyon, AZ: William Wallace Bass, 1920.

Beer, Bill. *We Swam the Grand Canyon: The True Story of a Cheap Vacation That Got a Little Out of Hand*. Seattle: The Mountaineers, 1988.

Belknap, Buzz, and Loie Belknap-Evans. *Grand Canyon River Guide*. Evergreen, CO: Westwater Books, 2001.

Selected Bibliography · 307

Bolton, Herbert E. *Pageant in the Wilderness: The Story of the Escalante Expedition to the Interior Basin, 1776. Including the Diary and Itinerary of Father Escalante Translated and Annotated.* Salt Lake City: Utah Historical Society, 1950.

Breed, William J., and Evelyn Roat, eds. *The Geology of the Grand Canyon.* Flagstaff: Museum of Northern Arizona and Grand Canyon Natural History Association, 1976.

Brew, J. O. "Hopi Prehistory and History to 1850." In *Handbook of North American Indians, Southwest,* edited by Alfonso Ortiz, 9: 514–23. Washington, DC: Smithsonian Institution, 1979.

Brian, Nancy. *River to Rim: A Guide to Place Names along the Colorado River in Grand Canyon from Lake Powell to Lake Mead.* Flagstaff, AZ: Earthquest Press, 1992.

Brooks, Juanita, and Robert Glass Cleland, eds. *A Mormon Chronicle: The Diaries of John D. Lee, 1948–1976,* vol. 2. Salt Lake City: University of Utah Press, 1983.

Brown, B. T., K. A. Butterfield, R. R. Johnson, and M. S. Moran. "An Inventory and Classification of Surface Water Resources in Grand Canyon National Park, AZ." Division of Resource Management, Grand Canyon National Park and the Cooperative National Park Resource Studies Unit, University of Arizona, n.d.

Brugge, David M. "Navajo Prehistory and History to 1850." In *Handbook of North American Indians, Southwest,* edited by Alfonso Ortiz, 10: 489–501. Washington, DC: Smithsonian Institution, 1983.

Bryant, Harold Child. "First Climbers Scale Vishnu Temple, Grand Canyon Peak." *Arizona Republic,* August 9, 1945, B-1.

Butchart, J. Harvey. *Grand Canyon Treks III: Inner Canyon Journals.* Glendale, CA: La Siesta Press, 1984.

———. *Grand Canyon Treks: A Guide to Inner Canyon Routes.* Glendale, CA: La Siesta Press, 1976.

———. "Summits Below the Rim: Mountain Climbing in the Grand Canyon." *Journal of Arizona History* 17, no. 1 (Spring 1976): 21–38.

———. *Grand Canyon Treks II: A Guide to the Extended Canyon Routes.* Glendale, CA: La Siesta Press, 1975.

———. "The Lower Gorge of the Little Colorado River." *Arizona Highways Magazine* 41 (September 1965): 34–42.

Calloway, Donald G., Joel C. Janetski, and Omar C. Stewart. "Ute." In *Handbook of North American Indians, Great Basin,* edited by Warren L. d'Azevedo, 11: 336–67. Washington, DC: Smithsonian Institution, 1986.

Carmony, Neil B., ed. "The Grand Canyon Deer Drive of 1924: The Accounts of Will C. Barnes and Mark E Musgrave." *Journal of Arizona History* 43, no. 1 (Spring 2002): 41–64.

Carmony, Neil B., and David E. Brown, eds. *The Wilderness of the Southwest: Charles Sheldon's Quest for Desert Bighorn Sheep with the Havasupai and Seri Indians.* Salt Lake City: University of Utah Press, 1993.

Casanova, Frank E. "Trails to Supai in Cataract Canyon." *Plateau* 39, no. 3 (Winter 1967): 124–30.

"Chronology of Grand Canyon Trails." Grand Canyon National Park, unpublished manuscript, n.d.

Collins, Robert O., and Roderick Nash. *The Big Drops: Ten Legendary Rapids.* San Francisco: Sierra Club Books, 1978.

Colton, Harold S. "Principal Hopi Trails." *Plateau* 36, no. 3 (Winter 1964): 91–94.

———. *Black Sand: Prehistory in Northern Arizona.* Albuquerque: University of New Mexico Press, 1960.

———. "Prehistoric Trade in the Southwest." *Scientific Monthly,* April 1941, 308–19.

Cordell, Linda S. "Prehistory: Eastern Anasazi." In *Handbook of North American Indians, Southwest,* edited by Alfonso Ortiz, 9: 131–51. Washington, DC: Smithsonian Institution, 1979.

Coues, Elliot, ed. *On the Trail of a Spanish Pioneer: The Diary and Itinerary of Francisco Garces (Missionary Priest) in His Travels Through Sonora, Arizona, and California, 1775–1776; Translated from an Official Contemporaneous Copy of the Original Manuscript, and Edited, with Copious Critical Notes by Elliot Coues.* 2 vols. New York: Francis P. Harper, 1900.

Crampton, C. Gregory. *Land of Living Rock: The Grand Canyon and the High Plateaus: Arizona, Utah, Nevada.* New York: Alfred A. Knopf, 1972.

———. *Standing Up Country: The Canyon Lands of Utah and Arizona.* New York and Salt Lake City: Alfred A. Knopf and the University of Utah Press in Association with the Amon Carter Museum of Western Art, 1964.

"Cross River Hiking." Grand Canyon National Park, unpublished manuscript, n.d.

Crumbo, Kim. *A River Runner's Guide to the History of the Grand Canyon.* Boulder, CO: Johnson Books, 1994.

Cushing, F. H. "The Nation of Willows." *Atlantic Monthly,* September–October 1882, 362–74, 541–49.

Davis, Dan. "A Traverse of the Colorado River from Lees Ferry to Lake Mead." Grand Canyon National Park, unpublished manuscript, November 19, 1957.

———. "River to Rim Routes." Grand Canyon National Park, unpublished manuscript, n.d.

———. "Voyages down the Colorado River." Grand Canyon National Park, unpublished manuscript, n.d.

Davis, Donald G. "Brahma Temple, First Ascent." Grand Canyon National Park, unpublished manuscript, May 15, 1957.

Dawson, Thomas F. *The Grand Canyon, An Article: Giving the Credit of First Traversing the Grand Canyon of the Colorado to James White, A Colorado Gold Prospector, Who It Is Claimed Made the Voyage Two Years Previous to the Expedition Under the Direction of Maj. J. W. Powell in 1869.* 65th Congress, 1st Session, Senate Resolution No. 79, June 4, 1917, Document No. 42. Washington, DC: U.S. Government Printing Office, 1917.

Dellenbaugh, Frederick S. *A Canyon Voyage: The Narrative of the Second Powell Expedition down the Green-Colorado River from Wyoming, and the Explorations on Land, in the Years 1871 and 1872.* New Haven, CT: Yale University Press, 1926.

———. *The Romance of the Colorado: The Story of Its Discovery in 1540, with an Account of the Later Explorations, and with Special Reference to the Voyages of Powell through the Line of Great Canyons.* New York: G. P. Putnam's Sons, 1906.

Dimock, Brad. *Sunk Without a Sound: The Tragic Colorado River Honeymoon of Glen and Bessie Hyde.* Flagstaff, AZ: Fretwater Press, 2001.

Dutton, Clarence Edward. *Tertiary History of the Grand Canyon District, with Atlas.* Department of Interior Monographs of the United States Geological Survey, vol. 2. Washington, DC: U.S. Government Printing Office, 1882.

Eiseman, Fred. B. "The Hopi Salt Trail." *Plateau* 32, no. 2 (October 1959): 25–32.

Euler, Robert C. "The People." In *The Mountain Lying Down: Views of the North Rim*, by Timothy J. Priehs. Grand Canyon, AZ: Grand Canyon Natural History Association, 1979.

———. "The Canyon Dwellers." *American West* 4, no. 2 (May 1967): 22–27, 67–71.

Euler, Robert C., M. E. Cooley, and B. N. Aldridge. "Effects of the Catastrophic Flood of December 1966, North Rim Area, Eastern Grand Canyon, Arizona." *Geological Survey Professional Paper*. Washington, DC: U.S. Government Printing Office, 1977.

Euler, Robert C., Richard W. Effland, Jr., and A. Trinkle Jones. *The Archaeology of the Powell Plateau: Regional Interaction at Grand Canyon*. Grand Canyon, AZ: Grand Canyon Natural History Association, Monograph no. 3, 1981.

Euler, Robert C., and A. Trinkle Jones. *A Sketch of Grand Canyon Prehistory*. Grand Canyon, AZ: Grand Canyon Natural History Association, 1979.

"Explorations in Grand Canyon, Mysteries of Immense Rich Cavern Being Brought to Light, Remarkable Finds Indicate Ancient People Migrated from Orient. Jordon Enthused." *Arizona Gazette*, April 5, 1909, 1, 7.

Farabee, Charles R. *National Park Ranger: An American Icon*. Lanham, MD: Roberts, Rinehart Publishers, 2003.

———. *Death, Daring, and Disaster: Search and Rescue in the National Parks*. Boulder, CO: Roberts, Rinehart Publishers, 1998.

Farmer, Malcolm F., and Raymond DeSaussure. "Split-Twig Animal Figurines." *Plateau* 27, no. 4 (April 1955): 13–23.

Fewkes, J. Walter. "The Snake Ceremonials at Walpi." *A Journal of American Ethnology and Archaeology*, vol. 4. Boston: Houghton, Mifflin and Co., 1894.

Flavel, George F., Neil B. Carmony, and David E. Brown, eds. *The Log of the Panthon: An Account of an 1896 River Voyage from Green River, Wyoming to Yuma, Arizona through The Grand Canyon*. Boulder, CO: Pruett Publishing, 1987.

Fletcher, Colin. "The Man Who Walked Through Time." *Arizona Highways Magazine* 61, no. 6 (June 1985): 12–21.

———. *The Man Who Walked Through Time*. New York: Alfred A. Knopf, 1967.

Ford, T. D., P. W. Huntoon, G. H. Billingsley, and W. J. Breed. "Rock Movement and Mass Wastage in the Grand Canyon." In *Geology of the Grand Canyon*, edited by W. J. Breed and E. C. Roat. Flagstaff, AZ: Museum of Northern Arizona and Grand Canyon Natural History Association, 1974.

Fowler, Don D., Robert C. Euler, and Catherine S. Fowler. *John Wesley Powell and the Anthropology of the Canyon Country.* U.S. Geological Survey Professional Paper 670. Washington, DC: U.S. Government Printing Office, 1969.

Fradkin, Philip L. *A River No More.* New York: Knopf, 1981.

Freeman, Lewis R. "Surveying the Grand Canyon of the Colorado: An Account of the 1923 Boating Expedition of the United States Geological Survey." *National Geographic Magazine* 45, no. 5 (May 1924): 472–548.

Ganci, Dave. "The Conquest of Mt. Sinyala, Deep in Grand Canyon." *Arizona Magazine, The Arizona Republic,* July 20, 1969, cover, 30–33.

———. "Successful Summit Attempt" (photographs by Jerry Robertson). *Arizona Days and Ways Magazine,* June 26, 1960, cover, 36–39.

———. "Zoroaster Temple." *Summit Magazine,* January 1959, 16–17.

———. "Zoroaster Temple." Backcountry Rangers Office, Grand Canyon National Park, unpublished manuscript, September 18, 1958.

Garrison, Lemuel A. "John Hance: Guide, Trail Builder and Windjammer." *Arizona Highways Magazine* 25, no. 6 (June 1949): 4–11.

Georges, Helen S. *Desert Awareness: An Informative Guide for Anyone Traveling in the Southwest.* Phoenix: DARES, 1989.

Ghiglieri, Michael P., and Thomas M. Myers. *Over the Edge: Death in Grand Canyon.* Flagstaff, AZ: Puma Press, 2001.

Goldman, Rosalie. "The Wrinkled Pink Walls of Kanab Canyon" (photographs by Melvin Goldman). *Arizona Highways Magazine,* July 1964, 17–18, 31–34.

Grand Canyon, The Guide. South Rim: May 22–September 6, 2004. National Park Service, U.S. Department of Interior, Grand Canyon National Park, Arizona.

Granger, Byrd H. *Grand Canyon Place Names.* Tucson: University of Arizona Press, 1960.

Hall, Joseph G. "Spotted Skunk on Shiva Temple in Grand Canyon." *Plateau* 40, no. 3 (Winter 1968): 98–100.

Hart, John. *Walking Softly in the Wilderness.* San Francisco: Sierra Club Books, 2005.

Hamblin, W. Kenneth, and Joseph R. Murphy. *Grand Canyon Perspectives: A Guide to the Canyon Scenery by Means of Interpretive*

Panoramas. Provo, UT: Brigham Young University Geology Studies, Special Publications no. 1, 1969.

Hoffmeister, D. F. *Mammals of the Grand Canyon*. Urbana: University of Illinois Press, 1971.

Hughes, J. Donald. *In the House of Stone and Light*. Grand Canyon, AZ: Grand Canyon Natural History Association, 1978.

———. *The Story of Man at the Grand Canyon*. Grand Canyon, AZ: Grand Canyon Natural History Association, 1967.

Huntoon, P. W., G. H. Billingsley, and W. J. Breed. *Geologic Map of Grand Canyon National Park, 1:62,500 scale*. Grand Canyon, AZ: Grand Canyon Natural History Association and Museum of Northern Arizona, 1976.

Ives, Joseph Christmas. *Report upon the Colorado River of the West: Explored in 1857 and 1858*. Washington, DC: U.S. Government Printing Office, 1861.

James, George Wharton. *The Grand Canyon of Arizona: How to See It*. Boston: Little, Brown & Co., 1905.

———. *In and Around the Grand Canyon: The Grand Canyon of the Colorado River in Arizona*. Boston: Little, Brown & Co., 1901.

———. *The Indians of the Painted Desert Region: Hopis, Navahos, Wallapais, Havasupais*. Boston: Little, Brown & Co., 1900.

Kelly, Isabel T., and Catherine S. Fowler. "Southern Paiute." In *Handbook of North American Indians: Great Basin*, edited by Warren L. d'Azevedo, 11: 368–97. Washington, DC: Smithsonian Institution, 1986.

Khera, Sigrid, and Patricia S. Mariella. "Yavapai." In *Handbook of North American Indians, Southwest*, edited by Alfonso Ortiz, 10: 38–54. Washington, DC: Smithsonian Institution, 1983.

Kolb, Ellsworth. *Through the Grand Canyon from Wyoming to Mexico*. New York: MacMillan Co., 1914.

Kolb, Ellsworth, and Emery Kolb. "Experiences in the Grand Canyon" (photographs by the authors). *National Geographic Magazine* 26, no. 2 (August 1914): 99–184.

Kolb, Emery. "The Discovery of Cheyava Falls." *The Grand Canyon Guide*, May 7–20, 1978.

Lavender, David. *River Runners of the Grand Canyon*. Grand Canyon and Tucson, AZ: Grand Canyon Natural History Association and University of Arizona Press, 1985.

Leavengood, Betty. *Grand Canyon Women*. Grand Canyon, AZ: Grand Canyon Association, 2004.

Lindford, Laurence D. *Navajo Places: History, Legend, Landscape.* Salt Lake City: University of Utah Press, 2000.

Lockwood, Frank C. "Captain John Hance, He Built Trails and Spun Yarns at Grand Canyon." *Desert Magazine,* July 1940, 15–17.

Lummis, Charles Fletcher. *A Tramp Across the Continent.* New York: Charles Scribner's Sons, 1892.

Marley, Bob. "Ultimate Grand Canyon Backpack," June 4, 1999, www.kwagunt.net/gctrek.html.

Marshman, Kevin. "Zoroaster Temple, Opting for Ascension Where Going Down Is Chic." *Summit Magazine* 29, no. 5 (September–October 1983): 2–5, 34.

Matthes, Francois E. "The Grand Canyon of the Colorado River." *Bright Angel Quadrangle,* U.S. Geological Survey, 1967.

McGuire, Thomas R. "Walapai." In *Handbook of North American Indians, Southwest,* edited by Alfonso Ortiz, 10: 25–37. Washington, DC: Smithsonian Institution, 1983.

McKee, Edwin. "Kanab Canyon: The Trail of Scientists." *Plateau* 18, no. 3 (January 1946): 33–42.

———. "On Canyon Trails." *Grand Canyon Nature Notes* 8 (1933): 173–77, 191–94.

Merriam, C. Hart. "Results of a Biological Survey of the San Francisco Mountain Region and Desert of the Little Colorado, Arizona." *North American Fauna* 3 (September 11). U.S. Division of Agriculture, Division of Ornithology and Mammalogy. Washington, DC: U.S. Government Printing Office, 1890.

Muir, John. "The Grand Canyon of the Colorado." *Century Magazine* 55 (November 1902): 107–16.

Murberger, Nell. "Trail-Blazer of the Grand Canyon." *Desert Magazine* 21, no. 10 (October 1958): 5–9.

Myers, Tom. "The Last Hand Hold, Harvey Butchart 1907–2002." *Grand Canyon River Guides, Boatman's Quarterly Review* 15, no. 3 (2002): 8–9.

Nash, Roderick. *Grand Canyon of the Living Colorado.* San Francisco: Sierra Club Books, 1970.

Ohlman, Jim. "Good Grand Canyon Climbs." From the George Bain collection, with his comments, unpublished manuscript, 1988.

Peattie, Roderick, and Weldon F. Heald, eds. *The Inverted Mountains: Canyons of the West.* New York: Vanguard Press, 1948.

Plog, Fred. "Prehistory: Western Anasazi." In *Handbook of North American Indians, Southwest*, edited by Alfonso Ortiz, 9: 108–30. Washington, DC: Smithsonian Institution, 1979.

Powell, J. W. *Canyons of the Colorado*. New York: Flood & Vincent, 1895.

Powell, Walter Clement. "Journal of Walter Clement Powell." Edited by Charles Kelly. *Utah Historical Quarterly* 16–17 (1948–49): 257–478.

Rahm, David. *Reading the Rocks: A Guide to the Geologic Secrets of the Canyons, Mesas, and Buttes of the American Southwest*. San Francisco: Sierra Club, 1974.

Reiche, Parry. "The Toreva-Block: A Distinctive Landslide Type." *Journal of Geology*, no. 5 (January–December 1937): 538–48.

Reilly, P. T. "How Deadly Is Big Read." *Utah Historical Quarterly* 37, no. 2 (Spring 1969): 244–60.

Reisner, Marc. *Cadillac Desert: The American West and Its Disappearing Water*. New York: Penguin Books, 1986.

Roessel, Robert A., Jr. "Navajo History, 1850–1923." In *Handbook of North American Indians, Southwest*, edited by Alfonso Ortiz, 10: 506–23. Washington, DC: Smithsonian Institution, 1983.

Roosevelt, Theodore. *A Book-Lover's Holidays in the Open*. New York: Charles Scribner's Sons, 1916.

———. New York *Sun*, May 7, 1903.

Rusho, W. L., and C. G. Crampton. *Desert River Crossing: Historic Lee's Ferry on the Colorado River*. Salt Lake City, UT: Peregrine Smith, 1975.

Schwartz, Douglas W. "Havasupai." In *Handbook of North American Indians, Southwest*, edited by Alfonso Ortiz, 10: 13–24. Washington, DC: Smithsonian Institution, 1983.

———. "Split-Twig Figurines in the Grand Canyon." *American Antiquity* 23, no. 3 (January 1958): 264–74.

Smith, Robert L. *Venomous Animals of Arizona* (illustrations by Joel Floyd). Tucson: University of Arizona, College of Agriculture, 1982.

Stanton, Robert Brewster. *Colorado River Controversies*. Boulder City, NV: Westwater Books, 1982.

Steiger, Lew. "Kenton Grua." *Grand Canyon River Guides, Boatman's Quarterly Review* 11, no. 1 (Winter 1997–98): 37–47.

Stevens, Larry. *The Colorado River in Grand Canyon: A Comprehensive Guide to Its Natural and Human History.* Flagstaff, AZ: Red Lake Books, 1999.

Stewart, Kenneth M. "Mohave." In *Handbook of North American Indians, Southwest,* edited by Alfonso Ortiz, 10: 55–70. Washington, DC: Smithsonian Institution, 1983.

Stoffle, Richard W., et al. *Piapaxa 'Uipi (Big River Canyon).* Bureau of Applied Research in Anthropology. Tucson: University of Arizona, 1994.

Stone, Julius Frederick. *Canyon Country: The Romance of a Drop of Water and a Grain of Sand.* New York: G. P. Putnam's Sons, 1932.

Suran, William C. *The Kolb Brothers of Grand Canyon: Being a Collection of Tales of High Adventure, Memorable Incidents, & Humorous Anecdotes* (photographs by Emery Kolb and Ellsworth Kolb). Grand Canyon, AZ: Grand Canyon Natural History Association, 1991.

Talayesva, Don C. *Sun Chief: The Autobiography of a Hopi Indian,* edited by Leo W. Simmons. New Haven, CT: Yale University Press, 1948.

Teal, Louise. *Breaking into the Current: Boatwomen of the Grand Canyon.* Tucson: University of Arizona Press, 1994.

Thybony, Scott. *Official Guide to Hiking the Inner Canyon.* Grand Canyon, AZ: Grand Canyon Natural History Association, 1994.

Tillotson, M. R., and F. J. Taylor. *Grand Canyon Country.* Stanford, CA: Stanford University Press, 1929.

Titiev, Mischa. "A Hopi Salt Expedition." *American Anthropologist* 39, no. 2 (April–June 1937): 244–58.

Tower, Donald B. "The Use of Marine Mollusca and Their Value in Reconstructing Prehistoric Trade Routes in the American Southwest." *Papers of the Excavator's Club* 2, no. 3 (1945): 1–55.

Turner, R. M., and M. M. Karpiscak. *Recent Vegetation Changes along the Colorado River between Glen Canyon Dam and Lake Mead, Arizona.* U.S. Geological Survey Professional Paper 1132. Washington, DC: U.S. Government Printing Office, 1980.

"Water Sources in Grand Canyon N.P." Grand Canyon National Park, unpublished manuscript, n.d.

Wheeler, Lt. George Montague. *A Report upon United States Geographical Surveys West of the 100th Meridian.* Washington, DC: U.S. Government Printing Office, 1889.

Whitney, Stephen. *A Field Guide to the Grand Canyon* (illustrations by the author). New York: William Morrow and Quill, 1982.

Wilkerson, James A., M.D., ed. *Medicine for Mountaineering & Other Wilderness Activities,* 5th Edition. Seattle: Mountaineers Books, 1975.

Ziegler, Gary. "Second Ascent of Zoroaster Temple." *Trail and Timberline* 503 (November 1960): 166–68.

Index

About the Author

Author and photographer John Annerino was born on the edge of the desert and cut his teeth in the haunted canyons of the Superstition Mountains. He has been working in the frontier of Old Mexico and the American West for more than 20 years, documenting its indigenous people, natural beauty, and political strife. A veteran contract photographer for Liaison International, he has had his work published in *LIFE, Time, Newsweek,* the *New York Times, People, Scientific American, Travel & Leisure,* and many other prestigious publications worldwide. Annerino's fifteen single-artist calendars, including *Desert Light* and *La Virgen de Guadalupe,* and his eleven books of photography illuminate his passion to document endangered places, peoples, cultures, and traditions. His recent assignment work includes *National Geographic Adventure* and *ABC News Primetime* and digital photo spreads in the best-selling *AMERICA 24/7: A One Week Time Capsule of American Life* and its sequel, *Arizona 24/7.*

Annerino has spent most of his life exploring the terra incognita of the American West and Old Mexico—as a photojournalist, adventurer, and wilderness runner. A scholar of Southwestern history, he has extensive firsthand knowledge of this mythic region, its spirited individuals, and Native Peoples. Among many explorations by foot, raft, and rope, Annerino has worked as a climbing guide, survival instructor, Helitac forest fire crew boss, and a boatman on the Upper Salt River and the Green and Yampa rivers. In his quest to explore the remote corners of the Grand Canyon, Annerino worked as a Colorado River boatman and paddle captain, logging more than 5,000 miles on the Río Colorado. Following the rugged routes of explorers and Native Americans, he canyoneered the length of the Grand Canyon's longest and deepest tributary chasms, including the Little Colorado River Gorge, Buckskin Gulch / Paria Canyon, Cataract and Havasu canyons, and Kanab Creek Canyon; pioneered ascents of magnificent temples such as the southwest face of Zoroaster Temple; hiked the canyon's most awe-inspiring trails; and, between 1980 and 1982, ran the length of the Grand Canyon by three different routes, recounted in *Running Wild*. These runs included a six-day, 170-mile run below the South Rim; a seven-day, 210-mile run along the ancient Hopi/Havasupai trade route atop the South Rim; and an 8½-day, 250-mile run below the seldom-explored North Rim. In 1988, Annerino ran 750 miles of daunting Arizona wilderness from Mexico to Utah, also along ancient Indian routes, and later led the first modern unsupported crossing of the treacherous Camino del Diablo, "Road of the Devil," on foot mid-summer, a trip recounted in his critically acclaimed book *Dead in Their Tracks*. To date, Annerino has explored on foot more than 50,000 recorded miles of primitive trails and Native American routes through the deserts, canyons, and mountains of the Great Southwest.